1/08

The Courtier
and the Heretic

ALSO BY MATTHEW STEWART

*Monturiol's Dream: The Extraordinary Story of the Submarine Inventor
Who Wanted to Save the World*

*The Truth about Everything:
An Irreverent History of Philosophy with Illustrations*

The Courtier and the Heretic

LEIBNIZ, SPINOZA, AND
THE FATE OF GOD
IN THE MODERN WORLD

Matthew Stewart

W. W. NORTON & COMPANY NEW YORK · LONDON

For information about permission to reproduce selections from this book, write to
Permissions, W. W. Norton & Company, Inc., 500 Fifth Avenue, New York, NY 10110

Manufacturing by The Maple-Vail Book Manufacturing Group
Book design by Chris Welch Design
Production manager: Andrew Marasia

Library of Congress Cataloging-in-Publication Data
Stewart, Matthew, 1963–
The courtier and the heretic : Leibniz, Spinoza, and the fate of God
in the modern world / Matthew Stewart. — 1st ed.
p. cm.
Includes bibliographical references (p.   ) and index.
ISBN 0-393-05898-0 (hardcover)
1. Leibniz, Gottfried Wilhelm, Freiherr von, 1646–1716. 2. Spinoza, Benedictus de,
1632–1677. 3. God—History of doctrines. I. Title.
B2599.G63S74 2006
211—dc22

2005019962

W. W. Norton & Company, Inc., 500 Fifth Avenue, New York, N.Y. 10110
www.wwnorton.com

W. W. Norton & Company Ltd., Castle House, 75/76 Wells Street, London W1T 3QT

1 2 3 4 5 6 7 8 9 0

For Katherine and Sophia

Contents

8   Contents

The Courtier
and the Heretic

1

The Hague, November 1676

It is our good fortune to live in an age when philosophy is thought to be a harmless affair. As the autumn of 1676 approached, however, Baruch de Spinoza had ample reason to fear for his safety. One of his friends had recently been executed, and another had died in prison. His efforts to publish his definitive work, the *Ethics*, had come to an end amid threats of criminal prosecution. A leading French theologian named him "the most impious and the most dangerous man of the century." A powerful bishop denounced him as "that insane and evil man, who deserves to be covered with chains and whipped with a rod." To the general public, he was known simply as "the atheist Jew."

Among those who seemed eager to bring the infidel philosopher to justice was a young courtier and polymath named Gottfried Wilhelm Leibniz. In a personal letter to that same French theologian, Leibniz described Spinoza's work as "horrible" and "terrifying." To a famous professor, he called it "intolerably impudent." To a friend he confided, "I deplore that a man of such evident culture should have fallen so low."

Yet, in the privacy of his study, Leibniz crammed his notebooks with meticulous commentaries on Spinoza's writings. He exchanged secret letters with his public nemesis, addressing him as "celebrated doctor and profound philosopher." Through mutual friends he pleaded for a chance to examine a manuscript copy of the *Ethics*. And, on or around November 18, 1676, he traveled to The Hague and called on Spinoza in person.

LEIBNIZ ARRIVED IN Holland by yacht. He was thirty years old and well on his way to claiming his title as the last universal genius of Europe. He had already discovered the mathematical method we call calculus (later than, but independently of, Isaac Newton). He carried in his luggage his arithmetical calculating machine—a small wooden box stuffed with gears and dials that may be counted among the earliest ancestors of the modern computer. He had begun to fill out the long list of his contributions to the fields of chemistry, chronometry, geology, historiography, jurisprudence, linguistics, optics, philosophy, physics, poetry, and political theory. "When one . . . compares one's own small talents with those of a Leibniz," wrote Denis Diderot in the *Encyclopédie*, "one is tempted to throw away one's books and go die peacefully in the depths of some dark corner."

He would have been wearing his trademark wig, an elaborate traveling coat, and the kind of ornate vest, knee-length breeches, and silk stockings that were then the latest fashion in Paris. "It is so rare for an intellectual to dress properly, not to smell, and to understand jokes," the Duchess of Orléans noted approvingly. He was of smallish frame, with an unavoidable nose and keen, scrutinizing eyes. He carried his head far forward of his hunched shoulders, and he never knew what to do with his arms. His limbs, it was said, were as crooked and ungainly as those of Charon—the old and sulky ferryman of the dead. As he lurched along the leaf-strewn canals of The Hague, his elaborate robes flapping in the autumn wind, he must have looked like an exotic, gilded bird of prey.

He made up for it all with an elegance of mind, or so his contemporaries thought. "He is a man who, despite his insignificant outward appearance, is in a position to perform what he promises," a German baron advised Louis XIV's foreign minister. To meet Leibniz was to be overwhelmed in a stream of consciousness. The writings that spilled from his plume fill over 150,000 sheets in the archives of Hanover, and have yet to be comprehensively edited. But there was something elusive in him, too—an air of restlessness that amounted to more than a young man's passing wanderlust. He occasionally left his listeners feeling that, after the dazzling show of words, something still remained unsaid. "I love this man," said a petulant princess. "But I am angry that he treats everything so superficially with me."

SPINOZA LIVED IN a redbrick house along a canal called the Paviljoensgracht on the northern outskirts of town, a few paces short of the kind of flat, windmilled landscape made famous by Dutch artists of the time. He was not quite forty-four years old and had three months left to live. The works on which his later fame rests were complete. With his *Tractatus Theologico-Politicus*, he established himself as one of the first great theorists of the modern, secular state and a forerunner of the framers of the Constitution of the United States. In the *Ethics*, he anticipated later philosophical and scientific developments by two and sometimes three centuries. "To be a follower of Spinoza," Hegel once said, "is the essential beginning of all philosophy." When Einstein was asked, "Do you believe in God?," he famously replied: "I believe in Spinoza's God."

He was of average height, with a "well-formed body," a "beautiful face," and a "pleasing physiognomy," or so several observers noted. He coughed frequently but otherwise gave little sign of his failing health. He had an olive complexion; frizzy black hair, cut to shoulder length according to the fashion of the times; a thin mustache; long, thick, arched eyebrows; and dark, languid eyes—"so that one might easily know by his looks that he was descended from Portuguese Jews," said one commentator.

Spinoza rented his room from an amiable painter and his boisterous family, who apparently got along quite well with the atheist upstairs. During the day, he ground lenses for microscopes and telescopes. At night, by candlelight, he polished his system of metaphysics. Once he remained in his lodgings for a stretch of three months, calling down at odd hours for meals that typically consisted of raisins and milk gruel. According to the inventory taken after his death, he owned two pairs of pants, seven shirts, and five handkerchiefs. His one luxury was a four-poster bed with red curtains, inherited from his parents.

Yet, Spinoza was hardly as simple as his manner of living might have suggested. Friends and visitors often found something deeply enigmatic in him, a strange mix of caution and boldness, of modesty and arrogance, of icy logic and rebellious passion. He was a heretic with the character of a true believer, a saint without religion. He had the kind of charisma that could inspire lifelong devotion; but he also had an exceptional talent for making enemies.

SPINOZA LEFT NO record of the event—or, in any case, he left none that survived the efforts of his posthumous editors, one of whom happened to be Leibniz's principal liaison in Holland at the time. Leibniz, in the forty years that remained to him, did his best to avoid the subject.

When pressed, Leibniz claimed that he had stopped in on his fellow philosopher while "passing through" The Hague. He added that they met for "a few hours"and merely exchanged "anecdotes concerning the affairs of those times." As for any philosophy he might have acquired on the trip, he said he thought it was so bad that he would not "waste time in refuting" it.

None of it was true. In fact, Leibniz traveled to The Hague for the specific purpose of meeting its most infamous philosopher and he remained there for at least three days. By his own admission, he conversed with his host "many times and at great length." The discussions strayed well outside the bounds of polite conversation on current events. The one piece of evidence to survive directly from the meeting consists of a single sheet of writing that, according to a note at the bottom of the page, Leibniz penned in Spinoza's presence and then read out to him. It contains a proof of the existence of God.

The most important clues concerning events in The Hague, however, are to be found in between the lines of Leibniz's philosophy. Analysis of his unpublished writings makes clear that a decisive change in the tone and substance of his reflections occurred within days of his visit with Spinoza. In the metaphysical system he first presented to the public ten years after his return from Holland, moreover, no influence is more important, more problematic, more strangely bipolar, and less acknowledged than that of Spinoza.

As he approached his sixtieth year, Leibniz finally seemed to let slip that his youthful interest in Spinoza had been more than circumstantial. "You know that I once went a little too far, and began to lean to the side of the Spinozists," he wrote in the voice of a fictional spokesperson in a dialogue that he ultimately chose not to publish. But even this belated and suppressed confession understates the depth, complexity, and duration of his relationship with his fellow philosopher. In fact, the meeting with Spinoza was the defining event of Leibniz's life. Everything before points toward it for resolution; and everything after points back for explanation.

THE SEVENTEENTH CENTURY was an age of glitter and strife; of spiritual awakenings followed by religious wars, civil wars, revolutions, invasions, and acts of ethnic cleansing; of explosive growth in international trade, the formation of global empires, rapid urbanization in the major capitals, inevitably accompanied by epic plagues and fires; and, at least in the eyes of a select few, of a new kind of science rising with all the promise of a slumbering god. Historians have since called it "the century of genius"; but informed opinion at the time generally held that it was an age of exceptional wickedness. If there is a single thread that runs through the rich and confusing tapestry of seventeenth-century life, it is that this was an age of transition—the time in which the theocratic order of the medieval era ceded to the secular order of modernity.

Spinoza did not invent the modern world, but he was perhaps the first to observe it well. He was the first to attempt to answer the ancient questions of philosophy from a distinctly modern perspective. In his philosophical system, he offers a concept of God befitting the universe revealed by modern science—a universe ruled only by the cause and effect of natural laws, without purpose or design. He describes what it means to be human after our pretension to occupy a special place in nature has been shattered. He prescribes a means to find happiness and virtue in an era when the old theologies have no credibility. And he advocates a liberal, democratic system of government suitable for an inherently fragmented and diverse society. His is the first and archetypal instance of the active response to modernity—an affirmation of the modern world that today we associate mainly with secular liberalism.

Leibniz was no less farsighted than his rival, and no less grand in his ambitions. He, too, put his faith in the guidance of reason, and it was this faith that impelled him on his journey to The Hague. But the two men who met in that windy November belonged to their age in very different ways. In circumstances of birth, in social position, in personal aspirations, in eating habits, fashion sense, and the infinity of small things that make up what we call character, the glamorous polymath of Hanover and the saintly revolutionary of The Hague were nearly perfect contraries. And there are no two finer examples of the dictum that character *is* philosophy.

In large part as a direct result of his meeting with Spinoza, Leibniz came to represent his own original and antithetical response to the challenges of the modern era. In his philosophical writings, he articulates a strategy for recovering something of the old ideas about God and man by means of an analysis of the limits of reason. He claims to discover the meaning and purpose of life in all that modernity fails to comprehend. He presents a vision of a modern society united to serve goals of justice and charity that transcend self-interest. His metaphysical system is the paradigm for the reactive response to modernity—or what today we associate mainly with religious conservatism.

In the most widely accepted versions of the history of philosophy, Spinoza and Leibniz are understood to represent a speculative metaphysical program that long ago succumbed to academic progress.* In

---

*The views offered in this book reflect a great debt to the work of a number of recent scholars. At the same time, some of the conclusions concerning Leibniz, Spinoza, their relationship, and its significance for modern thought will not be uncontroversial. In the interest of keeping the focus on the primary subjects, however, almost all discussion of the secondary literature has been saved for a note on sources at the end of the book.

fact, taking a broader view of events, it is clear that the two greatest philosophers of the seventeenth century remain unsurpassed, and should perhaps be considered the twin founders of modern thought. We live in an age defined by its reaction to Spinoza and to all that he recorded in his philosophy. And there is no more compelling expression of this reaction than the philosophy Leibniz developed in the long years after his return from Holland. Contemporary debates concerning the separation of church and state, the clash of civilizations, and the theory of natural selection, to name just a few examples, are all continuations of the discussion that began in November 1676. Even today, the two men who met in The Hague stand for a choice that we all must make and have implicitly already made.

2

Bento

Even among philosophers, first impressions count. Three facts about Spinoza's origin and circumstances are crucial in understanding the impact he had on Leibniz. The first is that he was a Jew; the second is that he was expelled from the Jewish community in his twenty-fourth year on account of his heretical views; and the third is that he was born and lived in the golden age of the Dutch Republic. For medieval-minded contemporaries, Spinoza's pedigree marked him as an alien creature—"the kind of monster our dear Holland produces," said one scandalized theologian. For modern observers, the story of Spinoza's youth is more apt to trace the image of an extraordinary individual—the kind of person who can change history. For Leibniz, who remained forever caught between two ages, Spinoza would be both—a freak and a world-historical personality—and therein lay the problem that would determine the course of their meeting and the subsequent development of Leibniz's philosophy.

Baruch de Spinoza was born in Amsterdam on November 24, 1632. His given name is Hebrew for "blessed one." The boy was known familiarly by the Portuguese equivalent, Bento. Later, for scholarly purposes, he adopted the Latin Benedictus. In his posthumous work, he was identified only by his already infamous initials, BDS. To the delight of the philosopher's future detractors, the family name, Spinoza (also written as Spinosa, Despinosa, d'Espinoza, and other variants), derives from the Spanish for "thorny" (as in the English "spines").

The circumstances of Bento's birth owed a substantial debt to the cruel and senseless acts of King Ferdinand and Queen Isabella, more than a century before. In 1492, the monarchs of Castile and Aragon ordered all Jews in their territories to convert to Christianity or leave the realm. At the time, Spain was home to about 800,000 Jews, who, despite suffering from systematic persecution over the preceding centuries—synagogue burnings, judicial murders, forcible conversions, and being sold off into slavery—had made a substantial contribution to the local economy and culture. A large number of the Spanish Jews responded to Ferdinand's decree by accepting Christ as their savior. Many of these "conversos," however, soon discovered that conversion did little to quench the fires of fanatical intolerance: tens of thousands were burned at the stake in the Spanish Inquisition. Others boarded a fleet of boats ordered up by Ferdinand and fled to North Africa, the Middle East, and southern Europe. The largest share—numbering perhaps 120,000—migrated to the neighboring kingdom of Portugal.

Their reception left something to be desired: 20,000 Jewish children underwent forcible baptism, and 2,000 Jews were massacred in Lisbon on one unfortunate day in 1506. But, in time, the immigrants established a thriving merchant community. Around the middle of the sixteenth century, however, the Vatican announced that the Inquisition should proceed "in a free and unimpeded way" in Portugal. After the union of the two Iberian monarchies under a single crown in 1580, the Portuguese authorities showed that they could outdo even the Spanish in their zeal to expose and burn the enemies of the faith.

Sometime around 1590, the Portuguese Inquisition caught up with the family of Isaac Spinoza, a merchant from Lisbon then living in the southern town of Vidigueira. In little doubt about the future that awaited them on the Iberian peninsula, Isaac and his brother Abraham gathered up their families and escaped to the north—or, as the records of the inquisitors have it, they "fled before pardon." Isaac's in-laws, on the other hand, chose to remain in Portugal and receive their pardon—which took the form of imprisonment and torture.

Isaac and Abraham settled in the French port city of Nantes, where the brothers resumed their international trading activities. Abraham soon moved on to Rotterdam and then Amsterdam, where he had a daughter named Rachel and participated in the founding of a Jewish community. Isaac and his family remained in Nantes. Among Isaac's brood was a young son, Michael, born in 1587 or 1588 in Vidigueira. Michael grew up to become a trader in Nantes, just like his father.

At the age of thirty-four or so, Michael joined his uncle Abraham in Amsterdam, most likely in order to take Abraham's daughter, Rachel, as his bride. Sadly, Rachel died childless a few years later. In 1628, at the age of forty, Michael took a new wife, Hanna Deborah Senior. Hanna's mother hailed from Oporto, where a number of her relatives, too, had come to grief at the hands of the Portuguese Inquisition.

The Seniors, like the Spinozas, can only have considered it their good fortune to have ended their travels in the Dutch Republic. The Dutch revolt against Spanish rule of 1572 marked the beginning of the kind of age that justifiably occasions both marvel at human capabilities and disappointment at the extent to which the rest of history falls short. In a single century, on a piece of land that lay largely below sea level, and a population of two million, which amounted to little more than a rounding error in the continent's total, the Dutch built a global empire, produced an improbable number of history's greatest artists, scientists, and philosophers, and set the standards in economic and political practice that shaped the modern world.

The glory of the Dutch golden age blossomed mainly where the money was: in the city of Amsterdam. Between 1572 and 1640, Amsterdam quadrupled in population and became the undisputed center of world trade. Its merchant ships creaked under a bounty of Brazilian sugar, Spanish wool, Portuguese salt, Baltic grain, Turkish mohair, Mediterranean fruit and wine, spices from the East Indies, a variety of Dutch manufactures, such as fine textiles, tapestries, ceramics, furniture, and tobacco pipes, and, of course, the dyestuffs required by the Republic's frenetic artists.

Many aspects of life in Amsterdam astounded seventeenth-century travelers. Visitors gushed about the magnificent public buildings, the elegant private mansions on tree-lined canals, the fanatical neatness of the inhabitants, the low crime rate, the plentiful and well-endowed hospitals, the innovations in military methods, the scientific and technological marvels, such as the newfangled street lamps, the clocks, the telescopes and the microscopes, and, inevitably, the universal obsession with the painted image. Spinoza's first biographer and friend, Jean-Maximilian Lucas, writing in 1677, called Amsterdam "the most beautiful city in Europe."

But the feature of life that left the most vivid impression on visitors to Amsterdam—sometimes favorable, more often not—was the extraordinary freedom enjoyed by its people. The Dutch "love nothing so much as their freedom," wrote a scandalized German traveler. Servants and their mistresses dress and behave so much alike, he added, that it is hard to tell them apart. Louis XIV, who saw freedom as a form of vulgarity, scoffed that Holland was "a nation of fishwives and tradesmen." Sir William Temple, the English ambassador in the 1670s, on the other hand, took a much brighter view:

> It is hardly to be imagined how all the violence and sharpness, which accompanies the differences of religion in other countreys, seems to be appeased or softened here, by the general freedom which all here enjoy. . . . Men live together like Citizens of the World, associated by the common ties of Humanity . . . under the impartial protection of indifferent laws, with . . . equal freedom of Speculation and Enquiry.

Leibniz himself could not but acknowledge this newfound spirit of Dutch freedom. "This *simulacrum* of liberty is one of the principal pillars of the Dutch State," he wrote, somewhat grudgingly, in 1671, five years before setting foot in the Republic. "Such is the manner by which the multitudes find contentment in their freedom of belief and speech," he added, "that the most miserable sailor, in the tavern where he drinks his beer, fancies himself a king, even though he must still bear the heaviest burden to earn his livelihood." Yet Leibniz, ever ambivalent, had to admit that "this imaginary liberty has something real in it: For justice is administered in a very praiseworthy manner, without regard for rank or riches."

The same "freedom of Speculation and Enquiry," as Sir William put it, made the Dutch golden age one of the most fruitful periods in the history of science. Among the pioneers of the time were Christiaan Huygens, the brilliant mathematician and physicist who invented the pendulum clock and discovered the rings of Saturn, and Antoni von Leeuwenhoek, the self-taught microscopist who discovered bacteria and observed firsthand the structure of human sperm.

Freedom also left its mark on the extraordinary artistic achievements of the age. Mannered representations of great princes in Arcadian settings were no longer in style; the newly liberated classes of Dutch society demanded a new kind of art. Thousands of painters shucked off their day jobs and rose to meet the new demand, and from the battling crowd of brush wielders emerged new masters of cloudy skies, windy seascapes, tousled hair, fleeting glances, rare moments of introspection, and close encounters with divinity over the kitchen table.

For many visitors, there was no clearer sign of this new freedom—nor any surer proof of the depravity of the Dutch—than the manner in which the Jews of Amsterdam lived. These Portuguese Jews numbered perhaps little more than one thousand at the time of Bento's birth and resided mainly in and around the island of Vlooienburg, a neighborhood of lumber warehouses lined by the Amstel and the Houtgracht. Unlike almost all other European cities, however, Amsterdam did not confine its Jewish population to a ghetto. A significant number of Jews—especially among the wealthier ones—made their homes in the city's tonier areas. Conversely, a number of non-Jews—notably, Rembrandt—lived in the (predominantly) Jewish neighborhood.

Behind Dutch tolerance of their new neighbors was something perhaps more durable than the love of liberty, namely, an enlightened understanding of commercial self-interest. The Portuguese Jews brought with them an extensive network of trading contacts in Iberia and South America—markets that had only recently opened to Dutch merchants. By midcentury, the Jewish community accounted for as much as 15 percent of Amsterdam's foreign trade.

Leibniz, for one, understood clearly that Dutch tolerance had a distinct profit motive and that it was responsible for an appreciable share of the nation's economic growth. Five years before his visit he articulated a seventeenth-century version of the "melting pot" theory:

> From Spain came the Portuguese Jews; from Poland, the Socinians expelled by the latest edicts; from England those exiled in the Restoration.... [Each] brought with him his knowledge: the arts, the commerce, the manufacturing industry of his country. ... Every time troubles start up in Germany and in Belgium (as earlier in France), Holland—the universal refuge of sects and exiles—sees its population and riches grow.

The Jews of Amsterdam, too, saw their population and riches grow through their participation in the Dutch economic miracle. An English visitor to the city on the Amstel wrote that the Jews were "Ritch merchants, not evill esteem'd off, living in liberty, wealth and ease." With economic success came a new synagogue, a vigorous system of education, a healthy measure of respect from the neighbors, and a desire to participate in, among other things Dutch, the euphoria about art. One Jewish family was said to have amassed paintings worth "a ton of gold."

Michael Spinoza was, just like his father before him, a prosperous merchant, occupying an unexceptional rank in the hierarchy of Amsterdam's new class of Portuguese Jewish traders. He lived with his family in respectable, rented accommodation in the center of the Jewish neighborhood, just a few doors down from the house of Rembrandt. Michael must certainly be counted an upstanding member of the community, for he served two terms on the board of the synagogue. He traded in Brazilian sugar, candied ginger, raisins, and other dried fruit. No doubt the family fortunes fluctuated. Caught between pirates and the English Royal Navy, which at the time was keen to complicate life for Dutch merchants, Michael's cargoes did not always make it into port; and when they did, the goods sometimes proved to be rotten on arrival.

Bento was the third of five children (as best as can be determined). The eldest was Miriam, born in 1629, and the second child was Isaac, named in honor of his paternal grandfather. After Bento came a son, Gabriel, and a daughter, Rebecca (although there is some doubt about Rebecca's place in the birth order and even about the identity of her mother). When Bento was six years old, his mother, Hanna, died, very possibly of the same chronic lung disease that would eventually claim his life. Two years later, Michael married Esther de Soliz, a native of Lisbon, with whom he (most likely) did not have any children.

At the age of seven or so—the year after his mother died—Bento enrolled in the local Jewish school, where the education was as deep as it was narrow. Pupils were divided by age into six large rooms, and they progressed through a program that consisted principally of memorizing the Bible, studying the Hebrew language, and learning Jewish customs. Classes were held for three hours in the morning and three hours in the afternoon; in between, during the three-hour lunch break, most of the pupils received instruction from private tutors hired by their parents.

By the time Bento matriculated, the school of the Amsterdam Jewish community had achieved an international reputation. A Polish scholar described his visit to the school in breathless terms: "I saw giants in scholarship: tender children as small as grasshoppers. . . . In my eyes they were like prodigies because of their unusual familiarity with the entire Bible and the science of grammar. They possessed the ability to compose verses and poems in meter and to speak a pure Hebrew."

There can be little doubt that Bento was one of these precocious "grasshoppers." Spinoza's friend Lucas, along with his other early biographer, Colerus, confirm what would be evident in any case from the philosopher's later achievements: that he was an exceptionally gifted student. "Nature endowed him with a keen wit and quick intelligence," Colerus says. "He was not yet fifteen years old when he raised difficulties that the most learned among the Jews found it difficult to solve," Lucas adds. Spinoza's early training stayed with him for life: well into middle age, he took time off his philosophical work to write a Hebrew grammar. In view of the philosopher's later critiques of the scriptures, his teachers might well have rued the trouble they took to get him to memorize the Bible.

The sparse and grainy snapshots remaining from this period of Bento's life reveal not just an infuriatingly intelligent boy, but also one with no lack of confidence in his own counsel. When he was around ten years old, the story goes, his father sent him to collect some money from a certain elderly widow. Bento called upon the woman, and she asked him to wait while she finished reading the Bible. After sighing over her prayers, the pious widow counted out the money owed on her table, making virtuous noises about what an "upright" man the young boy's father was and how "he has never departed from the Law of Moses." Then she scooped up the coins and dropped them into the boy's bag.

But Bento's father had taught him well to distinguish false piety from genuine worship; sensing that the Bible-thumping lady was conducting business on the wrong side of the line, the lad insisted over her strained objections on counting the coins himself. Sure enough, he found that he had to ask the crafty hag for two more ducats, which she had allowed to slip through a slit on top of the table. Bento was elated at his discovery, and so, too, was his father, who gave him praise. The episode apparently excited much favorable comment on the boy from other members of the community.

Bento's talents soon attracted the notice of his community's leaders, notably Rabbi Saul Morteira, a man who would figure prominently in later events. Lucas, perhaps echoing Spinoza's mixed opinion of his teacher, calls him "a celebrity among the Jews and the least ignorant of the rabbis of his time." He was born in Venice in 1596 and studied medicine under the tutelage of Doctor Montalto, a Marrano, or Jew from Spain, employed in the court of Maria de' Medici. When Montalto died, Morteira traveled to Amsterdam, bringing with him Montalto's body for burial, volumes of esoteric knowledge from the Venetian Jewish community, and, it was said, "a taste for court life." By the time Bento entered school, Morteira had risen to become the senior rabbi in Amsterdam.

Morteira was a man of hard discipline, an autocrat of the classroom—the kind of teacher whose passion in advancing the fortunes of those who followed him on the true path to salvation ceded only to his zeal in persecuting those who failed to heed his instruction.

Students who raised inappropriate topics (e.g., the trinity) he promptly expelled; and for those Jewish men who remained uncircumcised he reserved an even worse fate, namely, eternal punishment. When a doctrinal dispute arose with a fellow rabbi concerning guaranteed entry to heaven for all Jews (Morteira took the view that there were no guarantees), he engineered a humiliating demotion for his rival and did not rest until he had hounded the offending rabbi off to Brazil.

Morteira cherished the view that Bento was one of his followers, and a good one at that. "He admired the conduct and the genius of his disciple," says Lucas. Morteira evidently failed to grasp that Bento was not the kind of pupil who seeks a master. With the kind of self-sufficiency that perhaps marks the beginning of all philosophical journeys, the young pupil set out to examine the Bible on his own, deciding to consult no one but himself in this matter. Very soon, it seems, he found he had no need of Morteira's services in interpreting the scriptures.

It was around this time that Bento began to perplex his betters with questions that they could not answer. When he perceived that his doubts embarrassed his teacher, however, Bento—showing the uncanny reserve and the aversion to scandal so evident in his later life—simply nodded his head and pretended to be very satisfied with the answers he received.

The pretense apparently succeeded. Morteira, says Lucas, particularly liked the fact that Bento was "not at all vain. . . . He did not understand how a young man of such penetration could be so modest." Morteira—like others to come—would learn too late that the source of the philosopher's modesty lay not in a low opinion of himself but rather in the low value he attached to the opinions of those who praised him.

In Bento's late teenage years, a series of blows to the Spinoza family fortunes prevented him from pursuing the most likely fate of a bright young scholar—to become a rabbi—and thereby altered the course of the history of western philosophy. In 1649, when Bento was in his seventeenth year, his older brother, Isaac, died, and Bento was called to take his place at his father's side. At the same time, Michael's trading business reeled from several disastrous misadventures. In 1650, a ship laden with wine fell into English hands. The following year, a consignment of Brazilian sugar was again lost to the Royal Navy. Barbary pirates made off with another 3,000 guilders' worth of goods, and Moorish corsairs soon plundered still more of Michael's cargoes.

Family tragedy added to the business catastrophes. In 1651, Bento's elder sister, Miriam, died in childbirth. Two years later, his stepmother, Esther, passed away. The thrice-widowed Michael had only five months to grieve before following her into the grave. By the age of twenty-one, Bento had lost the entire older half of his immediate family and was in charge of a merchant business that was rapidly sinking into bankruptcy.

Together with his younger brother, the budding philosopher now traded under the name of Bento and Gabriel Spinoza. In view of his new responsibilities, it is no surprise that Bento failed to enroll in the advanced courses for training rabbis. It seems, however, that he did continue his studies informally through a yeshiva group led by Rabbi Morteira.

To what extent the man who would later rewrite the history of western thought enjoyed trading in raisins and sugar is not known. The scattered evidence concerning his business activities suggests that he took his duties seriously and was not incapable of pursuing the family's interests through the normal legal and commercial channels. In any case, the experience as a merchant undoubtedly did make an important contribution to his philosophical development, for it exposed him to a much wider community in his home city.

As a merchant of Amsterdam, Bento frequented the city's mercantile exchanges, its warehouses, and the port. He worked alongside brokers, bankers, fellow merchants, and shipmasters. A number of the open-minded, spiritually hungry gentiles he first met in the course of his business activities in fact became lifelong friends. Jarig Jelles, for example, who would write the preface of the philosopher's posthumous works, was a successful grain merchant who retired in early middle age in order to pursue wisdom.

On one of his forays into town, the young trader made his first, fateful visit to a bookshop. Amsterdam in the seventeenth century was a city of bookshops. There were at the time as many as four hundred establishments dedicated to spreading the printed word. Under the tolerant eye of the civil authorities, authors from across Europe sent their wares to Holland for publication, and, as a result, Dutch publishers outproduced their continental rivals in several languages. An important part of the Amsterdam adventure for intellectual visitors as diverse as Leibniz and John Locke was a visit to one or more of the city's bookshops, where one had the opportunity not just to browse the aisles for contraband literature, but also to sniff out new ideas among the freethinking bibliophiles, who with the stimulus of coffee and Dutch-made pipes—for smoking had become a national sport— would while the afternoon away discussing novel theories, plotting revolutions, and bantering about the latest developments in the republic of letters.

It was in this nicotine-laced atmosphere of intellectual excitement that Bento one day met Frans van den Enden. Bookseller, Latinist, medical doctor, amateur thespian, champion of radical democracy, outspoken advocate of free love (until caught *in flagrante*), ex-Jesuit (erroneous beliefs), author of the play *Lusty Heart* (banned from the stage), accused of "sowing the seeds of atheism" among the youth of Amsterdam (guilty as charged), van den Enden was the bad boy of the early Dutch Enlightenment. One pupil who later repented his own youthful errors described him as "entirely without God." A widower at fifty, he raised his brood of children according to his own, unorthodox principles of education. His eldest daughter, Clara Maria, was among the very few young women in Europe at the time who could claim to be a master of Latin, music, painting, and theater. "She was rather frail and deformed," says Colerus. "But she made up for it with her keen wit and outstanding learning." She was just the kind of girl, perhaps, who would have attracted the eye of a young philosopher.

When van den Enden's bookshop went out of business in the late 1640s, he decided to set up a school in his own house, offering instruction in Latin, Greek, and other subjects. Despite his eyebrow-raising reputation, Frans managed to lure students from good families, some coming from as far away as Germany. In order to foster the thespian spirit among his students, he organized them into productions of Roman comedies and other plays.

Frans introduced Bento to a thrilling world of learning he had hitherto glimpsed only from a great distance. It was Frans, no doubt, who told the young man that "it was a pity that he knew neither Greek nor Latin." Having devoted much of his childhood exclusively to the Hebrew Bible, Bento must have felt left behind in the tumultuous progress of the wider republic of letters. The aspiring scholar promptly enrolled in van den Enden's school for scandal, accepting Clara Maria as his tutor in Latin. At some point in his early twenties, Bento moved in with Frans and his family. Now a master of Latin in his own right, he offered tutorials in exchange for his room.

By all accounts, Bento exhibited a ruthless passion for learning. The focus of his intense desire to know was Descartes, the great French philosopher whose ideas had sparked controversy throughout the European intellectual world. Descartes resided for two decades in Amsterdam before his death in 1650, and possibly Bento saw the philosopher himself strolling along the canals. With his short stature and unusually unprepossessing face, the Frenchman cut a recognizable figure in city life. In any case, Bento soon established a reputation as a formidable expositor and critic of the Cartesian philosophy. According to Colerus, he adopted as his guiding maxim the words of his French master: "That nothing ought to be admitted as True, but that which has been proved by good and solid reasons." It wasn't long before he concluded that this maxim ruled out most of the Bible, not to mention Descartes's own philosophy.

The young radical was drifting ever farther from the Jewish community in which he was raised. Back on the other side of the Houtgracht, the tongues wagged. Some of Bento's peers began to whisper that the wandering merchant was retailing some truly execrable ideas. They said that he believed that the books of Moses were made by man; that the soul dies with the body; and that God is a corporeal mass. For Jews of the time, just as much as for Christians, such notions were frightening heresies.

The rumors were indeed true, at least in some sense. In his mature works, Spinoza does in fact suggest that the Bible is a human invention, in a manner of speaking; and he explicitly rejects the doctrine of personal immortality. While he nowhere says that God is a part of the corporeal world, he does indeed claim that the corporeal world is a part of God (to put it crudely), and the rumormongers should probably be pardoned for failing to worry the difference. The available evidence, furthermore, strongly suggests that the philosopher formed these dangerous convictions well before he wrote them down for posterity—and certainly before his twenty-fourth year. Lucas confirms that Spinoza was "under the age of twenty" when he first conceived of "his grand project."

The crisis began with one of those encounters that, as Lucas puts it, "one cannot decently avoid, even if they are often dangerous." A pair of young men who professed to be his most intimate friends approached Bento and begged him to share with them his real views. They promised him that he had nothing to fear from them, for whatever his opinions were, they had no other motive in their questions than the desire to arrive at the truth. Bento, always reticent in such situations, said nothing at first. Then, feigning a smile, he suggested that they could always look to Moses and the prophets for answers.

This time, the pretense did not work. The youths persisted with their questions. If one reads the Bible carefully, said one, it would seem that the soul is not immortal, that there are no angels, and that God has a body. "How does it appear to you? Does God have a body? Is the soul immortal?" he asked, according to Lucas.

Bento responded with the kind of guilelessness he invariably manifested whenever he found himself among those he took to be fellow philosophers.

"I confess," he said, "that since nothing is to be found in the Bible about the immaterial or incorporeal, there is nothing objectionable in believing that God is a body. All the more so since, as the prophet says [Psalm 48:1], God is great, and it is impossible to comprehend greatness without extension and, therefore, without body."

"As for spirits, it is certain that Scripture does not say that these are real and permanent substances, but mere phantoms."

"With regard to the soul, wherever Scripture speaks of it the word Soul is used simply to express Life, or anything that is living. It would be useless to search for any passage in support of its Immortality."

Having revealed his hand, Bento abruptly ended the conversation.

The two friends left only after he agreed to resume the discussion at a later time. But, suspicious of their motives, he subsequently refused to return to the subject, and after a while broke off all contact with the pair.

When they saw that he shunned them, the two young men developed an extreme animus toward Bento and decided to exact revenge. They went around the community repeating and embellishing the rebel scholar's comments, murmuring that he "had nothing but hatred and contempt for the law of Moses," that Rabbi Morteira was wrong to think that he was pious, and that, far from being one of the pillars of the community, he would be its destroyer.

It did not help matters that Bento soon struck up an association with Juan de Prado, a physician twenty years his senior, who arrived in Amsterdam in 1655 with an unenviable reputation for failing to get along with his fellow Jews. Prado was a tall, thin, dark-haired man with a large nose, and he did not appear to generate any income from his activities as a doctor. Instead, he lived off handouts from an increasingly reluctant community, which suspected him, too, of disseminating heresies.

Sentiment in some quarters apparently turned homicidal around this time: an attempt was made on Bento's life. As he stepped out of a theater (or possibly the synagogue—reports conflict), he saw an unknown man approach him. He glimpsed the flash of a knife and stepped back just as the blade came swooping down toward him. The knife penetrated his overcoat but missed his body. The assailant fled the scene. The philosopher kept the coat, tear unmended, for the rest of his life, a souvenir of the incident and a reminder of the perils of a life of the mind.

It would be far from the last time that he incited this kind of extreme hatred in others—a fact that must reflect some aspect of his character or of the way that he moved in the world. Maybe it was a certain look in the overexpressive eyes, maybe it was a subtle curl in the lips—who knows? In his mature writings, it shows up as a chilling frankness in tone as he dismembers unsatisfactory philosophical views with a peremptory chop of the logical cleaver. Clearly, Bento was more transparent than he believed himself to be; he had some not altogether conscious way of conveying the contempt with which he beheld his philosophical inferiors. He exuded an absolute indifference to the judgments of others, and it was this air of inaccessibility, perhaps, that fueled unending conflagrations of loathing on the part of those who, in all likelihood, had suffered only minor slights.

Bento's former friends, not satisfied with peddling rumors retail, took their case to the community headquarters. On a hot summer day in 1656, in the old, wooden warehouse that then served as the synagogue, they repeated to a panel of judges their allegations concerning the young man's heresies. The judges were horrified. Inflamed with indignation, they prepared to excommunicate Bento without delay. After they cooled down, they decided upon a more pragmatic approach. They summoned the deviant for a hearing, to give him a chance to repent or, if not, to see if at least he would be amenable to negotiation.

The extreme anxiety and trepidation of leaders of the synagogue were understandable. More than theology was at stake: when the Dutch authorities permitted the Jews to live and worship in Amsterdam, they did so under the condition that the newcomers stick to their beliefs and not pollute the atmosphere of the city with any additional heresies. The Jewish leaders knew that the survival of their community depended on avoiding scandal.

Bento went "cheerfully" to the synagogue, says Lucas, certain in his heart that he had done nothing wrong. In the makeshift chamber of the Jewish community's place of worship, the young man with the dark, curly hair quietly took his place before the splenetic panel of judges. One witness after another took the stand before him and testified about his loathsome deeds and opinions.

At some point in the parade of denunciations, perhaps during a recess, one of the elders evidently pulled Bento aside in an effort to solve the problem in a different way. He offered the young man a financial incentive to renounce his heretical views in public. According to Colerus, the philosopher later reported that he was promised one thousand guilders for the service—enough money in those days to commission half a dozen portraits from Rembrandt.

Bento refused. He said that even if they offered him ten times as much, he would not accept, for to do so would make him a hypocrite.

When Morteira got wind of the hearing against his disciple, he rushed to the synagogue to see for himself, still clinging to the notion that Bento was destined to be his spiritual heir. Elbowing his way on to the sweltering panel, the rabbi demanded sternly of Bento, in Lucas's words: "Whether he was mindful of the good example he had set him? Whether his rebellion was the reward for the pains he had taken with his education?"

Evidently, Morteira still failed to understand the nature of his "disciple." Seeing that conflict was now unavoidable, Bento dropped the pretense of modesty and, if Lucas is to be believed, delivered a blast of icy sarcasm. "I am aware of the gravity of the threats," he said. "And in return for the trouble you have taken to teach me the Hebrew language, I am quite willing to show you how to excommunicate me."

Morteira was apoplectic. His rage multiplied with the humiliation of such a public betrayal. He "vented all his spleen" at the young monster and then stormed out of the synagogue, saying that he would not return "except with a thunderbolt in his hand."

With Morteira's "thunderbolt" we at last clear the sometimes choppy seas of secondhand accounting and arrive at a piece of solid fact, for there is ample evidence that a "thunderbolt" is pretty much what the rabbi delivered. Spinoza's excommunication, preserved in the Amsterdam archives, was among the harshest ever issued by his community.

On July 27, 1656, this verdict was read out before the ark of the synagogue of Amsterdam:

> The lords of the Mahamad . . . having long known of the evil opinions and deeds of Baruch de Espinoza, have endeavored by various ways and promises to turn him from his evil ways. But having been unable to reform him, but rather, on the contrary, daily receiving more information about the abominable heresies which he practiced and taught and about the monstrous deeds he did, and having for this numerous trustworthy witnesses who have deposed and born witness to this effect in the presence of said Espinoza, they . . . have decided . . . that the said Espinoza should be excommunicated and expelled from the people of Israel. . . . Cursed be he by day and cursed be he by night; cursed

be he when he lies down and cursed be he when he rises up.
Cursed be he when he goes out and cursed be he when he comes
in. The Lord will not spare him, but then the anger of the Lord
and his jealousy shall smoke against that man, and all the curses
that are written in this book shall lie upon him, and the Lord
shall blot out his name from under Heaven.

The sting of the excommunication came in its tail. It banned all
members of the community from any intercourse with the con-
victed, under pain of the same penalty. Even his family could not
speak, conduct business, or share a meal with him. He was, in effect,
dead to them.

Excommunication, or *cherem*, was a severe but not unknown practice in the Jewish communities of Amsterdam and elsewhere of the
period. In some cases, it was viewed as a warning more than a punishment, intended to last for a day or a week, and reversible under
appropriate conditions and behaviors. In other cases, the intentions
were less benign.

The best measure of the seriousness of Spinoza's situation is the fate
of his friend Juan de Prado. Prado was excommunicated in the same
year as the philosopher, and it seems clear that, in the eyes of the rabbis, Prado and Spinoza both stood for the same set of heresies. One
of Morteira's supporters later lauded the rabbi for clearing the synagogue of the "thorns" (*espinas*) in its "meadows" (*prados*).

Yet Prado's *cherem* was considerably milder in tone than Spinoza's.
Furthermore, while Spinoza seems to have been offered a bribe to
return to the straight and narrow, Prado was not. Clearly, the younger
man was the bigger fish, in the eyes of the rabbis. Most telling of all,
while Spinoza made no effort to appease the leaders of the synagogue, Prado did in fact recant. Later that summer, he confessed
before an assembly of judges that "on my own free will . . . I have
sinned and erred." Had Spinoza been willing to mount the platform
of the synagogue and make this sort of statement, he might well have
returned to the future for which he was raised. But it seems that the
aspiring philosopher had not the least intention of doing so.

Instead, the evidence suggests, he wrote an *Apology*. The text—

which has since been lost—would have had nothing to do with saying he was sorry. On the contrary, it would have been an elaboration and defense of the very opinions for which he had been excommunicated. The title of the *Apology*, in fact, could only have served to remind readers of the parallels between his excommunication and the case of Socrates, whose unsuccessful attempt to answer charges of impiety is represented in Plato's dialogue of the same name. A contemporary who saw the document reports that its contents were quite close to those of the *Tractatus Theologico-Politicus* of 1670, in which Spinoza lays out his heretical critique of the Bible and argues for the establishment of a secular state founded on the principle of toleration.

Spinoza never looked back. In the twenty years of life that remained to him, he left no hint that he ever regretted the actions that led to his expulsion from the Jewish community of Amsterdam. At the time, when informed of the verdict against him, according to Lucas, he was serene. "I enter gladly on the path that is opened to me," he said, "with the consolation that my departure will be more innocent than was the exodus of the early Hebrews from Egypt."

SPINOZA'S EXCOMMUNICATION was the defining event of his life. It determined, in the first instance, the circumstances in which he would live. When he crossed the bridge over the Houtgracht for the last time, Spinoza threw himself at the mercy of the newly tolerant Dutch society. He no longer saw himself as a Jew, but as a citizen in a free republic. His mature philosophy became a celebration of the spirit of freedom that characterized his parents' adopted country. His first published work of original philosophy, the *Tractatus Theologico-Politicus*, opens with something like a letter of thanks to his new home:

> Since we have the rare good fortune to live in a commonwealth where the freedom of judgment is fully granted to the individual citizen and he may worship God as he pleases, and where nothing is esteemed dearer and more precious than freedom, I think I am undertaking no ungrateful or unprofitable task in

demonstrating that not only can this freedom be granted without endangering piety and the peace of the commonwealth, but also the peace of the commonwealth and piety depend on this freedom.

This same spirit of freedom radiates from the core of Spinoza's metaphysics. God—the beginning and end of all his thought—is "the only free cause"; and the philosopher's highest aspiration is to participate in this divine freedom: to become, in his own words, "a free man."

In his new status as an apostate Jew, however, Spinoza would soon test the limits of the same Dutch freedom that made his new life possible. The vituperations of the rabbis would come to seem like mild admonishments in comparison with the vitriol the Christian theologians had in store for him. Indeed, after his expulsion from the Jewish community, the philosopher entered into a kind of double exile—he was an outcast twice removed. To the Jews he was a heretic; to the Christians he was, moreover, a Jew.

Henry Oldenburg—the secretary of the Royal Society of London and one of Spinoza's principal correspondents—expressed an attitude typical of the time when he described Spinoza as "that odd philosopher, yet lives in Holland, but no Hollander he." The blue-blooded physicist Christiaan Huygens—who traded optical secrets with the philosopher—referred to Spinoza in private correspondence as "our Israelite" and "our Jew." When the religious authorities of the Netherlands fingered Spinoza as "one who mocks all religions" and likened him to a form of "gangrene" in the Republic, they rarely failed to point out that he was, in addition, a Jew. And Leibniz, with his inimitable finesse, called him "that discerning Jew."

This position of the double exile, too, would become a part of the essence of Spinoza's philosophy. It was because his vantage point lay on the extreme margins of society that Spinoza could see clearly that the old God was dying and that his theocratic rule on earth was crumbling. It was from this position, too, that he conceived of his remedy for the modern condition. In his political philosophy, he advocated the kind of tolerant, secular society in which he himself would no longer count as an exile. In his metaphysical speculations, he discovered a divinity far removed from the constraints of tradition, orthodoxy, superstition, and all the other sources of majority opinion, a God stripped of the power to make arbitrary decrees, answerable only to the universal light of the mind, the guidance of reason.

No less than it defined his philosophy, Spinoza's excommunication shaped and displayed an extraordinary personality—one as rare as it was rich in paradox and insight. To be expelled from one's community in the bitterest terms on account of one's unpublished opinions by the age of twenty-three is an unusual accomplishment; to go on to become recognized as "the most impious man of the century"— and after that one of the most influential philosophers in history— confirms that it was no accident.

Spinoza never lost the innate sense of superiority and the almost clinical level of self-sufficiency that led to the bare-knuckle confrontation with his entire community. "We see therefore that all the notions whereby the common people are wont to explain Nature are merely modes of imagining," he writes with typical disdain in his *Ethics*, "and denote not the nature of anything but only the constitution of the imagination." When asked by a hostile correspondent how he could be so sure that his philosophy was the true one, he replied: "I know it in the same way that you know that the three angles of a triangle are equal to two right angles." Beneath the cool surface of his arguments seethed a rebellious passion—the fierce rejection of any authority that did not emanate entirely from within, perhaps even a protest against the element of submission to an external power that seems central to all religious experience.

And yet, the humility that Rabbi Morteira glimpsed in the young Bento would continue to impress friends and adversaries throughout his life. Colerus says that the philosopher was universally regarded as "courteous and obliging" and "troublesome to nobody." Saint-Évremond, a highborn adventurer and free spirit of the time who lived in Holland in the late 1660s, reports that "his knowledge, his modesty, and his unselfishness made all the intellectual people in The Hague esteem him and seek his acquaintance." When Spinoza compared his own fate to the exodus of the Hebrews from Egypt, furthermore, he clearly intended to suggest that he was in some way more true to the word of God than his antagonists. When he titled his self-defense an *Apology*, he signaled his belief that he, like Socrates, would ultimately be exonerated in the name of a higher kind of justice. The most impious man of the century transparently took himself to be the most pious. He rejected the orthodoxy of his day not because he believed less, but because he believed more.

The peculiar combination of humility and pride, of prudence and valor, of icy rationalism and zealous passion; the guilelessness that opened doors to his adversaries; and the indifference bordering on insouciance that could drive them to extreme rage—all of these startling juxtapositions of character were present on the day of Spinoza's excommunication, and all would remain with him throughout his life. Even today, his character represents something of an enigma, a problem more philosophical than biographical. No less than his metaphysics, it raises a question about the possibility of faith in a world without religion. Did Spinoza find a secular path to salvation, or did he merely invent a new form of superstition? Was he misunderstood or a misfit? a rarity or an oddity? At the time, only a subtle few understood the problem embodied in Spinoza's very way of being. Among these, as it happens, the best was also the first: Leibniz.

3

Gottfried

hile the Dutch celebrated the new freedoms of their golden age, the inhabitants of central Europe were busy killing one another in a festival of holy violence that came to be known as the Thirty Years War. The troubles began in Bohemia in 1618, when the Catholic authorities shut down one Protestant church and destroyed a second. Protestants responded by tossing a pair of Catholic deputies out the windows of a government office. The Catholics turned around and quashed the revolt, but not before igniting a series of conflicts that spread from the Baltic to the River Po. The Thirty Years War was in many ways the military continuation of the struggle between the Reformation and the Counter Reformation that began in the previous century, but the venal motives of the kings and princes involved can hardly be discounted.

During the three decades of conflict, the population of Germany declined from 21 million to 13 million—a ratio of destruction that surpasses even that of the world wars of the twentieth century. In his novel *Simplicissimus*, the writer Grimmelshausen catalogues the horrors of the war, which, aside from the usual quota of rapes and murders, included the application of thumbscrews, the forced eating of feces, and the torching of whole villages along with their inhabitants. The bumper harvest of death, however, was mostly the result of collateral damage: mercenary armies destroyed livelihoods more than lives as they rampaged across the countryside, and helped to create ideal conditions for the spread of the plague.

With its disastrous failure to control the course of the conflict, the Holy Roman Empire demonstrated conclusively that its power was now a matter of historical fiction. France and Sweden gobbled up large tracts of German territory, and sovereignty of the rest devolved to hundreds of princes and bishops, each the master of a region, town, or, at least, a castle. The war represented a catastrophe for intellectual life in the German lands, too. Many scholars fled before the violence, and those left behind retreated into the safety of a sterile conservatism. A full century would pass before Germany recovered its pride of place in the republic of letters, during which time, as the historian Lewis White Beck has noted, Leibniz alone would fly the flag of higher learning from his precarious perch in Hanover.

As the war ground its way to an end free of glory or purpose, Germany discovered within itself a grim tolerance of religious differences, a hankering for security, and the heartfelt conviction that the unified order of medieval times was not such a bad thing after all. A popular poem of the time, penned by the satirist Johann Michael Moscherosch, summed up the political thinking of the time in its title: "Germany Which Sighs for Peace." The hostilities eventually came to an end with the Peace of Westphalia—known to contemporaries as the Peace of Exhaustion.

It was amid such craving for a good night's sleep that, on July 1, 1646, Gottfried Wilhelm Leibniz first opened his eyes. Gottfried's origins, no less than those of Bento, may serve to demonstrate that a considerable amount of philosophy takes place before birth, and that much of the rest happens not long thereafter. But the past that Leibniz inherited and the future into which he was born could hardly have been more different from those of the man whose path he would cross in his thirty-first year. Fourteen years younger than his rival, Gottfried came into a world that was in many ways much older. He never quite got over the sense of loss that was his birthright as a child of the Thirty Years War, and he never quite satisfied the hunger for peace and security that gnawed at his age. It should come as no surprise that he devoted the better part of his life to rebuilding a glittering empire that seemed to have vanished before he was born.

GOTTFRIED WAS FORTUNATE at least in his city of origin. Leipzig escaped the worst of the Thirty Years War, and may have even turned a profit during the conflict, for it was able to maintain its famous annual trade fair throughout the hostilities. Not coincidentally, Leipzig was a city with few doubts about its religious identity; since the time of the Reformation, it had basked in renown as a center of Lutheran studies.

Gottfried's father, Friedrich Leibniz, occupied a prestigious position in the town's theological infrastructure. He was vice chairman of the faculty and professor of moral philosophy at the University of Leipzig. Thrice married and twice widowed at the time of Gottfried's birth, Friedrich had a son and a daughter from his first marriage. His latest wife, Catharina Schmuck, was of perhaps even higher social standing than he; she was the daughter of a famous lawyer. Two years after Gottfried's birth, she bore a daughter, Anna Catharina, whose son eventually became the sole heir to the fortune his uncle, the philosopher, accumulated in the course of his remarkably profitable career.

Gottfried first distinguished himself when he was three days old, or so the story goes. At his baptism, "to the astonishment of the bystanders," the infant opened his eyes and lifted his head toward the officiating priest, as if to welcome the holy water on his brow. Friedrich was ecstatic. The event was "a most sure token, that this my son will walk through life with his eyes upturned to heaven," he noted in his journal.

According to some personal recollections that the philosopher himself committed to paper much later in life, the pace of his spiritual development did not let up. When he was two years old and "full of pranks," the future inventor of the calculus was playing on a table one day in the presence of his father and a maid. The maid tried to grab hold of the mischievous tot, but he stepped backward and crashed to the floor.

"My father and the maid scream out: they look, they see me laughing at them, unhurt."

Once again, Friedrich recognized the special favor of the Almighty, and immediately dispatched a servant to church with a note of thanks. The proud head of the household took pains to advance his son's intellectual development, too. When Gottfried was four, Friedrich gave him a history book to read and took time to recite many of its narratives himself—"with such a favorable result, as led him to indulge the brightest anticipations of my future progress."

Sadly, the doting father died in his fifty-fifth year, when Gottfried was only six years old. The grief and the yearning for paternal affirmation are still palpable in Leibniz's recollections, many years later: "My father . . . conceived of such high hopes for me that he often exposed himself to the playful satire of his friends. Unfortunately, however, I was not destined long to enjoy his friendly assistance, nor he to rejoice in my continued progress." Gottfried and his sister grew up in the care of their mother. The sparse record left to us suggests that Catharina was an intelligent and pious woman whose devotion to her children was more than equal to the standard set by her husband.

At seven Gottfried enrolled in a prestigious Leipzig school, and—just like Bento fourteen years earlier—he immediately dazzled all with his brilliance. While his classmates were plodding through their alphabet primers, Gottfried taught himself Latin by decoding the picture captions in an illustrated edition of Livy. By the age of twelve he was fluent in Latin and "stammering" in Greek. He was able to compose verses in Latin "with so much readiness and felicity," he later wrote, that once, at the age of thirteen, he prepared a poem in three hundred perfectly rhyming hexameters on just three days' notice. When he read the work before the school assembly, his teachers apparently swooned with delight. How his fellow students felt about the matter is not known. Gottfried was not the type to make friends on the playing fields of youth. "I preferred books to games," he later explained.

Naturally, he was already deep into Aristotle. Notes he wrote at thirteen concerning the latter's philosophy of logic, he fondly recalled, "sometimes filled my teachers with astonishment. I not only applied with ease the rules of logic to examples—a feat performed by none of my schoolmates—but I also ventured to express doubts about the principles of the science and made many original suggestions which . . . were read by me in later life with no little gratification."

At fourteen the prodigy matriculated to the University of Leipzig, where he continued his intensive study of Aristotle and the scholastics. The thesis he produced at the age of seventeen, *On the Principle of Individuation*, intimates some of the central themes of his mature philosophy, and even includes the word "monadic"—a term that would play so great a role in his later work.

There can be little doubt that Gottfried's star shone just as brightly as Bento's in those early schooldays, if not more so. Yet, even in the distant and partial reflections of a mostly lost past, it is easy to see that they represented very different types of schoolboy prodigy. Bento was reserved, concerned more to conceal than to reveal his thoughts—the kind of boy wonder, perhaps, who might be overlooked but for a certain glint in the eyes and a rapierlike word let slip here or there. Gottfried, on the other hand, showed no inclination to diminish the impact of his supreme intelligence on others, neither in childhood nor later: "I invariably took the first rank in all discussions and exercises, whether public or private, as not only my teachers testified, but also the printed congratulations and *carmina* of my school-fellows."

While Bento was the kind of pupil who gives his teachers heartache, Gottfried was the kind who causes his teachers to rejoice in their choice of profession. At the University of Leipzig, Gottfried latched on to the first in a series of powerful men who would help to guide his advance through life. Jacob Thomasius was a prominent professor of philosophy whose ambition it was to revive the study of Aristotle in a manner consistent with the practice of orthodox Lutheran theology. Gottfried's letters to his mentor could well serve as models for just the kind of feedback any teacher would wish to receive from his pupils. An example:

> The "foretaste" of the history of philosophy that you have written has set all our mouths watering more than I can tell you. . . . You know that I am no flatterer. But, truly, whenever I hear

people who understand these matters speak of your work, they are unanimous in saying that there is no one from whom we can better hope for a universal history of philosophy than from you.

One can scarcely imagine how different the subsequent history of philosophy might have been had such a letter passed from Bento to Rabbi Morteira.

Leibniz spent his entire life attached to one authority figure or another. Usually it was a duke or a count; sometimes it was a queen or an emperor. It would not be ungracious to presume that he was always seeking the kind of protection that he lost when his father passed away at such a tender age; and that perhaps the occasional wavering of his moral compass in later years was attributable to the same unfortunate circumstance. In any case, his guardians almost always returned his compliments with interest. Professor Thomasius, his first great champion, declared that the young scholar was "already equal to the investigation of the most abstruse and complicated controversies."

Upon completing his first course of studies at Leipzig, Gottfried was required to choose his profession. On the advice of teachers and relatives—including among them some distinguished lawyers—he opted to pursue a degree in jurisprudence. It was a happy choice, in view of both his later career and his personal talents. He would deploy his juridical knowledge and his legalistic frame of mind not just in his political career but in his philosophical work as well. He became "God's attorney," writing legal briefs in the form of metaphysical works intended to defend his omnipresent client against charges of evildoing.

The prospective jurist, sadly, was soon called to apply his legal training in a more mundane matter. His mother died in his eighteenth year, just as he was completing his master's degree. An uncle who shared an interest in her estate promptly disputed the terms of her will, and Gottfried chose to represent himself in the ensuing legal wrangle. Unfortunately, the judicial authorities failed to see the wisdom of his arguments, and they ruled in favor of the uncle. Gottfried's relations with the maternal branch of the family dissolved in acrimony. To compound the misfortune, his sister had only a few years left to live, and from his half siblings he would always remain separated by age, geography, and interests. Gottfried, like Bento, would have become an orphan, had he not graduated into a solitary adulthood.

Forced to make his own way in the world, the young scholar focused his superabundant energy on acquiring a doctorate in jurisprudence. In preparation for the degree, he produced several treatises on legal theory, and in particular on Roman law, which were of sufficient quality and interest to be published a few years later. In order to keep the possibility of an appointment in the philosophy faculty open, he also produced a tract on *The Art of Combinations*, a remarkable piece of work that he later cited as evidence that his ideas about calculus had been germinating in his mind from a very early age. In that essay, he first mooted the cherished dream of a "universal characteristic"—a symbolic logic of such universality and perspicuity that it would someday reduce all philosophical disputes to mere mechanical calculations.

In 1666, Gottfried applied to receive his doctoral degree from the University of Leipzig. This was the moment toward which his twenty years of life had been directed, his opportunity to take a position in the local academic community befitting the son of one of its late, distinguished professors. He was confident that his pioneering work in jurisprudence and mathematics met the appropriate requirements.

His application was refused.

It was a stinging rebuff, and—in view of the groundbreaking nature of his work—grossly unjust. The fault, he later claimed, lay with some older students who, jealous of their precocious rival's early success, persuaded the faculty to suspend approvals on all applications from younger students. According to comments recorded by his faithful assistant Eckhart, however, it seems that the wife of the dean of the faculty may also have been in on the plot. For reasons unclear, she had conceived a grudge against the aspiring doctor.

The details of the episode are lost to history, but the pattern of events is one that will become all too familiar in the course of the philosopher's long life. On the one hand, Leibniz evidently possessed an easy and winning charm, as is abundantly confirmed in his fluid rise to power and by the fact that he eventually sustained fruitful relations with literally hundreds of individuals across the continent. Eck-hart says that he mingled well with people of all types and back-grounds, for he "always looked for the best in others." On the other hand, he had a peculiar talent for making enemies—a talent of which he seems to have been largely oblivious. The sneak attack at Leipzig would be far from the last time that, without the least hint of fore-shadowing, a sudden burst of hostility would overturn the happy applecart of the philosopher's life.

Faced with such a rejection from the hometown establishment, another man might have retreated into a fortress of self-sufficiency. Perhaps, in the time-honored way, he might have turned to philoso-phy as a consolation. Or, at the very least, he might have waited around a few more years and applied for his degree when the faculty judged that it was his turn. Gottfried promptly showed that he was different. On the morning after his private Waterloo, he packed his bags and set off in search of a brighter future. For the rest of his life, he would live by his wits, ransacking the world for friends and influ-ence, accumulating successes and anxieties in equal measure, more dependent on the favor of others and yet more alone than ever before, beating ceaselessly against the inevitable stream of setbacks, yet never giving up hope on winning back the love he lost in the city of his birth.

To the end of his days, he never looked back at Leipzig except in anger. Despite a travel schedule that regularly took him from one end of his native country to the other, he avoided returning to his home-town. The philosopher concealed it well, but the rage was there, dif-fused into the background of his life, registering as a permanent, unspoken complaint against the injustices of life. Eckhart notes that toward domestic servants he was "inclined to fits of passion, but quickly pacified." In a curious piece written in the third person, Leib-niz himself provides a somewhat ambivalent analysis of his personal disposition in terms of traditional medical categories of the time: "His own temperament appears to have been neither purely sanguine, choleric, phlegmatic, nor melancholic. . . . The choleric tendencies, however, seem to have the ascendancy."

• • •

ON A WINTER day in 1667, the pillars of the academic community of Nuremberg assembled in the chambers of the nearby University of Altdorf. Before the panel of esteemed professors stood a small-framed, shortsighted twenty-year-old man with awkward limbs, an all too obvious nose, and a toff of dark hair, already thinning. Only a few months had passed since the youth had matriculated from Leipzig, and yet now he had the temerity to present himself for a doctoral degree. By appearances alone, he would not have been judged a promising candidate—a fact with which the philosopher would have to grapple for the rest of his life.

In a voice "bright and clear rather than strong"—for his lungs had always been weak—the candidate began to deliver in Latin a defense of his thesis. His performance was—by his own reckoning—outstanding: "I expressed my thoughts so clearly and felicitously, that not only were the hearers astonished at this extraordinary and, especially in a jurist, unexpected degree of acuteness; but even my opponents publicly declared that they were extremely satisfied." He followed his impeccable oration with the recitation of some verses he had prepared for the occasion. When it came to the poetry, the myopic scholar had to hold his notepaper up close to his eyes, which somewhat slowed his delivery. He had already formed the habit of writing in tiny, cramped script, his nose almost touching the paper.

A pair of querulous examiners, strangely unmoved by the candidate's manifest genius, interrupted him peevishly to ask why he had not bothered to memorize the verses, as he had obviously done with the preceding discourse. Whereupon Gottfried corrected them: he had not memorized the speech, he said, but rather had delivered it entirely extemporaneously.

There followed a rather awkward public inspection of the manuscript on which the candidate's discourse had been based. After comparing the manuscript with what they remembered of the speech, all parties concurred that the young man had indeed been speaking off the top of his head in Latin as fluent as the River Tiber.

To ecstatic applause, the homely but silk-tongued scholar was anointed Doctor of Laws. Some time after the spectacle, the local minister of education approached Herr Doctor Leibniz and whispered into his ear that the honor of a professorial chair at the university was his for the asking. But Leibniz politely declined, for he had already developed much greater expectations for himself. "My thoughts were turned in an entirely different direction," he recalled.

Leibniz discovered his future with the help of a Nuremberg society of alchemists. Later in life, he gave a humorous account of how he happened to fall in with such questionable company. He had been studying the writings of some local alchemists, he said, but remained baffled by their bizarre symbols and opaque texts. So, he composed a parody of their efforts, making incomprehensible claims by means of unintelligible symbols, and forwarded it to the president of the society. The president, apparently understanding the paper not at all, drew the obvious conclusion that its author was a genius. He not only invited the budding alchemist to join the society, but also offered him a paid position as secretary, which Leibniz accepted.

The story of the nonsense paper may have been part of the philosopher's later effort to distance himself from the somewhat off-color association with alchemy. In private, however, he exhibited an avid interest in the subject throughout his life—as did many of his contemporaries, such as Isaac Newton. Indeed, he was so certain that he would one day soon discover the means to turn lead into gold that at one point he fretted that the resulting oversupply of the yellow metal might drive down the price and thus deprive him of hard-earned profits.

In Nuremberg, his ulterior motive for joining the alchemist's society soon became evident. For, it was through the group that he made the acquaintance of the man who would do more than any other to advance his career: Baron Johann Christian von Boineburg.

The former (and future) first minister to the powerful Elector of Mainz, Boineburg was a recent Catholic convert whose head teemed with so many political and religious schemes that he might well have kept European civilization busy for centuries had he managed to stay in office for more than a few years at a time. It seems that he was a gregarious man, intelligent rather than intellectual, assiduous in the care of his own finances, enthusiastic if not always well informed about his adopted religion, and unapologetically ambitious. At the very first conversation he had with the young Leibniz, over dinner in

a Nuremberg hotel, the forty-five-year-old baron took the full measure of the junior alchemist's prodigious intellectual gifts. His latest
protégé, Boineburg soon advised his colleagues, "is learned beyond all
credence," "of excellent judgment and tremendous capacity to work,"
and "full of stamina": "Being familiar with the whole history of
philosophy, he is a good mediator between the old and new systems." Leibniz, conversely, saw in the baron a golden skyhook on
the slippery pole of life. By late 1667, the pact was made, and the
twenty-one-year-old academic-cum-courtier moved to Boineburg's
hometown of Frankfurt, where he served his master as secretary,
librarian, and policy adviser.

Even before he reported for duty to Boineburg, however, Leibniz
had raised his sights to his employer's employer, the Elector of Mainz,
Johann Philipp von Schönborn. On the journey to Frankfurt, he produced a booklet, *A New Method for Learning and Teaching Jurisprudence*,
which he capped with a lavish dedication to the Elector. He later presented the text to his excellency in person, together with prescribed
gestures of self-abasement. Though penned in bumpy carriages and
on dinner tables at roadside inns without the aid of reference books,
the essay contains valuable insights concerning the practice of law at
the time along with many well-considered proposals for reform. It
was published immediately to great acclaim, and then republished
half a century later.

In Frankfurt, Leibniz's first major assignment brought him into the
world of high politics, where he would remain for the duration of his
life. The Polish king had abdicated and the matter of succession was
in dispute. The wily Boineburg plotted to install a German aspirant
on the Polish throne. He assigned Leibniz the task of writing a treatise in support of his preferred candidate. In this, the first of many
such policy papers, Leibniz demonstrated in quasi-geometrical fashion that Boineburg's man had in his favor not just the genealogical
tables but also the accumulated wisdom of the greatest philosophers
in history. The case for the Polish Succession, it seems, ran through
several dozen rigorously deduced propositions, such as "A true friend
desires his friend's good for its own sake," which Leibniz proved with
the assistance of Plato, Epicurus, and Gassendi. The same talent for
uncovering links between eternal, philosophical truths and some

rather temporal proposals would become a hallmark of the philosopher-diplomat's later style.

Leibniz agreed with his mentor that the Polish treatise would be more likely to achieve its desired effect if it were believed to be the work of someone with a less German-sounding name. So, playing with the real author's initials, they put it out under the name of Georgius Ulicovius Lithuanus. The world did not learn for several decades that the Baltic-sounding Mr. Lithuanus was in fact Leibniz; nor would it be the last time that the philosopher published his work under a false name.

The Polish paper failed to achieve its stated purpose—the Poles picked a Pole in the end—but Leibniz got something of what he wanted. Nobles such as the Prince of Durlach and the Duke of Hanover heard of the young man's political acumen and savvy, and beseeched him to take up positions in their courts. But Leibniz—his eye on the even nobler Elector of Mainz—turned them down. The young counselor seems to have had few doubts about his worth in the market for courtiers. When introduced to the Duke of Hanover, the freshly minted doctor of laws—never one to let false modesty stand in the way of helping an aristocrat in need—offered to write letters of recommendation to other nobles in support of the forty-six-year-old Duke.

Boineburg's next assignment for his protégé marked the beginning of Leibniz's lifelong involvement in church politics. As a recent Catholic convert, Boineburg found himself ensnared by Protestant theologians in doctrinal controversies that he was ill equipped to understand. Naturally, he asked his able deputy to enter theological combat on his behalf. Leibniz obliged. "In the confusion of an inn," once again, the itinerant man of letters sat down with paper and plume and drafted an incomplete set of essays under the rubric of *Catholic Demonstrations*, in which he defended such typically Catholic doctrines as transubstantiation, the trinity, the resurrection, the incarnation, and the immortality of the soul against attacks from wayward philosophers and theologians.

In 1670, the Elector of Mainz finally invited Boineburg back into his court, and appointed Leibniz privy counselor of justice. Only twenty-four years old, Leibniz now occupied one of the highest civil ranks in one of the most powerful principalities in Germany. He had become the ultimate insider, the very antithesis of a double exile. In Mainz he took up lodgings in the home of a fellow courtier and immediately implicated himself in the most important political issues of the day.

The chief problem of Germany at the time was France. The fragmentation that followed the Thirty Years War had left Germany woefully exposed on its western front, and Louis XIV had shown no inclination to overlook the weakness. The Germans were convinced that the Sun King's diabolical plan was to gobble up their territory and declare himself master of all of Europe. That summer, the Elector of Mainz and his top advisers convened a meeting to discuss the French menace with the Elector of Triers and the Duke of Lorraine in the spa town of Bad Schwalbach.

The Duke of Lorraine argued that the Germans should join the Triple Alliance of England, Holland, and Sweden in order to fend off the ravenous French. But Leibniz, on behalf of Boineburg and the Elector of Mainz, produced a pamphlet in support of a different plan. Joining the Triple Alliance, he declaimed, would needlessly antagonize France, and might bring about precisely the invasion that was feared. Instead, the Germans should maintain a friendly face toward their nemesis. At the same time, while taking care to avoid raising Louis XIV's suspicions, the assembled princes should band together in a league and raise a standing army of 20,000 men to defend against possible attack. It was a bold and cunning plan and, in view of the later history of Germany, perhaps two centuries ahead of its time.

Unfortunately, the meeting ended without agreement, and the princes neither joined the Triple Alliance nor formed a German league. Within weeks, Louis XIV delivered his verdict on the matter. He sent an army of 20,000 of his own men on a rampage through the Lorraine. Back in Mainz, Leibniz fretted that the squabbling princes and bishops of Germany might never unite to achieve the goal of peace and prosperity under a single church. His homeland, he feared, "rejoiced in a freedom that was soon to be destroyed."

On a sunny autumn day in 1671, the youthful privy counselor of justice idled on the deck of a ferry on the Rhine. He was returning from a visit to Strassburg, where he had carried out an errand on behalf of Boineburg's son. As he gazed at the verdant banks of his nation's most symbolic river, he later wrote, it seemed to him that "the very hills skipped like lambs for delight . . . and the nymphs of the Black Forest danced joyfully their airy dances." To the sound of water lapping on the side of the riverboat, the elegantly dressed courtier turned over in his mind a most improbable plan, one that would solve all the problems left behind by the war that had ended just as he was born. It was a vision that had been maturing in his brain for several years. It involved Louis XIV, the entire French Army, and a new crusade. It would satisfy Germany's craving for security, it would unite the rest of Europe, and it would set the stage for a splendid reprise of medieval civilization. He called it the Egypt Plan.

LEIBNIZ WAS A great believer in plans. He should perhaps count as one of history's greatest multitaskers, a master of solving any number of problems at a single stroke. The resilience, energy, and almost untethered optimism he demonstrated in his youthful political schemes would stay with him for life. But the problem with which all of his plans in some way or other remained always connected was the problem of Leibniz himself—a problem that perhaps first came into focus in his twenty-first year, in the wake of his stunning defeat at the University in Leipzig.

With Leibniz, just as with Spinoza, the youthful experience of rejection marked a crucial test of character. Earlier than is perhaps usually the case, he was forced to ask himself: How can life be so unfair? In his later work, the same question would be transfigured into the one to which all of his philosophical labors were consecrated: Why is there evil? And all of the many answers Leibniz provided later in life were in some sense just iterations of the response he offered on that morning in Leipzig. Rather than walk away gladly into the wilderness—as Spinoza did, in a manner of speaking—he threw himself back at the mercy of society with an even greater desperation to succeed. In failing to win approval, he only tried harder to please. In discovering evil, he only worked harder to show that it was all part of the plan.

From the vantage point of a wizened twenty-five-year-old, Leibniz looked back on his decision to leave Leipzig and justified it thus: "I believed it unworthy of a young man to remain fixed in one place like a stake in the ground, and my spirit burned with the desire to win great fame in the sciences and to see the world." But his restlessness was more than a young man's passing wanderlust. Throughout his life, Leibniz was a man on the move, his existence tied to no one point on the planet. The yen to explore, the reckless curiosity, the conviction that any living arrangement is just a way station to someplace better, and the ability to find happiness only in ceaseless activity became part of his very way of being in the world. "The human mind cannot rest," he wrote around the time of his voyage down the Rhine. "To be motionless, that is, without movement toward further perception, is to torment the mind." In his mature philosophy, he would explicitly identify the principle of activity in all things with the soul itself.

There was something remarkable in Leibniz's kinetic philosophy of life, an uncorked passion for knowledge and experience worthy of admiration and imitation; but, on more than one occasion, it would raise the suspicion that all this movement was an exuberant froth without substance; that the man from everywhere was really from nowhere at all; that he was just running away from himself, always planning for tomorrow in order to flee from today, desperately seeking shelter from the present on the road between an imaginary future and a reconstructed past.

The craving for affirmation and longing for security that Leibniz evinced as a young man only grew more insistent as he met with ever louder approbation in his grand tour of the universe. When it came to loving Leibniz, as far as Leibniz was concerned, enough was never enough. It was this insatiable and very human—perhaps all too human—*neediness* that ultimately came to define his philosophy, and that made it so representative for the rest of the species. And it was this same neediness that would determine the nature of the reception he received from and his subsequent reaction to the man he met in The Hague in November 1676.

4

A Life of the Mind

S ome philosophers merely *argue* their philosophies. When they finish their disputations, they hang up the tools of their trade, go home, and indulge in the well-earned pleasures of private life. Other philosophers *live* their philosophies. They treat as useless any philosophy that does not determine the manner in which they spend their days, and they consider pointless any part of life that has no philosophy in it. They never go home.

Spinoza belonged unambiguously to the latter group. When he crossed the bridge over the Houtgracht in 1656, he consecrated his entire life to philosophy. Not since the days when Socrates stalked the agora in order to alert his fellows that the unexamined life is not worth living, and when Diogenes took up residence in a barrel in order to make a somewhat different point about the nature of the good life, had the world seen a philosopher so dedicated to his quest as Spinoza.

The five years following his traumatic expulsion from the Jewish community are sometimes called "the dark period" of Spinoza's life—a label that refers to the quality of our knowledge rather than the state of his mind. The most likely story is that the renegade philosopher moved to a house somewhere on the outskirts of Amsterdam, although some evidence—such as a reference by an English visitor in 1661 to a certain "Jew who is an impudent atheist"—suggests that he left quite an impression in the city itself.

Notwithstanding the biographical uncertainties, there is a remarkable piece of semi-autobiographical philosophy that sheds much light on this shadowy period of Spinoza's life. *The Treatise on the Emendation of the Intellect*, which most likely dates from the year or two following his excommunication, records Spinoza's first attempt to explain and justify his choice of life. It presents the "philosophy of philosophy," as it were, that would guide him through the rest of his days.

It opens with an intimate confession:

> After experience had taught me that all the things which regularly occur in ordinary life are vain and futile; seeing that none of the objects of my fears contained in themselves anything either good or bad, except insofar as the mind is affected by them, I resolved at last to find out whether there was anything which would be the true good, which would affect the mind singularly, to the exclusion of all else: whether there was something which, once found and acquired, would give me continuous, supreme, and everlasting happiness.

For Spinoza, philosophy originates in the very personal experience of a sense of the futility of ordinary life—a feeling of emptiness that in the philosophical tradition has earned the distinguished name of *contemptu mundi*, the contempt for worldly things, or, better, *vanitas*. The indictment of everyday existence here extends beyond the misfortunes and adversities of life and includes even the so-called good things in life. Spinoza says that the goods things are not good enough—that success in life is just the postponement of failure; that pleasure is just a fleeting respite from pain; and that, in general, the objects of our striving are vain illusions.

Of sensual pleasure, for example, the philosopher says: "The mind is so caught up in it . . . that it is quite prevented from thinking about anything else. But after the enjoyment of sensual pleasure is past, the greatest sadness follows." Equally futile, he reasons, is the craving for fame that dominates so many lives: "Honor has this great disadvantage, that to pursue it, we must direct our lives according to other men's power of understanding." As for money: "There are many examples of men who have suffered persecution even to death for the sake of their riches."

The feeling of *vanitas* Spinoza describes is not just a fleeting sense of dissatisfaction. It goes well beyond the sort of postcoital depression to which he seems to allude above or the melancholy thoughts that often follow when we at last get what we claim we always wanted. *Vanitas* rises to philosophy when it becomes intolerable—when one feels in one's bones, as Spinoza did, that one is "suffering from a fatal illness . . . foreseeing certain death unless he employs a remedy." It is a dire encounter with the prospect of a descent into absolute nothingness, a life without significance coming to a meaningless end.

The experience Spinoza records in his early treatise establishes a new and much more interesting sense for the label "the dark period" of his life. It is an experience very much akin to that which, in traditional spiritual narratives, is called "the dark night of the soul"—the moment of extreme doubt, fear, and uncertainty that precedes the dawn of revelation. Indeed, the journey through the void that Spinoza recounts is one trodden by poets, philosophers, and theologians too numerous to mention, who for millennia have recorded this feeling that life is a useless passion, a wheel of ceaseless striving, a tale told by an idiot, full of sound and fury, signifying nothing, and so on. But the sentiment is not universal; it does not attain prominence in the work of Leibniz, to name one example.

In Spinoza's case, the feeling of *vanitas* apparently lingered for a lengthy period in his mind before he chose to act upon it. "For although I perceived these things so clearly in my mind," he writes, "I still could not, on that account, put aside all greed, desire for sensual pleasure, and love of esteem." That Spinoza ever led a genuinely debauched life of lust and lucre is doubtful; and one must bear in mind his treatise is a stylized work, intended to connote a familiar internal experience more than to record a life history. But it is likely that he refers here to the period in his life just before the excommunication, when he pursued a career in international trade and was at least nominally an upstanding member of his community of birth.

The philosophy that originates in *vanitas*, Spinoza makes clear, aims directly for its opposite: "supreme, continuous, and everlasting happiness." This is no ordinary, soft-focus kind of contentment. It is as extreme as the dread from which it arises, and Spinoza defines it in terms taken from traditional religious experience: "blessedness" or "salvation." Philosophy, as Spinoza understands it, does not peddle in temporary cheer, modest improvements in well-being, or chicken soup for the soul; it seeks and claims to find a basis for happiness that is absolutely certain, permanent, and divine. The principal—indeed, the sole—purpose of his mature philosophy, as expressed in his masterwork, the *Ethics*, is to achieve this kind of blessedness or salvation.

Having established the archetypal condition of absolute darkness from which much of philosophy originates and the archetypal goal of unbounded blessedness for which it strives, Spinoza next commits himself to the archetypal means with which philosophy proposes to achieve its end, namely, the life of the mind—that is, the pursuit of wisdom in a life of contemplation. This is the point at which the philosophers and the theologians traditionally part ways. Whereas religious thinkers ultimately find sanctuary in the absolute certainty of revealed truth—passed on by word of mouth from God to us, via the scriptures and their interpreters—philosophers such as Spinoza take for granted that absolute certainty can come only from one's own internal resources. The philosophers further eliminate the possibility of achieving this kind of certainty through the experience of things in the physical world, for such things by their nature always come and go. That which is indubitable, insist Spinoza and his ancient brethren, must lie on the "inside," which is to say, in the *mind*. Like Socrates, Spinoza avers that blessedness comes only from a certain kind of *knowledge*—specifically, the "knowledge of the union that the mind has with the whole of Nature."

In his early treatise, Spinoza articulates a further, final element of the archetypal philosophical project: that the life of contemplation is also a life within a certain type of community—specifically, a fellowship of the mind. Like Socrates with his circle of debating partners, or Epicurus in his garden with his intellectual companions, Spinoza imagines a philosophical future in which he and other individuals of reason nourish their wisdom through ongoing, mutually enlightening dialogue. In fact, upon achieving blessedness for himself, he announces in his first treatise, his first step will be "to form a society of the kind that is desirable, so that as many as possible may attain it as easily and as surely as possible." For, "the highest good," he claims, is to achieve salvation together with other individuals "if possible."

Even as one consecrates one's life to the pursuit of continuous, supreme, and everlasting happiness, of course, as Spinoza himself points out, "it is necessary to live." He therefore rounds out the introductory sections of his *Treatise on the Emendation of the Intellect* with three proposed "rules of living," intended to serve as a practical guide to life for himself and his fellow philosophers. The first rule of living is, in brief, to *get along* with the rest of humanity. That is, fellow seekers should follow the accepted social customs and behave amicably with ordinary people and otherwise avoid trouble that might jeopardize the overriding mission of attaining philosophical blessedness. The second rule is that one should enjoy sensual pleasures to the extent that they are required to safeguard health and thereby serve the all-important end of leading a life of the mind. The third rule is that one should seek money and other worldly goods just so far as is necessary to maintain life and health—again, for the purpose of maintaining a vigorous mind.

In the summer of 1661, Spinoza emerged from his dark night of the soul and took up residence in a rented room in a small cottage on the outskirts of the village of Rijnsburg, about six miles west of the university town of Leiden and thirty miles south of Amsterdam. Sixteen years of life remained to be lived. All the evidence suggests that the philosopher adhered rigorously to the rules he enunciated in his first treatise.

IN HIS *ETHICS*, even more than in his earlier *Treatise*, Spinoza piles on his contempt for money and the kind of people who covet it. "The masses can scarcely imagine any kind of pleasure without the accompanying idea of money as its cause," he scowls. "Those who know the true value of money set the limit of their wealth solely according to their needs, and live content with little."

He practiced what he preached. In his choice of accommodations, for example, the philosopher showed complete indifference to the value of good real estate. In Rijnsburg from 1661 to 1663, in Voorburg from 1663 to 1670, and in The Hague from 1670 to 1677, he always boarded in small rented rooms in other people's houses on the less expensive side of the canals.

When it came to feeding the body, too, the philosopher kept to a rather austere economy. Colerus, who had the opportunity to peruse some of his receipts, reports that on one day he ate only "gruel made with raisins and butter." On another day he survived entirely on "milk soup with butter" washed down with "a pot of beer." (Beer was like water in those days—that is to say, it was watery, and it was much safer to drink than the stuff they pumped out of the brackish wells. Georg Hermann Schuller, Leibniz's friend and liaison in Holland, incidentally, is on record as having sent Spinoza a keg of beer as a gift.) The philosopher's wine consumption peaked at "only" two and a half pints of wine in the course of one month. "It is scarce credible how sober and frugal he was all the time," Colerus concludes. His one indulgence was tobacco, which he consumed avidly from a pipe.

His enthusiasm for sartorial fashions seems to have been no less restrained than that for the pleasures of the palate. Colerus says that his wardrobe was "plain and common" and that "he paid no heed to his dress." Lucas is perhaps more credible when he insists that Spinoza was modest but not careless in his appearance: there was something about his clothes "which usually distinguishes a gentleman from a pedant," he says, adding that the philosopher maintained that "the affectation of negligence is the mark of an inferior mind." The inventory taken after the philosopher's death seems to confirm Lucas's account: Spinoza's wardrobe was small and efficient (the two pairs of trousers and seven shirts suggest a rigorous schedule for laundry); but some of it, at least, was of fine quality (e.g., his shoe buckles were silver).

Nor was the philosopher much of a saver. "My relatives shall inherit nothing from me, just as they have left me nothing," he once claimed.

Upon his death, his sister Rebecca—who very likely had not seen her brother for twenty years—swooped down to The Hague just to be sure. True to his word, he left behind an estate of so little value that, after the funeral expenses were paid and other debts settled, there was nothing left over for greedy relatives. Rebecca hastily withdrew her claim for fear that she might actually lose money in the bargain.

Of course, according to the rules of the early treatise, a philosopher must acquire at least enough money to survive in good health. During his dark period, therefore, Spinoza learned a trade: lens making. In the late seventeenth century, the fabrication of lenses for telescopes and microscopes was an art more than a craft. The lens maker began by placing a slab of glass on a foot-powered lathe. Then, feet pumping, he applied an abrasive cloth to the spinning slab, sending glass dust billowing into the room, coating the machine, the floor, his clothes, and his lungs. After shaving the lens down to within fractions of a millimeter of a precisely specified curve, he vigorously buffed the rough surface in order to achieve a transparent finish. The process required patience, meticulous attention to detail, and a taste for solitary work. It was perhaps ideally suited to Spinoza's skills, temperament, and economic needs. Sadly, the constant exposure to glass dust very likely aggravated the chronic lung disease that would eventually claim his life.

By all accounts, Spinoza was a superb lens maker. Leibniz himself referred several times to the Dutchman's "fame" in the field of optics. Christiaan Huygens, an expert in the field himself, wrote to his brother that "the Israelite achieves an admirable polish." The lenses found among Spinoza's possessions after his death sold at high values in the auction of his estate.

As he grew older, Spinoza possibly came to rely more on another source of income: the charity of philosophical friends and admirers. The most generous benefactor was Simon de Vries, the scion of a merchant family and the philosopher's friend from his days as a trader in Amsterdam. De Vries died young in 1667, and in his will he provided for an annuity to the philosopher in the amount of 500 guilders. Spinoza refused to accept so large an amount, for, according to Lucas and Colerus, he did not wish to be seen as dependent on the largesse of another man. Instead, he insisted on reducing the grant to 300 guilders per year (or 250, depending on the source). Whether he collected the amount every year thereafter is not altogether certain; Leibniz in 1676 formed the impression that Spinoza's patron was the merchant Jarig Jelles, a friend of the philosopher from his Amsterdam years.

In a curious letter to Jelles, Spinoza uses a story about Thales of Miletus to illustrate his own attitude toward money. Fed up with being reproached for poverty by his friends, it seems, the ancient philosopher one day used his superior meteorological knowledge to make a killing in the market for olive presses. Then, his point proved, he donated all of the profits to good causes. The moral of the story is that "it is not out of necessity but out of choice that the wise possess no riches." There can be no doubt that Spinoza, like Thales, had little concern for money. But it should not be overlooked that, as the very fact that he wrote this letter suggests, he was quite concerned to make sure that others were well aware of his lack of concern.

HAVING LEARNED TO live with little money, Spinoza may have managed to get by with no love at all. According to the story handed down by Colerus, the young philosopher conceived of an amorous passion for his tutor in Latin, Clara Maria, the eldest daughter of Frans van den Enden. Smitten by the sprightly yet malformed lass, says the biographer, Spinoza declared many times that he intended to marry her.

Alas, a rival soon darkened the philosopher's star of love. Thomas Kerkering, a native of Hamburg and Spinoza's fellow student at the van den Enden school, also succumbed to Clara Maria's peculiar charms. The young German apparently knew better than the philosopher how to play the game of love. He courted the nubile Latinist assiduously, amply proving his ardor with the gift of a pearl necklace of great value. Clara Maria gave her heart and her hand—and, one presumes, her neck—to Kerkering, while Spinoza was left to taste the bitter fruit of rejection.

The story is perfectly plausible, but far from confirmed. Clara Maria was in fact Spinoza's Latin tutor, and she did marry a man named Thomas Kerkering, who was a pupil in the van den Enden school. The marriage took place in 1671, however, and the bride was listed as twenty-seven years old at the time—which would make her twelve to fourteen in the years when Spinoza, then in his early twenties, lived under the family roof. It is possible, of course, that Clara Maria lied about her age on the event of her wedding; but it would be unwise to discount the possibility that Spinoza's first chroniclers, having raised their eyebrows over the unseemly fact that his tutor in Latin was a girl, relied on their imaginations to supply the rest of the story of his unrequited love.

In any case, whether or not Spinoza's interest in Clara Maria went beyond her formidable Latin skills, the fact remains that his life story offers nothing but a thwarted and possibly fictional student affair in the way of romance or carnal love. Some modern interpreters take Spinoza's abject refusal to provide entertaining material for future filmmakers as proof that he was a misogynist, homosexual, or both, and that his philosophy therefore represents a hyperrationalistic refuge from the demands of sexuality. However, there is no meaningful evidence in support of any such claims.

More to the point, Spinoza's failure to marry or at least tell us more about his sex life seems to have no very deep connection with his philosophical program. In the *Ethics* he declares that marriage is "in harmony with reason." Lucas confirms that "our philosopher was not one of those austere people who look upon marriage as a hindrance to the activities of the mind." If he decided to forgo the charms of Clara Maria or any other possible love object, it was presumably because he did not view such relations as the best way to advance his own life of the mind. It should also be pointed out that his choice of a low-income lifestyle, his chronic illness, and his unenviable social status as an apostate Jew would hardly have made him an appealing prospect for the girls of Holland.

More generally, the position Spinoza takes in his philosophical works toward sensual pleasure is not at all that of a traditional ascetic. Far from denying the value of pleasure, sexual or otherwise, he comes closer to advocating its maximization. In the *Ethics*, for example, he writes:

... it is part of the wise man to recreate and refresh himself with pleasant food and drink, and also with perfumes, with the soft beauty of growing plants, with dress, with music, with many sports, with theatres, and the like, such as every man may make use of without injury to his neighbor. For the human body is composed of numerous parts of diverse nature, which continually stand in need of fresh and varied nourishment, so that the whole body may be equally capable of performing all the actions which follow of necessity from its own nature; and consequently, so that the mind may also be equally capable of understanding many things simultaneously.

Here Spinoza seems positively hedonistic in his celebratory list of sensual goodies—until, that is, one gets to the end of the passage. For the central point, as in the earlier *Treatise*, is that sensual pleasure is all well and good—but its only real purpose is to contribute to the all-important project of sustaining the mind for a life of contemplation. A few pages later, Spinoza makes the point explicitly: "Things are good only insofar as they assist a man to enjoy the life of the mind."

There is in Spinoza's thought on this point an illuminating paradox—one that ultimately sheds light more on questions of philosophy than biography. On the one hand, there can be no doubt that Spinoza lived a "life of the mind." Dress, music, sports, and carnal love always took a backseat to his "studies" (specifically, his "late-night studies," as he puts it in a letter to de Vries, for his lens-grinding activities occupied the daylight hours). Like so many philosophers before and after, he seemed to exhibit a certain alienation from the hurly-burly of ordinary life, a detachment from the body, a degree of otherworldliness. Following Plato, one might be tempted to say that he lived in the world of ideas—a world that exists outside the cave within which ordinary experience takes place. If his domestic arrangements were ever to be reviewed in a contemporary lifestyle journal, we can be sure that they would be described as "spiritual."

On the other hand, in the philosophical system that emerged from those candlelit nights, there is no space for an "other" world. There are no spirits, and there is no "mind"; there is nothing outside the cave. Everything that we take to be a mental operation, in Spinoza's considered view, has its basis in a material process, and all of our decisions are rooted in our desires. Indeed, with his claim that "desire is the essence of man," he articulates the foundations of the very conceptual framework that latter-day therapists, among others, might use to analyze his lifestyle as "repressed." The paradox with which modern interpreters must grapple, as it turns out, is the same one that would bedevil Leibniz. How can one who denies the very existence of the mind lead a life of the mind? Or, as the contemporary magazine reader might ask, can a materialist be spiritual?

PERHAPS THE MOST complex and fraught aspect of the "rules for living" that Spinoza adopted as a young excommunicant was that which concerned his dealings with other people—with society in general and, above all, with those friends he took to be his fellow philosophers.

At first glance, Spinoza appears to be a philosopher in the mold of Heraclitus, the ancient sage who retreated to a mountaintop so that he could escape the contaminating presence of his fellow human beings. Lucas says Spinoza moved to Rijnsburg for "love of solitude," and that when two years later he decamped to Voorburg, he "buried himself still deeper in solitude." Jarig Jelles, in the preface to the philosopher's posthumous works, recounts that "once he did not go outside his lodgings during three whole months." Even when stepping out, adds Lucas, the philosopher "never quitted his solitude except to return to it soon afterwards." A visiting counselor to the Duke of Holstein named Greiffencrantz (who, no surprise, was also a correspondent of Leibniz) reported that Spinoza "seemed to live all to himself, always lonely, as if buried in his study."

But a closer look at Spinoza's life reveals a different side of his social character, something much more akin to the gregarious and humane disposition of Epicurus, the ancient guru who cultivated a tranquil garden for the specific purpose of entertaining his fellow philosophers. Spinoza retreated to Rijnsburg not because he had no friends, but, as Lucas points out, because he had too many. And, even in the safety of his cottage, writes the biographer, "his most intimate friends went to see him from time to time and only left him again with great reluctance." Likewise, although Spinoza reportedly moved to Voorburg to escape his friends again, those friends "did not take long to find him again and to overwhelm him with their visits." Colerus, too, says that Spinoza had "a great many friends . . . some in the military, others of high position and eminence." In The Hague, it was said that the philosopher received attentions even from "*filles de qualité*, who prided themselves on having a superior mind for their sex." It is also not the case that Spinoza's friends were always the ones making the effort; in several of the extant letters, the philosopher mentions trips planned or made to Amsterdam, where presumably he sought the company of his friends.

Nor was Spinoza lacking in social skills. Colerus says that many persons of distinction "took a great delight in hearing him discourse." The most endearing portrait, not surprisingly, comes from his admirer Lucas:

> His conversations had such an air of geniality and his comparisons were so just that he made everybody fall in unconsciously with his views. He was persuasive although he did not affect polished or elegant diction. He made himself so intelligible, and his discourse was so full of good sense, that none listened to him without deriving satisfaction. . . . He had a great penetrating mind and a complacent disposition. He knew so well how to season his wit that the most gentle and the most severe found very peculiar charms in it.

The apparent tension between the Heraclitean and Epicurean sides of Spinoza's character is one that has trailed philosophers since ancient times. On the one hand, philosophy by its nature seems to be an essentially solitary activity. It is the individual's lonely voyage of discovery through the eternal truths of the cosmos—a journey that would seem to place the seeker at ever greater removes of knowledge and abstraction from the rest of humankind. On the other hand, in practice, philosophy is a very social activity. It involves dialogues, debates, competition for recognition, and the dissemination of wisdom to the ever needy human race.

Spinoza's own writings embody something of this ancient paradox

about philosophy. On the one hand, his works read like the monologue of a solitary traveler into the heart of things. He disdains references as pointless; philosophy, he implies, does not concern itself with
the error of others. On the other hand, his works are soaked in higher
learning. Provided one knows where to look, one can find in them a
raucous conversation with a whole society of earlier thinkers, from
the ancient Stoics to Maimonides and Descartes.

In his dealings with living people, too, Spinoza practiced a similarly
ambivalent sociability. He distinguished firmly between ordinary
humankind and the "fellowship of reason." With the multitudes, he
proposed, one should be Heraclitean. One must keep them at a
respectful distance, as one might an unruly herd of buffalo. Specifically, one should not to seek to share with them philosophical views
that they will not understand and may only cause them harm. "The
free man who lives among the ignorant strives as far as he can to
avoid receiving favors from them," he counsels. When he disdains the
pursuit of honor as a form of slavery to "the opinions of other men,"
as he does in his earliest *Treatise*, the "other men" Spinoza has in mind
are ordinary, ignorant members of the species at large.

In the presence of fellow philosophers, on the other hand, one may
allow oneself to be positively Epicurean. One should join with such
individuals in order to form a common front in the search for truth
and virtue, for "there is nothing in nature more useful to man than a
man who lives by the guidance of reason." He adds: "Man is a God
to Man"—on the assumption, of course, that the other Man in question is a philosopher, too. One should embrace one's fellow thinkers,
then, as one might a fellow God. Among men of reason, "honor" is
as noble as its name. In the *Ethics*, in curious juxtaposition with the
attitude expressed in the earlier *Treatise*, he defines "honor" as "the
desire to establish friendship with others, a desire that characterizes
the man who lives by the guidance of reason"; and he defines "honorable" as that which "is praised by men who live by the guidance of
reason."

Spinoza's policy with respect to the masses, at least, seemed to
work. Even the relentlessly hostile Pierre Bayle, famous for his ency-
clopedic *Dictionnaire historique et critique*, reports that the villagers

where Spinoza lived invariably considered him "a man good to associate with, affable, honest, polite, and very proper in his morals." The
philosopher's relations with his landlord in The Hague, Hendrik van
der Spyck, and the man's family, provide the most touching example
of his success in mixing with the great unwashed. When he needed
to take a break from his philosophical labors, it seems, the apostate
Jew would descend to the parlor and chat with his house companions about current affairs and other trivia. The conversations often
revolved around the local minister's most recent sermon. On occasion
the notorious iconoclast even attended church service in order to
better participate in the discussions.

Once, Ida Margarete, Hendrik's wife, asked Spinoza whether he
thought that her religion served no purpose. "Your religion is all
right," he replied. "You needn't look for another one in order to be
saved, if you give yourself to a quiet and pious life."

Spinoza's quest for honor among his fellow men of reason, not surprisingly, proved far harder to manage within the confines of his
stated policy. In fact, his life affords a rich field of study in the complex topic of philosophical communion, and perhaps serves best to
demonstrate how difficult it is to extricate even the most rarefied
philosophical partnerships from the instinctive, imaginative, and often
debilitating bonds of ordinary friendship.

Perhaps the closest Spinoza came to his ideal of philosophical
community was with his early merchant friends, who formed a loose
band of radical seekers united in their disdain for orthodox religion
as well as in their esteem for their master's works. A taste of life as an
early Spinozist comes from this letter from Simon de Vries, the
philosopher's great benefactor:

> As for our group, our procedure is as follows. One member
> (each has his turn) does the reading, explains how he under-
> stands it, and goes on to a complete demonstration, following
> the sequence and order of your propositions. Then, if it should
> happen that we cannot satisfy one another, we have deemed it
> worthwhile to make a note of it and to write to you so that, if
> possible, it should be made clearer to us and we may, under your

guidance, uphold the truth against those who are religious and Christian in a superstitious way, and may stand firm against the onslaught of the whole world.

Evidently, there was an underground sensibility to the movement. One pictures de Vries and company drawing the curtains, lighting the candles, and then poring over the manuscripts from their hermit rebel leader, reveling all the while in their vaguely illicit freedoms. Even so, in de Vries's reference to "those who are . . . Christian in a superstitious way" one may espy an awkward glimmer of daylight between the master and his followers. Most of Spinoza's sympathizers were members of liberal Protestant sects—of which there was no shortage in number and variety in the Dutch Republic at the time. They often interpreted his views in highly religious terms, making little distinction between "the guidance of reason" and the "inner light" of radical Protestantism. Spinoza showed considerable sympathy for some aspects of Christianity, and even suggested that Jesus was perhaps the greatest philosopher who ever lived; but he never called himself a Christian.

The case of Willem van Blijenburgh offers a quite different and highly cautionary example of the consequences of mistaken identity among alleged men of reason. Blijenburgh, a grain merchant at Dordrecht, first wrote to Spinoza in December 1664 as a stranger, having chanced upon a copy of his book on the philosophy of Descartes. In his first letter, the grain merchant politely asks the philosopher to comment on the matter of whether God is the cause of evil in the world. From what he had gathered of Spinoza's philosophy, he says, he had stumbled upon an obscurity in his thought: "Either Adam's forbidden act, insofar as God not only moved his will but also insofar as he moved it in a particular way, is not evil in itself, or else God himself seems to bring about what we call evil."

Spinoza's reply is courteous and informative, clearly inviting future correspondence: "I gather . . . that you are deeply devoted to truth, which you make the sole aim of all your endeavors. Since I have exactly the same objective, this has determined me not only to grant without stint your request . . . but also to do everything in power con-

ducive to further acquaintance and sincere friendship." It seems that
Spinoza assumed that one who claimed to have read his book on
Descartes and who then approached him with a philosophical ques-
tion was, by definition, a fellow man of reason.

The philosopher should perhaps not be faulted for being unaware
that Blijenburgh had already published a short book whose long title
begins: *The Knowledge of God and His Worship Affirmed Against the Out-
rages of the Atheists*. But one is entitled to wonder how he could not
have perceived that Blijenburgh's question about evil—phrased with
copious references to Adam and his apple—was motivated by some
highly orthodox theological concerns.

In his next letter, in any case, the man from Dordrecht puts forward what in Spinoza's mind could only count as a whopper. In the
midst of an otherwise interesting discussion of the problem of evil,
Blijenburgh asserts that Spinoza's views cannot be entirely correct
because they contradict the Bible.

Spinoza now understands that his grain merchant is not in fact a
man of reason. In his reply he bluntly suggests that they part ways: "I
hardly believe that our correspondence can be for our mutual
instruction. For I see that no proof, however, firmly established
according to the rules of logic, has any validity with you unless it
agrees with the . . . Holy Scripture." The black-and-white character
of Spinoza's first two letters to Blijenburgh—in the first, his correspondent is "deeply devoted to truth," while in the second he is
essentially a waste of time—illustrates how firm in Spinoza's mind
was the dichotomy between "men of reason" and the rest of humanity. In this case, though, Spinoza evidently could not resist getting in
the last word with his putatively unreasonable interlocutor. After
indicating that there is no point to further correspondence, he goes
on for several pages clarifying his views and defending them from
Blijenburgh's criticisms.

But Blijenburgh was like a wart, more easily acquired than
removed. In his next letter, he complains that Spinoza's missive is
"besprinkled with sharp reproofs" and proposes that the two meet
when business takes him next in the vicinity of Voorburg. Spinoza
responds politely to the proposal, although he perhaps hints at some

impatience when he insists that any meeting would have to take place soon, before he travels to Amsterdam.

From Blijenburgh's subsequent letter, it is evident that the dreaded meeting took place, for the grain merchant regrets that "when I had the honor of visiting you, time did not allow me to stay longer with you." He then poses a series of questions whose answers, as Spinoza could see, would have required him to divulge the entire contents of his unpublished *Ethics*.

At this point, Spinoza decided that enough was enough. Presumably, the meeting only confirmed what the philosopher had suspected, that the grain merchant was emphatically not a member of the fellowship of reason. Spinoza let the matter languish for two months, then grudgingly penned the philosophical equivalent of a Dear John letter: "I hope that when you have thought the matter over you will willingly desist from your request," he signs off. There the correspondence ends.

But Blijenburgh just would not go away. Nine years later, following the publication of Spinoza's *Tractatus Theologico-Politicus*, the man from Dordrecht published a five-hundred-page wrath-filled tract, the short version of whose title reads: *The Truth of the Christian Religion and the Authority of the Holy Scripture Affirmed Against the Arguments of the Impious, or a Refutation of the Blasphemous Book Titled "Tractatus Theologico-Politicus."* In that screed, Blijenburgh finds several hundred ways to express his singular conviction that his former host's work is "a book full of studious abominations and an accumulation of opinions which have been forged in hell."

Nine years and five hundred pages are big numbers in the context of a philosophical grudge. Yet such was the nature of the response Spinoza evoked among his contemporaries in more than just this instance. There was something about the way he interacted with those he deemed his philosophical inferiors—a look of contemptuous indifference? a sneer?—that they could not erase from memory; something that affected Rabbi Morteira and the philosopher's young friends from the synagogue; and something that might prove relevant in considering the effect that Spinoza would have on Leibniz.

The most poignant of Spinoza's unexpectedly troublesome

encounters with men of reason involved the man who supplied the first link in the chain of events that ultimately led to his encounter with Leibniz. Henry Oldenburg, twelve years Spinoza's senior, was a native of Bremen, Germany. After he became the secretary of the Royal Society of London in 1661, he corresponded with almost every major scientist and thinker in Europe at the time. When he eventually began publishing his far-flung correspondence under the title of *Philosophical Transactions*, he effectively invented the modern scientific journal. He was a great communicator and liberal spirit, at least in his younger years, and thirsty for scientific knowledge. No one regarded him as an original thinker in his own right, however, and he was quite conventional in his religious views.

In 1661, on his way to take up his new post in London, Oldenburg passed through the university town of Leiden. Sources there told him of the philosophical prodigy living in nearby Rijnsburg. The twenty-eight-year-old Spinoza, incidentally, had published nothing at the time; Oldenburg's decision to travel the extra six miles to visit him testifies to the youthful philosopher's powerful charisma—and perhaps serves to remind us how different the world was then.

On a summer day, the two men met in the dappled sunlight of the tranquil garden outside Spinoza's cottage. For several hours they conversed "about God, about infinite Extension and Thought, and about the union of soul and body." The humble sage of Rijnsburg mesmerized the expatriate German scholar. In the first of his many letters to Spinoza, Oldenburg writes:

> With such reluctance did I recently tear myself away from your side when visiting you at your retreat in Rijnsburg, that no sooner am I back in England than I am endeavoring to join you again. Substantial learning, combined with humanity and courtesy—all of which nature and diligence have so amply bestowed upon you—hold such an allurement as to gain the affection of any men of quality and of liberal education.

In a sign of misunderstandings to come, however, he adds, "We then spoke about such important topics as through a lattice window and

only in a cursory way." In this and subsequent letters, he asks Spinoza
to clarify his views on God and the like. He also repeatedly encourages
the philosopher to publish his work: "I would by all means urge you
not to begrudge scholars the learned fruits of your acute understanding both in philosophy and theology"; "I urge you by our bond of
friendship, by all the duties we have to promote and disseminate truth."

In his replies to Oldenburg, Spinoza dutifully elaborates on his
doctrines about God and Nature, assuming all the while that his correspondent is taking it all in. Oldenburg, Spinoza decided, was a man
of reason. In this it seems that the lattice may have blocked Spinoza's
view as well. To a fellow member of the Royal Society, Oldenburg
writes on one occasion that Spinoza "entertains me with a discourse
of his on the whole and parts etc . . . which is not un-philosophical
in my opinion." But he does not deem it worth his colleague's time
to read. Elsewhere, he refers to Spinoza as "a certain odd philosopher."

In 1665, four years and eighteen letters after it began, the correspondence between Oldenburg and Spinoza came to an abrupt end.
The initial cause may have been a domestic crisis for Oldenburg—
his wife of two years died, leaving him an inheritance, and he married
his sixteen-year-old ward, all of which caused some twittering in London society. The following year London burned, and then, in the political turmoil of 1667, Oldenburg was imprisoned for two months in
the Tower of London. He emerged a chastened man, perhaps more alert
to deviations from religious orthodoxy than before. But the last straw,
for Oldenburg, was the publication of Spinoza's *Tractatus Theologico-
Politicus* in 1670. Oldenburg suddenly grasped something of meaning
of Spinoza's beautiful words about God, Thought, and Extension. The
lattice was ripped asunder, and Oldenburg was evidently horrified by
what he saw. He fired off an angry letter, since lost, in which he
accused Spinoza of intending to "harm religion."

Yet the Oldenburg story does not end there. The correspondence
resumed at a moment of great peril for the philosopher. For it seems
that the personal bond forged in the garden of the Rijnsburg cottage
somehow survived—against all reason, perhaps.

Spinoza's imperfect relationships with fellow philosophers seem to
confirm the plain truth that, notwithstanding the ideals of the *Ethics*,

even the purest friendships always harbor some level of conflict. The Oldenburg affair perhaps shows that the best are those that can survive it. Both of these lessons, too, will prove valuable in understanding the link between Spinoza and Leibniz, the last known and by far the most important of his philosophical callers.

SPINOZA'S LIFE, in sum, was of the sort where all the drama takes place in the mind, where the lifting of an eyebrow counts as a major twist in the plot and the days tumble down like so many leaves of paper in the wind. Yet, as Spinoza's name began to reverberate around the world, the simple and modest lifestyle he inaugurated in Rijnsburg and pursued to the end of his days became the subject of far-flung controversies. The interpretation of its meaning became the center of one of the most passionate dramas in the European republic of letters.

According to the seventeenth-century way of thinking, an atheist was by definition a decadent. If there is no God (or, at least, no providential, rewarding-and-punishing God of the sort worshipped in all the traditional religions), the reasoning went, then everything is permitted. So a non-believer would be expected to indulge in all manner of sensual stimulation, to fornicate regularly with the most inappropriate partners, to lie, cheat, and steal with abandon, and then to suffer an agonizing death once the Almighty caught up with him, but not before mawkishly recanting his heresies in the presence of a clucking man of the cloth.

Spinoza, according to all the seventeenth-century interpreters, rejected all the traditional ideas about God; he was indisputably a heretic. Yet his manner of living was humble and apparently free of vice. Then, as now, the philosopher seemed like a living oxymoron: he was an ascetic sensualist, a spiritual materialist, a sociable hermit, a secular saint. How could his life have been so good, the critics asked, when his philosophy was so bad?

To complicate matters further, it seems that Spinoza was keenly aware of the philosophical significance of his reputation as a clean-living man of the spirit. In response to a Dutch critic who charged him with atheism, for example, he writes: "Atheists are usually inordinately fond of honors and riches, which I have always despised, as is known to all who are acquainted with me." Even the biography by Lucas, who undoubtedly received many of his anecdotes from the master himself, seems like part of an effort to mold his image beyond the grave. Did Spinoza disdain honor and riches because he genuinely despised them—or was he in search of some higher kind of renown and a different species of capital?

Spinoza's contemporaries, by and large, had at their disposal a convenient means to resolve the thorny difficulties raised by his egregiously virtuous lifestyle. For the most part, they could simply overlook the facts. Some went so far as to invent new twists in the story, more suitable for a wholesome narrative. The atheist Jew, they insisted, was indeed a craven, worm-eaten syphilitic who paid for his heresy in hideous coin. For, to allow that Spinoza led a good life was to suggest that the belief in God is not a necessary element of virtue.

Among Spinoza's contemporaries, however, Leibniz for once stood at a disadvantage. He was, in the first place, too clearheaded to accept the simple fictions of his peers. More to the point, as of November 1676, he would see it all with his own eyes. He took in the tiny, attic room, with the lens-grinding lathe at one end and the old, inherited, four-poster bed on the other. He smelled the cheap tobacco. He must have noticed that his host wore the same pair of silver shoe buckles every day. Perhaps he was offered a treat of gruel made from raisins and butter, or a cup of watery beer from a donated keg. In the end, Leibniz would know too much.

5

God's Attorney

In his early twenties, even while bounding up the ladder of courtly success in Frankfurt and Mainz, Leibniz somehow found the time to produce an impressive suite of philosophical writings: a lengthy letter on metaphysics to his mentor, Jacob Thomasius; the *Catholic Demonstrations* issued at Baron von Boineburg's request; a pair of essays on the physics of motion forwarded to Henry Oldenburg of the Royal Society; and sundry other missives to notables and papers delivered in the course of academic studies. These early exercises anticipate almost all of the central themes of Leibniz's mature philosophy, though often in partial or confused form and adulterated with notions that eventually went out with the wash. More interesting than the mixed bag of doctrines in these early works, however, is the overall attitude to philosophy that they embody. In his first philosophical efforts, Leibniz establishes the "philosophy of philosophy" that would explain, justify, and guide his work throughout his life. It is an approach that could not have been more different from that of the author of the *Treatise on the Emendation of the Intellect*.

In his twenty-fifth year, Leibniz drafted an essay in support of one of his most enduring ambitions: to establish an academy to promote the arts and sciences in Germany. In the course of his arguments on behalf of the project, he provides a name for just the kind of person he wishes to become: a *rector rerum publicarum*—a director or guide of public affairs. He goes on to describe in lyrical terms just what such directors do:

> They are those who honor God not only with praise and remembrance, or with words and thoughts, but rather also with good works. . . . They are those who apply as best they can the discovered wonders of nature and art to medicine, to mechanics, to the comforts of life; to finding work and food for the poor; to saving people from the vices and sloth; to the dispensation of justice; to reward and punishment; to the maintenance of the common peace; to the prosperity and advancement of the fatherland; to the extermination of famines, plagues, and wars insofar as it is in our power . . . ; to the propagation of the true religion and the fear of God—in brief, to the greater happiness of the human race.

Leibniz wanted very badly to do good. He turned to philosophy not in order to solve an essentially personal problem—as Spinoza, for example, did—but rather in order to solve *other* people's problems. He measured his results not in terms of his own salvation but rather by the general happiness of the human race. Philosophy for him was not a way of being but one of many instruments to be used in service of the general good. The maxim that guided him throughout his long and colorful life—and that he later made the explicit foundation of his entire system of philosophy—was "Justice is the charity of the wise." His vaulting ambition was to unite in his own practice the virtues of wisdom, justice, and charity. And if, as was inevitable in the course of such a long and productive life, he seemed to fall short of his ideal at times, it should always be remembered just how high he had set the bar for himself.

Leibniz's to-do list of "good deeds" was extraordinarily long and detailed, but it is worth pausing first to consider the general shape his philosophical work took, for the principle of charity dictated not just the content of his philosophy but also its form. Philosophers such as Leibniz do not address their works to God, the soul, or the fellowship of reason in general—as Spinoza perhaps did. Rather, they aim their works at very particular individuals—the kind with first and last names (and, in the case of Leibniz, often with imposing titles, too). Leibniz's early philosophical exercises, just like almost all of his later work, consist principally of letters written to some person of importance, supplemented by the occasional essay or treatise commissioned by some such person. His goal, as ever, was not necessarily to reveal the truth, but to get something done—not to change his own mind, but to change someone else's mind.

The other people in question, for Leibniz, included not just the recipients of his letters, but the fellow philosophers and writers he discussed within them. The lengthy missive he posted to Professor Thomasius in the spring of 1669 is a case in point. In that work, the young Leibniz floats some of his own ideas on a torrent of names of fellow thinkers. Among those still familiar to us, he mentions Aristotle, Averroës, Bacon, Robert Boyle, Descartes, Epicurus, Gassendi, Hobbes, Hooke, and Spinoza. From among those who have since dropped from the canon, he cites an even greater number: Andrae, Bodin, Campanella, Clauberg, Clerke, Clerselier, Conring, Denores, Digby, Durr, Felden, Gilbert, Guericke, du Hamel, Heerbord, van Hoghelande, Marci, Piccart, Raey, Regius, Trew, Viotti, Weigel, White, Zarbella.

In Leibniz's view, it seems, philosophy is something like a giant playing field—an intellectual "scene," perhaps—in which all the participants compete and collaborate on a vast, collective project. The practice of philosophy, he implies, consists largely in mastering the writings of a vast range of other authors; and its goal is the synthesis of the general pattern of thought of the time. The idea is in some ways very much like that which underlies modern academic practice (and Leibniz's habit of dropping names of authors he could not possibly have mastered would perhaps allow his work to pass unremarked in contemporary departments of literary theory); but it stands in striking contrast to the approach taken by Spinoza, to name one example.

Within the densely populated field of philosophy he beheld, Leibniz aspired to occupy a very special position. He did not wish to become the dictator of dictators, as Aristotle did, nor scoffer in chief, like Democritus. Instead, he sought to become the Great Peacemaker of All Thought. Always the child of the Thirty Years War, he was convinced that only peace could bring about a lasting intellectual prosperity. Just out of his teenage years, he adopted the pseudonym Guilielmus Pacidius. "Pacidius" is a Latin play on "Gottfried," and it means something like "peace-god," or perhaps "peacemaker." William the Peacemaker wanted everybody to stop fighting; he wanted to sew all the names and labels of philosophy into a "seamless mantle," as he puts it in his 1669 letter to Thomasius. A modern scholar calls him, aptly, a "conciliatory eclectic." An eighteenth-century observer, somewhat less generously, remarked that his ecumenical approach to fellow philosophers involved taking "their dogmas as his presuppositions." Eckhart attributed his accommodating approach to his personal style: "He always looked for the best in others."

In his later writings, Leibniz became only more universal in his irenic syncretism. In the *New Essays on Human Understanding*, for example, where he allows himself the luxury of commenting on his own philosophical system through a fictional spokesman, he writes:

> I have been astounded by a new system, of which I have read something in the learned journals of Paris, Leipzig, and Holland . . . and since then I believe I have seen a new face on the inside of things. This system appears to unite Plato with Democritus, Aristotle with Descartes, the scholastics with the moderns, theology and morality with reason. It seems to take the best from all systems and then advance further than anyone has yet done.

In his last years, Leibniz extended his conciliatory reach beyond the confines of the European continent, and sought to include Chinese thought as well. At one point he even pondered forming a common front with extraterrestrials, should they ever be discovered.

In his quest for intellectual peace, Leibniz always insisted on the virtue of clarity. If philosophers would only write clearly, he declared—no doubt speaking for generations of exasperated students—they would stop fighting with one another. Thus Leibniz inaugurated one of the leitmotifs of his mature "philosophy of philosophy." In *The Art of Combinations*, an academic paper he produced before he turned twenty, the brilliant young scholar first mooted the idea of a universal characteristic—a language of logical symbols so transparent that it would reduce all philosophical disputes to the mechanical manipulation of tokens. With possibly eerie prescience about the future of information technology, he envisioned encoding this logical language in an "arithmetical machine" that could end philosophical debates with the push of a button. In the future, he rhapsodized, philosophers reaching a point of disagreement will shout joyously, "Let's calculate!" Such a device, he assured his patron, the Duke of Hanover, would be the "mother of all my inventions."

Leibniz's universal characteristic, however, never amounted to more than the idea of an idea. It fascinates not on account of any results achieved, but as an expression of a certain kind of aspiration. Leibniz, like a number of more recent philosophers, cherished the notion that there are no genuine philosophical conflicts; there is only bad grammar. He wanted above all to believe in "the elegance and harmony of the world," and his quest to reconcile all philosophical positions in the placid movements of an inimitably baroque calculating device was at bottom an effort to confirm this belief. Philosophy, he seemed to assume, is not an end in itself; it is not the joyous experience of the union of the mind with God, as Spinoza would have it. It is instead just one more means of bringing about a tranquil silence. In Leibniz's ideal world, in fact, philosophy could just as easily be turned over to a beautiful machine. It could perhaps even run in one's sleep, just like a computer.

Leibniz's plans to promote universal peace and harmony, of course, involved some very specific and concrete "good deeds." In a later letter to his master, Duke Johann Friedrich of Hanover, he identifies the goal toward which much of his philosophy, early and late, was consecrated:

> It seems to me, as I have told Your Excellency on other occasions, that nothing is more useful to the general good than the authority of the universal church that forms one body of all

Christians united by the bonds of charity and that may hold in sacred respect the greatest powers of the earth. . . . This is why every good man should hope that the luster of the Church should be re-established everywhere.

Consistent with its altruistic orientation, Leibniz's philosophy began not with a personal program, as did Spinoza's, but with a political one. And his politics may be summed up in one word: theocracy. The specific agenda motivating much of his work was to reunite the Protestant and Catholic churches. His more general aim was, as one commentator aptly puts it, to establish "the religious organization of the earth." In his utopia, all peoples would be united under one church in a single *respublica Christiana*—a Christian republic.

Yet, in the political theory Leibniz began to develop in his earliest writings, unlike that of many of his medieval-minded contemporaries, theocracy is grounded in reason. That is to say, the ideal state derives its legitimacy not from the interpretation of the Holy Scriptures, nor from the "divine right" of kings, but from the eternal truths established by philosophy. Justice and the entire system of laws, no less than religion, according to Leibniz, have their foundation in the guidance of reason. Thus, in Leibniz's ideal world, the *respublica Christiana* is the same thing as "the Empire of Reason."

The Empire of Reason, conversely, embodies the principle of charity that Leibniz takes to be central to a Christian republic. Consequently, in his view, the ideal state has a duty not just to preserve the peace and security of its citizens, but also to improve their moral and physical well-being through charitable acts. The state is thus a form of institutionalized benevolence. He argues specifically that government leaders should take upon themselves the alleviation of poverty and the promotion of economic activity. It would not be at all amiss to see in Leibniz's political theory a first attempt to articulate the foundations of the modern welfare state.

Leibniz's immense political vision left him with a monumental philosophical task. Even as a twenty-something courtier in the German hinterlands, he held himself responsible for providing a synthesis of reason, justice, and the essential tenets of the dominant Christian theology. More specifically, as a first step, he believed he had to supply the rational foundations for a united Christian church. In the *Catholic Demonstrations*—which he took up at Boineburg's urging in 1668, at the age of twenty-two—he began his lifelong project to do just that. In that early and incomplete collection of essays, he defends a variety of controversial, mainly Catholic doctrines in a manner intended to make them acceptable to both sides of the principal schism in the western church.

Zeroing in on one particularly troublesome doctrine, he says: "I do not see anything that is more important for reunion than to be able to answer the apparent absurdities of transubstantiation. For all the other dogmas conform much more with reason." In the same text, he acknowledges that "transubstantiation implies a contradiction, if the philosophy of the moderns is true." By "moderns" here he refers loosely to all of those philosophers inspired by Descartes's mechanistic theories of physics. Leibniz's defense of transubstantiation against the dastardly "moderns" is subtle and ingenious; more to the point, it sheds much light on his underlying philosophy of philosophy.

In assessing the difficulties presented by the dogma in question, Leibniz, with his customary acuity, hits the nail on the head: transubstantiation implies, first, that a thing that has all the attributes of one type of substance (bread) suddenly becomes another substance (namely, the body of Christ); and, second, that, what with all the church services going on across the continent, the same substance appears to be found in many places at once. Little wonder, then, that the doctrine ran into trouble with the "moderns."

The argument against the transubstantiation deniers, in highly condensed form, goes something like this: First, the mechanistic physical theories of the modern philosophers, says Leibniz, are incoherent. Specifically, they fail to account properly for motion, or the origin of activity. Therefore, he contends, in order to explain motion, we must assume that there is in all bodies some incorporeal or nonmechanical principle of activity. This principle of activity must be embodied in a nonmechanical entity, specifically, a "concurrent mind." In the case of human bodies, the mind in question is the usual one—i.e., the one in the head. In all other bodies, however, the concurrent mind belongs to God. Since substance therefore necessarily has something non-physical or immaterial in it, he concludes, it is free from the "modern" constraints of appearing to be what it is and of having to be in one place at one time. (To put it crudely: God is free to change his mind, and when he does so, the substance of a thing changes with it, even if its physical attributes do not.) Ergo, transubstantiation (along with the immortality of the soul and a few other doctrines of note, as it turns out) is at least logically possible.

In his youthful defense of transubstantiation against mechanistically minded modern philosophers, Leibniz elevates an incorporeal, mindlike principle of activity to the status of primary reality, on a par with God. The implication is that the defining feature of human existence—the mind—is in some sense a (or perhaps *the*) essential constituent of all things, that everything in the world is "be-souled." Here we glimpse the first hint of the central doctrine of Leibniz's mature metaphysics, the idea that the human being—and more specifically, the human mind—occupies a very special place in the universe, that it is the indivisible atom from which all things are created. It is an idea that would put him at odds with the resolutely anti-anthropocentric Spinoza and yet, at the same time, paradoxically, would serve as an entirely unexpected bridge between his own, theocratic philosophy and the theory behind the modern, liberal political order championed by Spinoza.

On the face of it, Leibniz's approach to the defense of transubstantiation manifests his declared commitment to the search for truth by philosophical modes of argument. Unlike the vast majority of seventeenth-century commentators on this and related subjects, he cites neither the Bible, the Vatican, nor any authority other than reason itself in making his case. One of his principal stated aims in the text, in fact, is "to prove that philosophy is a useful and necessary beginning for theology."

At second glance, however, one may be forgiven for entertaining some doubt about the sincerity of Leibniz's commitment to reason. When he says of transubstantiation that "all the other dogmas conform *much more* with reason," for example, it is hard to escape the inference that he thinks that none of them conforms very much with reason—and transubstantiation least of all. Did Leibniz believe in the dogma he defended—or did he simply believe that its defense was necessary for the general good?

In fact, as a member of the Lutheran confession, Leibniz was nominally barred from subscribing to the dogma of transubstantiation, at least in its Catholic form. It further seems that Leibniz was never much of a Lutheran, never mind a Catholic. Eckhart reports that the villagers and the aristocrats of Hanover all agreed on one thing: that Leibniz was a non-believer. They had a nickname for him: Loewenix, meaning "believer in nothing." In the nineteen years he worked alongside the philosopher in Hanover, Eckhart adds, he rarely saw him in church, and he never knew him to take communion. Apparently, the great philosopher did not deem it worth his while to consume the bread that, according to his fine arguments, could very well have been the body of Christ.

In his *Catholic Demonstrations*, as elsewhere, however, Leibniz seems to evade questions about the truth of doctrines such as transubstantiation by adopting a legalistic pose. The nominal aim of his argument, in fact, is not to prove that transubstantiation is true, but that certain arguments against it are fallacious. That is, he takes an innocent-until-proven-guilty approach to the doctrine in question. Here Leibniz seems to practice philosophy much as one would practice law. Philosophical arguments are the moral equivalent of legal briefs: their purpose is to protect a client's interests, and their worth is measured in terms of *believability* and not belief—that is, in terms of what the jury decides, and not necessarily the truth.

The startling gap between the philosopher and his arguments in evidence here did not grow smaller in the course of Leibniz's long career. He would frequently exclaim, for example, that he had come into the possession of "some surprising arguments" in defense of various religiously or politically desirable doctrines, in much the same way that one might remark upon the chance discovery of some fine silverware in a neighborhood flea market. Even doctrines central to his own philosophy—such as the immortality of the soul and the goodness of God—he described more readily as "advantageous" and "useful" than as "true." In reducing philosophical arguments to the status of tools to be used in the pursuit of the general good, it seems, Leibniz could not avoid putting a disconcerting space between himself and his own philosophical propositions.

Leibniz's distance from his own arguments seems especially noteworthy when one considers that the courtier-philosopher, like most workaholics, had no life outside his work. There was no other self for whom the game of philosophical argumentation might have been understood as a game; no father struggling to provide a decent home for his kids; no husband grumbling affectionately about the fellow philosophers at the office; no member of the local chess club; no hunting aficionado or woodworking enthusiast. The game was all there was for Leibniz. He was nothing outside of his job; and yet he wasn't his job either.

Perhaps the most interesting feature of Leibniz's early defense of transubstantiation is the form in which he first presents what will turn out to be the central claim of his mature philosophy. His argument remains an argument *against* modern philosophy, and not *for* a particular metaphysical doctrine. That is, it is in the first instance a claim that modern philosophy is incoherent in some way (specifically, in this case, it fails to account for motion, which is why it fails to debunk transubstantiation). To put it in modern-sounding terms, Leibniz's argument follows the pattern of a "deconstruction," according to which modern philosophy is shown as failing to account for that which it promises to account for. Then, somehow—in a manner that will require much more investigation and that anticipates the sins of many of his latter-day imitators—Leibniz locates in this failure of modern philosophy the grounds for his own, purportedly antimodern (or perhaps better postmodern) doctrines. Because modern philosophy fails to account for motion, he infers, there must exist an incorporeal principle of activity, which he in turn makes the foundation for his ideas concerning all that is special about the human mind.

This sudden shift from critique to dogma—or, more bluntly, this confusion between exposing the errors of modern philosophy on the one hand and demonstrating the truth of his own philosophy on the other—is in some sense the founding gesture of Leibniz's metaphysical thought. In practical terms, it will always prove much easier to explain what Leibniz was against (namely, modern philosophy) than what he was for. Leibniz's philosophy—just like that of countless imitators in later centuries—is an essentially reactive one. It is defined by—and cannot exist without—that to which it is opposed. That to which it is opposed may go under many names—modern philosophy, mechanism, atheism, western metaphysics, and the like—but, as we shall see, one will eventually suffice for all: Spinoza.

EVEN WHILE PURSUING the general good into the realms of highly abstract philosophy and theology, Leibniz did not neglect to advance its claims within the greasy world of international politics. By the autumn of 1671, as his ferry carried him past nymphs dancing for joy on the banks of the Rhine, he had settled on the plan that, in his mind, would bring the greatest benefit to the human race in the immediate future: the Egypt Plan.

The idea was as unexpected as it was archaic. The German states could relieve themselves of the threat from France, Leibniz maintained, by persuading Louis XIV to divert his armies to the conquest of Egypt. Such a war would be a boon not just for the Germans but for all Europeans. Instead of Christians killing Christians—and thereby paving the road to Vienna for the Turks—Christians would be killing infidels. Europeans, of course, had a long and colorful history of such crusades; but it had been some time (four centuries or so) since anyone had thought to propose a new one. To make matters absolutely clear, Leibniz also sometimes referred to his proposal as "The Plan for a New Holy War."

Baron von Boineburg fell madly in love with the plan. He put his protégé to work immediately on drafting a lengthy elaboration and defense of the proposal. Leibniz prepared two hundred pages' worth of arguments in support of the conquest of the Nile. He compared the idea favorably with the other option that seemed to be on the Sun King's menu at the time, namely, the possible invasion of Holland. He proposed that the German princes should send a special, secret embassy to Paris in order to present the plan in all its splendor to Louis XIV himself. Boineburg and Leibniz, naturally, would lead the mission.

The plotters threw themselves fervently into promoting their call to Holy War. Boineburg organized another secret conference in the spa town of Bad Schwalbach. Leibniz's enthusiasm reached such a pitch that, on the occasion of the elevation of the successor to the Bishop of Mainz, he composed a lavish poem to celebrate the impending crusade.

As the zeal with which philosopher and his mentor pursued the trip to Paris attests, there were some ulterior motives at work in the plan to get Louis XIV to pillage an unsuspecting third country. Boineburg's reason for wanting to go to Paris, over and above patriotic duty, was straightforward: he was owed considerable back rent on some properties in France, and he believed that the only way to ensure the recovery of his investment was to make a personal appeal in the court of Louis XIV. Leibniz, too, may have had an ulterior motive—an even stranger reason for wanting to go to Paris to propose waging war on the infidel.

IN ORDER TO advance the general good of the human race (at least as he saw it), Leibniz believed that he would have to pursue his own personal good, too. To the famous Jansenist theologian Antoine Arnauld, the aspiring twenty-five-year-old philosopher made this confession:

> There is nothing, I think, upon which I have brooded more earnestly over the course of my life, however short, than the problem of assuring my security in the future, and I confess that by far the greatest cause of my philosophizing as well has been the hope of winning a prize not to be disdained—peace of mind—and the ability to say that I have demonstrated certain things which have heretofore merely been believed or even, in spite of their great importance, ignored.

Leibniz, no less than Spinoza, was keen to win philosophical honor. But, whereas Spinoza sought the kind of fame that accrues to leaders of underground revolutions, Leibniz went in search of a much more aboveground form of prestige. He unabashedly craved all those things that Spinoza disdained: titles, awards, salaries, tenure. "Great was his desire to shine," as one observer noted. And, indeed, without such trappings of fame, he reasoned, he would never be in a position to contribute to the general good of the human race. In Leibniz's mind, his own "security in the future" was sometimes difficult to distinguish from the general good of the human race.

The moment he had been elevated to privy counselor of justice in the court of Mainz in the summer of 1670, Leibniz launched an aggressive campaign to thrust himself into the limelight of the pan-European intellectual scene. The first phase of this campaign consisted of direct-mail approaches to leading figures in the republic of letters. Although he occupied a political position of some note, the young diplomat had not yet established his reputation in the intellectual world; these early letters were, in essence, cold calls.

Among the first recipients of Leibniz's introductory offerings was Thomas Hobbes, the aging and highly controversial materialist philosopher, then residing in London. "I know of no one who has philosophized more exactly, clearly, and elegantly than you, not even excepting that man of divine genius, Descartes himself," Leibniz tells Hobbes, just before going on to suggest that perhaps the widely reviled materialist might wish to rebut more forcefully those who say he does not believe in the immortality of the soul. The octogenarian Hobbes chose not to respond.

Leibniz next opened up communications with leading intellectuals in Holland, Italy, and France. He devoted special attention to Antoine Arnauld. His letter to the theologian runs to six thousand words and summarizes and refines many of the concepts examined in his earlier epistles to Thomasius.

That same summer of 1670 Leibniz also initiated a lengthy correspondence with Henry Oldenburg. "Pardon that an unknown one writes to one who is not unknown," he begins, with typical baroque flourish. The point of the correspondence soon becomes clear: Leibniz has produced a pair of essays on the philosophy of motion, under the title of *New Physical Hypothesis*, and he wishes to share his work with the members of the Royal Society.

Leibniz's essays on motion mark a significant stage in his philosophical development. They begin with some of the ideas about motion and activity that the philosopher first developed in the context of his work on the metaphysics of church reunion, and they go on to raise for the first time the problem Leibniz calls "the labyrinth of the continuum": loosely speaking, the problem of explaining how it is that infinitely small points can come together to constitute a line. The essays thus supply a link between Leibniz's earliest theological reflections and his later metaphysics. Intriguingly, they also hint at the study of mathematical infinitesimals that would soon lead him to his epochal discovery of the calculus.

The essays also offer some frankly bizarre speculations in physics. "Bubbles are the seeds of everything," the young scholar confidently maintains. Water is a mass of countless bubbles, he adds; and air is nothing but rarefied water. And what of the earth? "There can be no doubt that it, too, is made entirely of bubbles, for the basis of earth is glass, glass in a thick bubble."

The immediate aim of the essays was to inject its author into controversies raging between some of the major powers of the intellectual world of the time. The philosophy of motion was the site of a battle among such titans as Christiaan Huygens, Christopher Wren, and the ghost of Descartes. Leibniz's goal in drawing attention to himself in this way, in fact, was to secure membership in either the Royal Society of London, the Royal Academy of Paris, or both. Making little effort to disguise his ambition, he dedicated one essay apiece to each of those august bodies.

For those who had as yet no reason to be interested in Leibniz's personal philosophical development, unfortunately, his essays were mainly a source of bafflement. Leibniz showed some facility in his criticisms of Descartes, but his discussion otherwise suggested that his attempt to throw himself into the deep end of contemporary debates was premature. The English mathematician John Wallis offered a favorable review of the essays, but the cantankerous Robert Hooke was scathing about the "little work." Then as now, the consensus was that the less said about the bubble theory of the world, the better. A later critic described Leibniz's early essays on physics as the product of "proud ignorance." In his eagerness to establish his reputation among the members of the Royal Society, it seems that Leibniz ruffled a few too many feathers, the disastrous consequences of which would unfold several decades later in the dispute with Newton over the calculus.

THE IMMENSE AND variegated tableau of Leibniz's philosophy of philosophy came together in a letter he addressed to his future employer, Duke Johann Friedrich of Hanover, in the autumn of 1671. Johann Friedrich was the runt of the House of Brunswick. According to his mother, he was "horrifyingly fat, and much shorter than the others." Indeed, he was reportedly so obese that he rarely moved, and often preferred to rule his fiefdom from his well-appointed bed. On a journey to Italy that he had taken in the long, slow years before coming to power, he had converted to Catholicism. To the consternation of his family and peers, his conversion seemed to be motivated by a sincere belief in the truth of his new religion. He always had a soft spot for spiritual affairs, for philosophical speculation, and, more to the point, for Leibniz himself. The young philosopher pinned many of his hopes for future success on the pliable duke.

In the first pages of his October letter, Leibniz informed Johann Friedrich of his own principal achievements thus far in life, among which he numbered:

• *The universal characteristic.* If he is able to realize this idea, he says here, it will be the "mother of all my inventions."
• *The philosophy of motion.* "In natural philosophy, I am the first perhaps to have demonstrated completely that ... there is a vacuum, not by experiments, but by geometrical demonstrations, for I have proved some propositions on the nature of motion that no one else has thought of before. . . . A scholar from Italy wrote me that he had never yet seen any hypotheses that contented him more. From England I have received some quite favorable reviews."
• *Mathematics and mechanics.* "I have discovered some things that ... should be esteemed of no little importance." He refers here to an idea he has for building a calculating machine, one capable of performing

basic arithmetical functions. He also proposes a similar calculator for trigonometric functions.

• *Optics*. He lists three ideas: a "pandochal" lens, a "cata-dioptric" tube, and a surveying instrument able to measure distances from a single point. All of these, he says, have hitherto been "attempted in vain" by others.

• *The problem of longitude*. He says he has the idea for a solution to the problem of determining the longitude of ships at sea. If his experiments are not stopped, he warns, his method will shortly prove to be "the most accurate and universal of all those we now have."

• *Submarines*. He says he has "restituted" the idea behind the invention first attributed to Cornelius van Drebbel and described by the priest Marin Mersenne, for a vessel capable of traveling under the surface of the sea.

• *Pneumatics*. He has designed a machine capable of compressing air to 1,000 atmospheres—levels "for which hitherto there is nothing in the world to compare"—for possible use as an engine in ships or carriages.

• *Moral philosophy and jurisprudence*. His essay *Elementa Iuris Naturalae* (Elements of Natural Justice) is a "brief" work, he concedes, but "of such clarity and pithiness" that it has already exerted a profound influence on contemporary jurisprudence.

• *Natural theology*. He has demonstrated that "there must be an ultimate reason for things or for the universal harmony, which is God"; furthermore, he has adduced proofs that God is not the cause of sin, that punishment for sins is part of universal harmony, and that the mind is incorporeal; plus, he has solved the mind-body problem.

• *Revealed theology*. He has defended the "mysteries" of the church —such as transubstantiation—against the "insults of un-believers and atheists."

There can be no doubt that Leibniz was a universal genius—perhaps the last such genius in modern history. "In the same way that the ancients could manage eight horses simultaneously," said Fontenelle in his eulogy for the great thinker, "Leibniz could manage all the sciences simultaneously." Still, it would not be unkind to wonder whether the twenty-five-year-old who wrote this letter had perhaps a few too many horses in the race. Of all the world-beating inventions mentioned in his list, only one—the arithmetical calculating machine—later achieved any degree of physical reality. The rest went the way of most brilliant ideas. The lavish self-praise that characterizes the letter raises a quandary, too. Did Leibniz really believe that the English were head over heels for his allegedly groundbreaking physics? That he was, moreover, on the verge of cracking the centuries-old problem of longitude, not to mention that he already had the mind-body problem in the bag? Or was he just throwing everything he had at the Duke in a desperate hope that something would stick?

Fontenelle, as it turns out, was wrong only in the detail: the number of projects that Leibniz managed simultaneously was almost always an order of magnitude greater than eight. When an idea flared in his kinetic mind, he would grab it like a torch and run until the next bright light caught his eye, and then he would add that one to the bundle in his arms, too, dropping a few others in his haste and so leaving behind a trail of smoldering visions. In the 120 volumes' worth of material in the Leibniz archives, there are without doubt hundreds of sparkling inventions that have yet to be catalogued, let alone realized. He wrote about everything, to everybody, all the time. If Spinoza was the quintessential monomaniac—ruthlessly compressing a lifetime of insights into a single, adamantine volume—then Leibniz may be aptly described as an "omnimaniac."

There was in Leibniz a limitless energy, an enthusiasm for all things, and an almost desperate love of life that can only evoke wonder and admiration; but there was a certain recklessness, too, and maybe even an odd lack of seriousness. Though Leibniz's achievements in life were extraordinary by any measure, they were meager indeed in comparison with his plans. As he confessed to one of his later correspondents, "I can suggest much to others, but cannot alone execute all that occurs to me; and I would gladly give to others the fame of many of my inventions, if only the public welfare, the good of the race and the glory of God might thereby be promoted."

The epistle to Johann Friedrich does not end with the swollen list of the young Leibniz's intellectual triumphs. After summarizing his real or intended contributions to the sciences, the philosopher-diplomat turns to his work in politics. It is evident that the buildup of French armies will end badly, he tells the Duke. He foresees a "universal war" in which 100,000 men will die. But, praise God, he continues, he has devised a plan. He presents the essentials of the idea for a new holy war.

He intends to go to Paris to promote the plan, he says, and he is confident that the doors of the French capital will swing wide open before his advance. Louis XIV's all-powerful first minister, Jean-Baptiste Colbert, has expressed interest in his calculating machine; and he believes he can introduce himself to the Marquis de Pomponne, the secretary of state, on the strength of his ties with Pomponne's uncle, the great Arnauld.

At last, in the closing paragraphs of the letter, Leibniz gets to the point—for, whenever he wrote to the Duke of Hanover about his many achievements, there was always a point. He wants letters of introduction from the Duke to notables in Paris, especially people of the kind who may wish to "encourage through pensions" talented young men of learning—men such as Leibniz himself. For, he sees "no better opportunity" for advancing his scientific work than in journeying to Paris.

The Egypt Plan, as it turns out, is a brilliant means with which to further Leibniz's philosophical career. Paris, Leibniz gushes, "is the most knowledgeable and powerful city in the universe." It is the capital of the international republic of letters, home to the likes of Antoine Arnauld, Christiaan Huygens, and Nicolas Malebranche. Paris will provide the young courtier the opportunity to meet with and work alongside the great scientists and philosophers of his time. Just as important, it will allow him the opportunity to acquire titles, awards, and society memberships; it will thrust him on to the brightly lit stage of world history. If the feeling of *vanitas* that Spinoza describes in his earliest treatise has an opposite, it would have to be the sense of fervid anticipation with which the young Leibniz beheld the distant, tantalizing glitter of the City of Light.

Of course, it may seem strange that one of the two greatest thinkers of the seventeenth century should have made use of a proposal for a new holy war as a means to advance his philosophical career. But this rather unlikely circumstance may also serve as testimony to Leibniz's heroic skills as a universal mediator. In the eyes of William the Peacemaker, the Egypt Plan solved all the world's problems at a stroke: it solved the problem of German security, the problem of Europe's future as a Christian republic, the problem of Egypt (inasmuch as those Egyptians who weren't killed in the process would become Christians), and, *mirabile dictu*, it solved the problem of Leibniz, too. This would be far from the last time that the philosopher discovered, to his delight, such an unexpected but highly convenient concordance between the general good and his personal ambition. There is no reason to doubt, furthermore, that, as he labored to enact his bold plan to remake the Middle East and conquer the world of learning in one fell swoop, Leibniz remained convinced that the whole, multifarious operation was just one more proof of the "elegance and harmony of the world."

LEIBNIZ'S PHILOSOPHY WAS not yet fully formed; but his philosophy of philosophy—the attitude and approach he took to philosophy—was all in place by the time he turned twenty-five. The primary goal of contributing to the general good; the commitment to the chief good of defending the theocratic status quo (or, better, in view of the reunion project: the status quo *ante*); the altruism or other-orientation of his work, in both form and content; the perception of philosophy as a scene; the aspiration to thrust oneself on to center stage, to become the great conciliator of all thought; the emphasis on the utility of philosophical doctrines over and above their truth; the deconstructive approach to modern philosophy; the identification of philosophical merit with the rewards and recognition offered by the established authorities of the intellectual world; and the omnimania—all of this was present in Leibniz's earliest philosophical exercises, and all would remain with him throughout his long career.

Already evident, too, was the unexpectedly modern cast of Leibniz's mind. Notwithstanding the medievalism inherent in his ecclesiastical project, the young philosopher had already signaled the commitments to a form of humanism, the welfare state, and the primacy of reason that would link his thought to modernity. Even more telling, perhaps, the pragmatism—perhaps one may even call it relativism—that seems to underlie his approach to philosophy renders him more a figure of the present than of the past. "We must always adapt ourselves to the world," Leibniz once said, "for the world will not adapt itself to us." In the political ideal that he advocated, reason may have been the basis for empire; but in the real world in which he lived and acted, as Leibniz amply demonstrated in his practice, reason was just one more expression of power, and "the good" was just another name for "the useful."

Shadowing Leibniz from the start, too, were some of the question marks that inevitably arise over one who adopts such a quasi-modern approach to philosophy: the concern that in his relentless pursuit of the good, he perhaps lost sight of the truth; and the suspicion that in his failure to distinguish clearly between the general good and his personal interests, he perhaps confused the two.

The contrast with Spinoza, as always, seems definitive. There can be little doubt about the firmness of the convictions that motivated Spinoza's monomaniacal quest. In his case, the enigma lies rather in their source. How could he be so sure? Leibniz, on the other hand, presents us with a very different puzzle. In attempting to synthesize irreconcilable positions, in cavalierly defending doctrines to which he himself most likely did not adhere, and in spreading his attentions on all things so thinly as to seem superficial, he begs the question that troubled the villagers and nobles of Hanover alike: Did he believe in anything at all?

And so it is all the more curious that, at the very time that he was polishing up the Egypt Plan and burnishing his credentials as the in-house philosopher for a reunited Christian church—indeed, in the same month that he produced his lengthy self-analysis for the benefit of the Duke of Hanover—Leibniz made his first, secret contact with the philosopher of The Hague. But in order to make sense of his bewildering behavior in that regard and its many implications and ramifications, it is necessary first to catch up with Spinoza and the storm he had just unleashed on the republic of letters—a tempest of ideas that was to transform forever the landscape of the same world that the young man from Leipzig intended to conquer.

6

The Hero of the People

ommaso Aniello, an Amalfi fisherman, left this earth at the age of twenty-six in a strange and violent blaze of glory over ten hot days in the summer of 1647. Naples at the time was a dominion of the Spanish crown, which ruled the city with its customary blend of avarice, brutality, and incompetence. That spring the Spaniards had imposed a new tax on fruit, thus adding to the citizens' long list of grievances. On July 7, the fruit vendors rioted, the police fled under a hail of oranges, and the people arose in rebellion.

Masaniello, as the young fisherman came to be known, rowed his boat ashore and assumed leadership of the uprising. With his fishing net strung over his shoulder, he marched the rabble into the town palace and put their demands before the Spanish viceroy. For six days in that steamy July, Masaniello and his people's liberation army ruled the streets of Naples. From a wooden pavilion outside his home, the rebel fisherman held court, issuing edicts on behalf of the oppressed people of the city and dispensing justice to the friends and enemies of the revolution. On the seventh day, through the mediation of the Vatican, the captive viceroy signed a truce, according to which

Masaniello would assume the magnificent title of Captain-General and his followers would get the tax relief they sought.

The events of the next three days were lost in the haze of revolution. Some said that the young fisherman, overwhelmed by his sudden rise to prominence, succumbed to his own megalomaniacal fantasies; others said that the viceroy poisoned his drink; others that he was betrayed by his own followers. Whatever the case, on July 16, nine days after the winds of fortune swept him from his fishing boat to the people's pavilion, Masaniello was murdered in front of a church. The rougher elements of the mob hacked off his head, affixed it to the end of a lance, and presented it to the viceroy as a trophy.

A few days later, the people of the city suffered remorse for the foul deed. They put the slain hero's body parts back together again and interred him with great pomp.

The liberation of Naples was as brief as it was confused, but Masaniello ascended above the fog of history to claim a kind of immortality. "It wo'd stumble any one's belief," wrote a breathless commentator of the time, "that a young fellow, *a petty poor bare-footed fisherman*, shold draw after him . . . above *forty thousand armed men*, and shaking of his *linen flop, blue waistcoat*, and *red bonnet*, shold . . . command all of *Naples* . . . as absolutely as ever *Monark* did." The legend of Masaniello inspired poets, playwrights, and composers across the continent. The icon that seized the progressive imagination was that of a freedom fighter—a man who made the ultimate sacrifice for the liberation of his people from the cruel and corrupt theocratic order so ably embodied by the Catholic monarchy of Spain. Among radical painters, Masaniello became a stock figure, always represented in a fisherman's shirt, with a net strung over his shoulder and his eyes smoldering with fervor to save the oppressed people of the world.

AMONG THE PAINTERS Masaniello inspired was Baruch de Spinoza.

That the philosopher should have taken up painting as a pastime is perhaps not so surprising. The Dutch, after all, were in the throes of their art madness, and in the final fourteen years of his life Spinoza lodged with two artists—Daniel Tydeman in Voorburg and Hendrik van der Spyck in The Hague. His biographer Colerus, who had the opportunity to view a portfolio of charcoal and ink sketches left with van der Spyck, avowed that Spinoza was a fine draughtsman. Most of his drawings were portraits of individuals, presumably his friends, who included many prominent personages of The Hague.

The Masaniello sketch, according to Colerus, made use of the traditional iconography: the shirt, the net, and, one presumes, the fiery eyes. Obviously, the philosopher was among those caught up in the romance of the revolutionary fisherman. But the most astonishing thing about the work, according to Colerus, was that the face of the revolutionary hero did not look like that of a Neapolitan fisherman. It looked more like that of a Portuguese Jew. In fact, says Colerus, the man in the painting "bore a striking resemblance" to Spinoza himself. Hendrik van der Spyck—who himself produced several portraits of his lodger—insisted that the philosopher intended to depict himself in the role of rebel fisherman.

The Masaniello (self-)portrait marks a subtle yet decisive transformation in the self-image as well as the public image of the man whose journey toward personal salvation began in the safety of isolated cottages in remote villages. To be sure, the passion for freedom and the longing for glory had always been there; but those impulses had hitherto been well sublimated in his solitary meditations. With the publication of the *Tractatus Theologico-Politicus* in 1670, the humble raisin eater of The Hague made stunningly clear that he was an essentially political thinker. With his pen as well as his brush, he had appointed himself the spiritual leader of a global revolution.

THE FIRST SIGN of Spinoza's impending metamorphosis appeared in 1665, when the village of Voorburg stumbled into a typically vicious dispute over the selection of the next pastor for the town church. Petitioners in favor of the more conservative candidate enhanced their case by pointing out that among the progressives was Daniel Tydeman, in whose house lodged "a certain . . . Spinosa, born of Jewish parents, who is now (so it is said) an atheist, that is, a man who mocks all religions and is thus a pernicious element in this republic." Spinoza was, as always, deeply offended by the accusation of atheism; yet it seems that he was powerless to stop that word from consuming his reputation.

The ruckus in Voorburg may have prompted Spinoza to devote his energies to a new project. In October of that year he announced to Oldenburg his intention to publish a "treatise on my views regarding scripture." Three factors motivate him to go ahead with the plan, he explains:

1. The prejudices of the theologians. For I know that these are the main obstacles which prevent men from giving their minds to philosophy. . . .
2. The opinion of me held by the common people, who constantly accuse me of atheism. I am driven to avert this accusation, too, as far as I can.
3. The freedom to philosophize and to say what we think. This I want to vindicate completely, for here it is in every way suppressed by the excessive authority and egotism of the preachers.

In these first statements of his political manifesto, one may already detect glimmers of the radical politics of liberation to which the philosopher would shortly commit himself. But there is also a sense that his primary aim remains, as in his early *Treatise on the Emendation of the Intellect*, to safeguard his philosophical quest for salvation from possible political interference—rather than to promote philosophical interference in politics.

Three years passed, however, with no news on Spinoza's promised treatise. In 1668, the tragic fate of a pair of Spinoza's friends, the Koerbagh brothers, very likely prodded the reluctant revolutionary to apply himself to the project with renewed vigor. Adriaen Koerbagh and his younger brother Johannes were caught up in the whirl of ideas revolving around the figure of Spinoza. After a number of run-ins with the local theocrats, Adriaen published a work titled *A Garden of All Kinds of Loveliness Without Sorrow*. He wanted to enlighten the people of Holland; he wanted to free them from the oppressive rule of the theologians; and he claimed to prove that God is but one thing, an eternal being with infinite attributes that cannot be separated from its creation. Without question, Adriaen had spent too much time reading Spinoza's manuscript *The Short Treatise on God, Man, and His Well-Being*, which had been circulating underground for some time.

The theocrats saw little that was lovely and much that was sorrowful in Adriaen's garden. They accused him of blasphemy. The young heretic went into hiding, so the authorities arrested Johannes, who had been caught proselytizing on his brother's behalf. While Johannes languished in jail, the unrepentant Adriaen chose to multiply his sacrilege. From an undisclosed location, he issued another book, *A Light Shining in Dark Places*. The dark places in question were mainly to be found in the Catholic Church and the (insufficiently) Reformed Church, whose irrational doctrines, Adriaen argues, are deceptions deployed by the clergy to keep the people in abject submission.

With the help of a 1,500-guilder reward, the authorities learned that the author of *A Light* might be found wearing a dark wig and making a nuisance of himself on the streets of Leiden. They promptly located the poorly disguised iconoclast and brought him to justice. In a trial that was as short on facts as it was long on righteous indignation, the prosecutors pressed the young Koerbaghs to reveal the extent of their relations with Spinoza. But the Koerbaghs confessed only that they had met with the reviled atheist a few times, and that they had never talked philosophy with him. The magistrates didn't buy it, but in the absence of further evidence, they let the Spinoza connection drop. In the end, Adriaen was sentenced to ten years in the pestilent Rasphuis Prison, and to ten more years of exile— "should he survive."

He did not.

In the unforgiving autumn of 1669, after a few weeks in an unheated prison cell, Adriaen died of illness. Johannes was released, but his fate was no happier. He passed away three years later, ill, destitute, and alone.

Perhaps moved by the tragic fate of his fellow travelers, Spinoza finally released his *Tractatus* in 1670. In the subtitle he gives away the central concern of the treatise: *In which it is shown not only that the free-*

dom of philosophizing may be granted without harm to piety and civil peace, but also that such freedom is not possible except when accompanied by piety and civil peace. The words seem innocent enough to us now; but at the time they were shocking. Looming behind Spinoza's arguments was the vision of an entirely new political order, a recognizably modern one founded on the principle of toleration, according to which individuals have the inalienable right to express their own opinions about matters of conscience.

The bulk of the *Tractatus* is devoted to an analysis of the Bible. Spinoza sets out to demonstrate, among other things, that the Bible is full of obscurities and contradicts itself with abandon; that the Pentateuch manifestly did not come from the pen of God, Moses, or any other single author, but rather was the work of several very human writers over a long span of time; that the Jews were not God's "chosen people," except in the sense that they thrived in a specific place and time long ago; that the miracles reported in the Bible are always imaginary and often ill informed (how could Joshua say that the sun stopped one day, for example, when it is the earth that moves?); and that the prophets had no special powers to see into the future, but rather had only a talent for elaborating moral insights in a colorful language adapted to the preconceptions and the prejudices of the common people. In short, Spinoza presents a thoroughly secular and historicist reading of the scriptures—entirely unexceptional by modern standards—according to which the Bible is clearly the work of human hands, and the truths it relays are, in the main, not *factual* but *moral*.

What sounds unexceptional in the world Spinoza built, of course, was sacrilege at the moment of creation, and Spinoza knew it. At the heart of the philosopher's cool exegesis of the ancient texts lies a fiery political passion—the same one that fueled Bento's conflict with the rabbis at the synagogue. In the preface to his *Tractatus*, Spinoza barely conceals his revolutionary agenda: "the supreme mystery of despotism, its prop and stay, is to keep men in a state of deception, and with the specious title of religion to cloak the fear by which they must be held in check, so that they will fight for their servitude as if for salvation." Ultimately, Spinoza's aim in robbing the Bible of mystery is to destroy the theocratic order of his time. The established religion, Spinoza says, amounts to "the relics of man's ancient bondage"; and it is used by many "with an impudence quite shameless" to usurp the legitimate rights of civil authorities and to oppress the people. In his later *Ethics*, the philosopher repeats the charge: the theocrats denounce those who deny miracles, as he does, because "the dispelling of ignorance would entail the disappearance of that astonishment, which is the one and only support . . . for safeguarding their authority."

Here and in some of his private letters, Spinoza makes plain his view that organized religion—especially but not exclusively in the form of the Catholic Church—is really an organized fraud. It is deception on a massive scale, exploiting ignorance and fear in order to prey on the superstitious masses. Spinoza is no longer merely rising to the defense of the special interests of philosophers, nor does he limit his demands to the guarantee of certain individual rights by the existing state. Although he is careful to take a stand against violent revolution—which in his view causes more problems than it solves— he is in fact calling for the overthrow of an unjust and tyrannical system of oppression.

In the closing sections of his *Tractatus*, Spinoza sketches the outlines of a radical and quintessentially modern political theory. His fundamental aim is to replace the reigning, theocratic conception of the state with one founded on secular principles. According to the theocrats, the state is the temporal representative of a divine order. The purpose of the state, in other words, is to serve God; and the role of the ecclesiastics is to tell the people just what it is that God wants. Spinoza says, in a nutshell, that the purpose of the state is to serve humankind; and it is up to the people to tell the state what they want.

Spinoza, like most modern theorists, grounds the legitimacy of political authority in the self-interest of individuals. He argues not only that everyone, and every thing, for that matter, is driven by self-interest but that they ought to be as well. "The more every man endeavors and is able to seek his own advantage, the more he is endowed with virtue," he says in the *Ethics*. "To act in absolute conformity with virtue is nothing else in us but to act, to live, to preserve one's own being (these three mean the same) under the guidance of reason on the basis of seeking one's own advantage."

It turns out, of course, that self-interested human beings have much to gain from cooperation. Spinoza stresses that human beings in the absence of an ordered society live in miserable circumstances. Like Thomas Hobbes before him, he envisions something like a "social contract," according to which individuals cede their rights to a sovereign collective in order to acquire the benefits of living under the rule of law. The function of the state, in this view, is to provide the peace and security that enable naturally free individuals to cooperate with one another and thereby fulfill themselves. Spinoza, with the pithiness so characteristic of his work, condenses it all into a lapidary formula: "the purpose of the state is freedom."

Unlike Hobbes, however, Spinoza does not present this social contract as a one-off, absolutely binding surrender of all rights by the individual to the state. Rather, Spinoza says, the contract is constantly up for renewal; and should the state fail to live up to its end of the bargain, the citizenry has a right to revoke the agreement. Furthermore, he maintains, there are some rights that no one is able to cede—such as the right to think and hold one's own opinions, or what he calls "the freedom of conscience." Finally, whereas Hobbes concludes that the terms of the original contract are best realized in an absolute monarchy, Spinoza concludes (albeit with a number of caveats) that justice is most fully realized in a democracy, for a democracy is most apt to express the collective will that legitimizes the state in the first place.

Spinoza's advocacy of democracy on the basis of individual rights was extraordinarily bold for its time, and it qualifies him as the first truly modern political philosopher. He was indisputably the forerunner of the theorists who would later underwrite the Constitution of the United States, the French Revolution, and the rest of the secular, liberal, and democratic order of today.

Spinoza did not invent the idea of a secular state founded on self-interest; rather, he observed it clearly for the first time. In the late seventeenth century, the bewildering diversity of religious creeds that grew out of the Reformation, the variety of human experience on display in public life brought about by economic development and urbanization, and the manifestly secular quality of allegedly divine rulers who emerged at the top of national administrations—in other words, the same combination of developments that made Spinoza's own life as a double exile possible—had already rendered the old theocratic ideals *de facto* obsolete. The "problem of authority"—that is, the source of the legitimacy of political power—had already become the subject of intense concern among thinkers such as Hobbes and Machiavelli. The defining move of Spinoza's political philosophy was to affirm this new world of secular self-interest. He embraced modernity as the foundation of a new kind of ideal—the ideal of a free republic. The very features of modernity that were then and are still regarded by many as its signature evils—the social fragmentation, the secularity, and the triumph of self-interest—he enshrined as the founding virtues of the new world order. His political philosophy was, in essence, an active response to the challenges of modernity.

One aspect of Spinoza's free republic, however, sits a little uneasily with many modern conceptions of the secular state. According to Spinoza, getting the multitudes to behave rationally is no easy task, given the sway that religion has on the popular mind. One way to keep the masses in line is to allow them to divert their religious energies in commerce—so that they are too busy making money, in other words, to get caught up in theocratic shenanigans. The other way to ensure universal discipline is to develop and propound a popular religion that is consistent with the requirements of the state. In fact, says Spinoza, a "good" popular religion is very salutary for a well-functioning society. But this popular religion, he insists, must be under the strict control of civil (and not ecclesiastical) authorities. Its doctrines are to be supplied and its offices filled by the state, and not by priests or prophets.

In the eyes of the philosophers, it should be noted, this state religion will always have the character of a lie (or, at best, a half-truth). Indeed, says Spinoza, it is wiser to keep the whole truth from the man on the street: "If he knew that [the doctrines of faith] were false, he would necessarily be a rebel, for how could it be that one who seeks to love justice and obey God should worship as divine what he knows to be alien to the divine nature?"

Spinoza implicitly distinguishes between the exoteric and esoteric faces of philosophy. The exoteric message of philosophy is intended for public consumption. Its style is adapted to the popular understanding, and its contents are those deemed most suited to bring about desirable political results. The esoteric message, on the other hand, is aimed for the exclusive fellowship of reason. It reveals the truth.

THE *TRACTATUS THEOLOGICO-POLITICUS*, needless to say, did little to improve Spinoza's reputation. Rather, it ignited a conflagration of denunciations the likes of which would not be seen again perhaps until Darwin released *On the Origin of Species* two centuries later. At first the rage was concentrated on the book itself, for the philosopher had taken the precaution of publishing his work anonymously—and of gracing the title page with a false city of publication (Hamburg). But it was not long before the identity of the author became an open secret, and the attacks soon took a personal turn.

The theologians of the Netherlands were the first off the mark. Weeks after publication, the spiritual sheriffs of Leiden decried the "enormities, or rather obscenities" of the book and earnestly requested that "the same be seized and suppressed." In July 1670, one synod declared that the *Tractatus* was "the most vile and sacrilegious book the world has ever seen." Another assembly of Dutch preachers promptly resolved "to seek together the most suitable means to prevent the named Spinoza from continuing to disseminate his impiety and his atheism through these provinces." Their brethren in the southern Netherlands likewise urged the need for "remedies capable of stopping and extirpating this corrosive gangrene." Dozens of similar decrees rolled like thunder across the parishes of the lowlands.

Around the rest of Europe, too, defenders of the faith—of all faiths—were soon vying to outdo one another with condemnations of Spinoza and his book. Sadistic impulses often found release in the fulminations of the orthodox. In Paris, for example, Bishop Pierre-

Daniel Huet—tutor to the Dauphin and friend of Leibniz—suggested that Spinoza "would deserve to be covered with chains and whipped with a rod." Scatological expletives flowed fast and furious—Philip Limborch (later Spinoza's dinner companion) lambasted Spinoza for his "defecated erudition and masticated critique." Other critics tended to come out the front end of the digestive tract: Spinoza is "the most impious, the most infamous, and at the same time the most subtle Atheist that Hell has vomited on the earth" said one. The English philosopher Henry More, perhaps at a loss for evocative metaphors, simply stomped his feet and fumed: "you the most impudent of mortals . . . you most impudent imposter and hypocrite."

At the same time, naturally, an embarrassingly large number of people took the trouble to read Spinoza's satanic tract. Though it could be sold only under the counter and at some risk to both seller and purchaser, the book ran through several printings and was soon widely distributed across Europe. The English prelate Edward Stillingfleet (who later trained his theological guns on the nefarious John Locke) lamented that Spinoza's work was "mightily in vogue among many." Bayle wrote, with sarcasm intended, "All the strong spirits [*esprits forts*] flocked to him from all over." Although overt declarations of sympathy are scarcely to be found in writings of the period, the mere mention of Spinoza's influence could serve to fan the flames of his underground fame. The practice of the time, in fact, was to praise with faint damnation. Typical is the comment by Saint-Évremond, a man who visited Spinoza and who was thought to be "soft" on Spinozism: "In the humble and pensive solitary of [Rijnsburg] . . . French libertinism, which until now has been no more than a vague desire to be free, an impatience of rule, and a revolt against dogma . . . thinks it has found the required apologist for its unbelief, the right man to give a logical basis and formal expression to the aims it has most at heart."

IN THE AFTERMATH of his debut as a global revolutionary, Spinoza faced a very real threat of persecution. Indeed, one of his Dutch critics, a professor at Utrecht, all but demanded his blood—"for it is not for nothing that [the state] carries the sword in its hands." The fate of the Koerbagh brothers now hung like a glum signpost over Spinoza's own future. Lucas reports that the philosopher henceforth "could not live in security because he had discovered the key to the sanctuary." ("The key to the sanctuary" was the title of the French translation of the *Tractatus*.)

In his correspondence, Spinoza made use of a signet ring engraved with the image of a thorny rose and a single-word motto: *Caute*, or "Caution." "The virtue of a free man," he explains in the *Ethics*, "is as great in avoiding dangers as in overcoming them." At times, at least, he seemed to live in accordance with this maxim. When he learned of an effort to publish a Dutch translation of the *Tractatus*, for example, he stopped it in hopes of avoiding charges of spreading impiety among the non-Latinate masses. The same abundance of caution seems to have guided him in later withdrawing the *Ethics* from publication.

Taking a broader view of his behavior, however, it is evident that Spinoza's motto of "Caution" had the character of a prescription rather than a description of his actual practice. He was like a downhill skier who reminds himself that breaking a leg is no virtue; it never occurred to him to get off the slopes. The brute fact is that it took astonishing courage to publish such a work as the *Tractatus* in 1670. To appreciate the boldness of Spinoza's actions today, one would perhaps have to imagine a Jew propounding a skepticism such as his concerning the relevant sacred texts from within one of the modern world's existing theocracies—and then also imagine that there was no outside world in which he might seek asylum.

There was a kind of innocence, too, in Spinoza's political persona. In retrospect, the reaction to the *Tractatus* was eminently foreseeable. Yet, incredibly, Spinoza imagined that by publishing a book in which he debunks the prophets, denies the existence of miracles, and literally desacralizes the Word of God, he could somehow "avert [the] accusation" of atheism. The same hint of naïveté is evident in his presentation of the "esoteric" truth about popular religion in the "exoteric" form of a widely disseminated book. Despite his subtle analyses of the foibles of the human intellect, and notwithstanding his contemptuous assessment of the masses' capacity for rational thought,

Spinoza seems to have harbored the conviction that no one could find fault with him if he limited his writings to statements of reason and fact. In his responses to warnings from friends concerning the risks of his course of action, Spinoza repeatedly evinced a kind of bafflement, like that of a child who says, "But I am only telling the truth." He could not shake the conviction that the truth would win out; and in this he proved that he was no exception to the rule which says that in the breast of every good revolutionary beats the heart of an idealist.

Spinoza was also no exception to the rule which says that in the throbbing thorax of every good revolutionary there is a certain longing for glory. In his earliest treatise, as we know, the philosopher averred that honor is a thing of value only among men who live by the guidance of reason. But in the revolution he sought to bring about, he implicated the fates of many more individuals than a few fellow philosophers. With his ideal of a free republic, he flew his flag in the name of all the people. He had inserted himself into a grand, world-historical narrative. He had become, in his own mind at least, the Masaniello of a civilization-wide struggle for freedom.

And therein lies a still deeper version of the familiar paradox about Spinoza. According to the author of the *Ethics*, self-interest is virtue itself. The political order he intended to establish is one in which all social goals are secular, and so none may transcend the self-realization of the individual. In his magnum opus he baldly avowed that "no virtue can be conceived prior to this one, namely, the drive to preserve oneself." Any yet, there can be little doubt that when he sallied forth from his lodgings in Voorburg with the *Tractatus* in hand, Spinoza brazenly crossed the line that divides self-interest from the common good. Like his Neapolitan idol, he was prepared to sacrifice his own survival for the sake of bringing freedom to his people, in exchange for which he hoped to acquire the kind of glory that accrues to rebel heroes, whose lives tend to end with their decapitated heads being paraded around on a stick.

The questions that arise from Spinoza's inexplicably charitable actions offer a challenge for modern political theorists. More to the point, they would represent a particularly acute dilemma for Leibniz, who claimed a monopoly on the principle of charity for his own political theory. Can one who advocates a secular political order commit to a political goal that transcends his or her survival? Can one who believes only in the virtue of self-interest act from seemingly altruistic motives? In sum: Can a liberal be a hero?

7

The Many Faces of Leibniz

I n the dispersed and fractious republic of letters of late-seventeenth century Europe, Leibniz was something like a one-man intelligence agency. From operatives across the continent he regularly received discrete packets of information, which, like a savvy spymaster, he repackaged and distributed back to the network as he deemed appropriate. It is hardly surprising that he was among the first to pick up the alarming signals radiating from Holland about Spinoza.

Leibniz's first reference to his fellow philosopher predates the publication of the *Tractatus Theologico-Politicus*. In his letter to Thomasius of April 1669, he includes the name of Spinoza on a list of several expositors of Descartes. At the time, Spinoza's sole publication was his *Principles of the Cartesian Philosophy*, in which his stated aim is to present in logical form the master's chief doctrines. The book does include some strong hints of its author's personal views, however, and Leibniz's dismissive assertion that Spinoza, along with the other expositors, had done little more than repeat Descartes's arguments is hasty. (In fact, it suggests that the young German had not read the work he cites—which is not altogether surprising: at the age of twenty-two, Leibniz could hardly have been expected to master the works of all the authors he mentions in this letter to Thomasius.)

One year later, Leibniz copied the text of his letter to Thomasius almost word for word into the preface for another work. Among the various minor edits: Spinoza's name disappears entirely from the document.

The emendation is easy enough to explain. In between Leibniz's two versions of the text, Spinoza published his *Tractatus Theologico-Politicus*. The first of many to attack the book in print, as it turns out, was none other than Professor Thomasius. The "anonymous treatise on the freedom of philosophizing," Leibniz's tutor declaims in his review, is a "godless" work.

Leibniz did not hesitate to show his colors. In September 1670, he congratulates Thomasius: "You have treated this intolerably impudent work on the liberty of philosophers as it deserves."

From one of his Dutch agents, Leibniz soon learned—if he did not know already—the identity of the anonymous author of the *Tractatus*. In April 1671, Professor Johann Georg Graevius of the University of Utrecht informs him that "last year was published a most pestilent book, whose title is *Discursus TheologicoPoliticus* [*sic*] . . . which opens the window wide to atheism. The author is said to be a Jew, name of Spinoza, who was thrown out of the synagogue on account of his monstrous opinions."

Leibniz promptly replies: "I have read Spinoza's book. I deplore that a man of such evident erudition should have fallen so low. . . . Writings of this type tend to subvert the Christian religion, whose edifice has been consolidated by the precious blood, sweat, and prodigious sacrifices of the martyrs."

Evidently, Leibniz was keen to join the chorus of informed opinion on Spinoza. But here in his reply to Graevius he strikes two notes that seem slightly out of tune in the symphony of denunciation. Unlike most of his outraged colleagues, Leibniz indicates with phrases like "a man of such evident erudition" that he has high regard for the intellectual gifts of the author of the *Tractatus*. Second, typically, Leibniz focuses his concern on the effects of Spinoza's arguments (e.g., subverting the Christian religion), and not on their truth.

Leibniz continued the assault on Spinoza in correspondence with the great theologian Antoine Arnauld. In a letter of October 1671, he complains about "the terrifying work on the liberty of philosophizing" and "the horrible book recently published on the liberty of philosophizing"—both unambiguous references to Spinoza's *Tractatus*. As he so often did, Leibniz here simply held up a mirror to his addressee: Arnauld, as Leibniz would easily have guessed, thought that the *Tractatus* was "one of the most evil books in the world." Interestingly, in his letter Leibniz carefully picks his way around the actual name of Spinoza. Evidently, he did not want the powerful Parisian to know that he knew the identity of the anonymous author of the revolting treatise—although Professor Graevius had in fact passed along that information six months previously.

There was little that was unusual or unexpected in Leibniz's first official responses to Spinoza and his *Tractatus*. The two philosophers, after all, were nothing if not natural enemies. One was the ultimate insider, the other a double exile; one was an orthodox Lutheran from conservative Germany, the other an apostate Jew from licentious Holland. Above all, one was sworn to uphold the very same theocratic order that the other sought to demolish. It would have been very surprising indeed if Leibniz had not declared Spinoza's work "horrible" and "terrifying," as he did to Arnauld.

And yet, Leibniz's next move *was* very surprising. Six months after denouncing Spinoza to Graevius, and in the very same month he wrote to Arnauld pretending he didn't even know the name of the author of the *Tractatus*, Leibniz took the first step into the labyrinth that would soon come to define his life and work. On October 5, 1671, he addressed a letter to "Mr. Spinoza, celebrated doctor and profound philosopher, at Amsterdam." (He was apparently unaware that the worthy sage now lived in The Hague.)

"Illustrious and most honored Sir," he writes. "Among your other achievements which fame has spread abroad I understand is your remarkable skill in optics." He goes on to raise some obscure questions in optical theory, and encloses for Spinoza's comment a recent treatise of his on the matter. He asks that Spinoza send any reply through a certain "Mr. Diemerbroek, lawyer" in Amsterdam.

Spinoza's reply is prompt, courteous, and not particularly encouraging about Leibniz's problems with optical theory. In fact, Spinoza seems to understand very well that the discussion of optics is merely an excuse to make contact. In the postscript to his reply, he gets to the point:

> Mr. Dimerbruck [sic] does not live here, so I am forced to give this to the ordinary letter-carrier. I have no doubt that you know somebody here at The Hague who would be willing to take charge of our correspondence. I should like to know who it is, so that our letters can be dispatched more conveniently and safely. If the Tractatus Theologico-Politicus has not yet reached you, I shall send a copy if you care to have it.

Spinoza here shows that he is willing to conduct any future correspondence in a clandestine way, according to Leibniz's wishes, so that both may avoid the risk of publicly exposing their relationship. It is also quite evident that Spinoza clearly assumes that his correspondent is well aware of the fact that he is the author of the Tractatus, and that the point of their exchange is to discuss its contents, and not optics.

Leibniz soon wrote one or more letters to Spinoza. In later correspondence, their mutual friend Georg Hermann Schuller reminds Spinoza that Leibniz "paid great attention to your Tractatus Theologico-Politicus and wrote you a letter on the subject, if you will recall." (The surviving letter, of course, says nothing about the Tractatus.) In reply, Spinoza says: "I believe I know Leibniz through correspondence. . . . As far as I can tell from his letters, he seems to me to be a man of liberal spirit and versed in all the sciences [emphasis added]." In correspondence since destroyed, then, Leibniz evidently praised the book he elsewhere qualified as "intolerably impudent" and managed to make Spinoza think he was a "liberal spirit." And he did all of this through clandestine communications, so that no one else might discover the exchange.

Curiously, the only one of his colleagues at the time who seems to have sensed something of Leibniz's hidden sympathies was his partner in political adventures, Baron von Boineburg. On the back of a recently discovered copy of the *Tractatus*, in Boineburg's hand, is a list of individuals divided into those deemed "pro" and "contra" Hobbes. To be pro-Hobbes, at the time, was to be edgy: a freethinker, a materialist, and possibly a heretic—just like Spinoza, in other words. In Boineburg's estimation, Leibniz was on the side of the pros.

With Professor Thomasius, Leibniz remained much more circumspect. Inexplicably, he waited ten months after learning the identity of the author of the *Tractatus* before letting his erstwhile tutor in on the news. On January 31, 1672, he finally wrote to Thomasius: "The author of the book . . . you exposed, in your brief but elegant refutation, is Benedict Spinoza, a Jew thrown out of the synagogue on account of his monstrous opinions, as one writes to me from Holland. For the rest, [he is] a man of very great learning, and above all, an eminent optician and maker of remarkable lenses." Here Leibniz suggests that he knows the identity of the author of the *Tractatus* only through his contacts in Holland. He neglects to mention to his former mentor that he recently had the matter confirmed by the author himself, who some months previously offered to send him a copy of his book.

Leibniz presented yet another, even more parsimonious version of the truth about Spinoza to Albert van Holten, a fellow defender of the faith. In late 1671, van Holten writes: "The Jew Spinoza, who bears a most inauspicious name . . . will be thrashed by the intellectuals, as he deserves." In his response of February 27, 1672, Leibniz says: "That Spinoza is the author of [the *Tractatus*], it seems to me, is not certain." But, of course, Leibniz—writing a month after his last letter to Thomasius and four months after hearing back from Spinoza—knew beyond a shadow of a doubt that Spinoza was the author of the *Tractatus*. Why did he suddenly deploy yet another subterfuge, this time apparently to protect the atheist from the man who wanted him "thrashed"?

A missive to another of his friends quickly belies the notion that Leibniz secretly wished to shield the celebrated and profound philosopher of The Hague from attack. On March 8, 1672, just days after fending off the thrasher, Leibniz writes to Professor Spitzel, a stalwart Calvinist, to encourage him to savage the *Tractatus*:

You have seen without doubt the book published in Belgium, of the title: *Libertas philosophandi*. The author, one says, is a Jew. He puts forward a critique, learned, to be sure, but full of venom against ... the authority of the sacred Scriptures. Piety urges that he should be refuted by a man of solid learning in oriental letters [i.e., Hebrew], such as you. . . .

Again, the incorrect citation of the title of Spinoza's book, like the implication that Leibniz knows that Spinoza is a Jew only because "one says" it is so, is intended to suggest that the writer's relation with the Jew in question is far more distant than is in fact the case. Furthermore, it now appears that Leibniz believes that Thomasius's refutation of Spinoza was not "elegant" enough and altogether too "brief," contrary to what he had earlier told his tutor, for, now he wants someone else to wield the hatchet with greater vigor. Spitzel, it turns out, was not interested in the assignment; in his reply, he refers Leibniz back to Thomasius's review.

WHY DID LEIBNIZ write to Spinoza? Why would he have risked his job—and perhaps more—in this way?

In part, Leibniz approached Spinoza in the same spirit that he first contacted Hobbes, Arnauld, Oldenburg, and all the other luminaries of the republic of letters. His self-appointed mission was to become the grand conciliator of the entire known universe of thought, the chief *érudit* of Europe. Spinoza, whatever the critics said, had suddenly emerged as a very large part of that universe, and Leibniz could not afford to forgo contact with the latest supernova in the intellectual firmament. Nor could he avoid seeing Spinoza as something of a rival in the quest for recognition. Leibniz's overture to the philosopher of The Hague, in brief, was the fruit of his ambition and his careerism.

Yet there was more to it than that. There is good reason to suspect that Spinoza's hardheaded critique of revealed religion found a sympathetic listener in Leibniz. It is a fact worthy of notice that, although he lived in a century noted for its Bible thumping, Leibniz rarely bothered to cite the scriptures in his philosophical works. His grandest aim, after all, was to build the *respublica Christiana* on a foundation of pure reason, not of biblical interpretation. According to Eckhart, furthermore, the philosopher often claimed that he saw nothing in the New Testament "that is not part of simple morality," and he frequently described himself as a "priest of nature"—sentiments that are clearly in tune with those of the author of the *Tractatus*.

Perhaps the most intriguing link between the two philosophers may be found in those sections in the *Tractatus* in which Spinoza outlines the contents of a desirable "popular religion." The essence of the creed Spinoza proposes to sell to the masses is the belief that "there is a Supreme Being who loves justice and charity and whom all must obey in order to be saved, and must worship by practicing charity and justice to their neighbor." Spinoza's exoteric religion, it turns out, bears a striking resemblance to the theological doctrines concerning God, justice, and charity that Leibniz so strenuously advocates in his own work as "advantageous" and "useful" to humankind. In fact, though Spinoza himself stops short of providing the details, it would not be implausible to suggest that the central tenet of the exoteric "religion" most suitable for ensuring good behavior within Spinoza's modern ideal of a free republic might well be the principle of charity combined with the doctrine of metaphysical individualism—i.e., the belief in the sanctity of the individual—that lies at the core of all of Leibniz's thought.

Behind the unexpected exoteric parallels, too, one may glimpse some further, esoteric links between the two philosophers who first exchanged letters in the autumn of 1671. Leibniz's very way of thinking—in particular, his unalterable commitment to the guidance of reason—compelled him to embrace some of the radical notions first expressed in an oblique way in the *Tractatus*. In May 1671—the same month in which he informed Professor Graevius that he had read Spinoza's deplorable book—Leibniz penned a thoughtful letter to a friend named Magnus Wedderkopf concerning the nature of God. If we accept that God is omniscient and omnipotent, he writes, then we are bound to conclude that God "decides everything," that is, that he is "the absolute author of all." In the book Leibniz had just finished reading, Spinoza writes that "whatever occurs does so through God's . . . eternal decree" and that as a result "Nature observes a fixed and immutable order" and "nothing happens in Nature that does not follow from her laws."

In thinking along such lines, Leibniz recognizes that he now faces a "hard conclusion": He must acknowledge that the sins of a sinner—he names Pontius Pilate—are ultimately attributable to God: "For it is necessary to refer everything to some reason, and we cannot stop until we have arrived at a first cause—or it must be admitted that something can exist without a reason for its existence, and this admission destroys the demonstration of the existence of God and of many philosophical theorems." There is no clearer statement of one of Leibniz's core commitments: the world must be *reasonable*, that is, everything must have a reason, and even God must participate in this chain of reasons. The principle of sufficient reason binds everything together in a chain of necessity; its iron grip must begin with God and include even all those things we call evil, too.

But the same commitment to reason, understood in a certain way, is the very foundation of Spinoza's philosophy, too. The challenge of showing that his own conception of God does *not* lead directly to Spinozism would come to dominate all of Leibniz's mature philosophy. Even in his letter to Wedderkopf, he indicates an awareness of the danger he courts. In the closing paragraph he warns his friend: "But this is said to you; I should not like to have it get abroad. For not even the most accurate remarks are understood by everyone." Many years later, perhaps fearing that his earlier remarks might be too well understood, Leibniz took the trouble to dig up the letter and scrawl in the margins: "I later corrected this."

Leibniz spent his life trying to correct the error, yet he never quite erased the suspicion that he was just showing the pretty side of some hideous ideas borrowed from another. To be sure, it would be naïve to imagine that Leibniz and Spinoza fell neatly into putative roles as, respectively, the exoteric and esoteric philosophers of modernity. But, even in the days of their first exchange, there was already at least a hint of the possibility that, far from being pure contraries, Leibniz and Spinoza were two very different faces of the same philosophical coin, always looking in the opposite directions as they spin through the air, yet always landing in the same place.

• • •

LEIBNIZ'S BEHAVIOR AROUND the time of his first contact with Spinoza inevitably raises a question about the extent of his duplicity. That Leibniz was practiced in deceit and manipulation seems undeniable. When he praised the *Tractatus* to Spinoza and damned it to Arnauld, he must have been lying to someone. Was he pathological?

Leibniz is almost unequaled among the great philosophers of western history in the degree of mistrust that he has inspired. Some historians have concluded that he was indeed a scoundrel—a self-serving careerist masquerading as one of humanity's great benefactors. Bertrand Russell, for example, accuses him of debasing his genius in the quest for "cheap popularity." Eike Hirsch's recent biography opens with a depressing confession: "The more I got to know Leibniz, the more he seemed to me all-too-human, and I quarreled with him. For he often struck me as boastful, sometimes downright petty, and at those times he seemed to me to be driven by ambition or even addicted to money and titles." The suspicions have afflicted not just historians, but some of the philosopher's contemporaries, too. Leibniz had a talent for making enemies. Many (though certainly not all) of his peers thought there was something sneaky about the man.

In recent times, however, a phalanx of Leibniz scholars has risen to the philosopher's defense, explicitly rejecting the portrait drawn by Russell and others. The same biographer who laments Leibniz's crass ambition, for example, claims to see in his "weaknesses" a way to know his "greatness" as a "visionary of the truth." What Russell describes as pandering the scholar Christia Mercer now labels "the rhetoric of attraction"—that is, the noble effort to adjust one's message to one's listeners' needs and abilities so as to "attract" them to the correct view. "It is always risky to speculate on motives," concludes the scholar Nicholas Rescher, "but in my own mind there is no doubt that the aspirations which actuated [Leibniz] were, in the main, not those of selfishness but of public spirit."

Guessing motives, however, is not just risky, as Rescher says; in this case, it may miss the more interesting point. With Leibniz, there were always ulterior motives. He almost never made explicit all of the reasons for any of his actions. The aspiration to promote the general good; the desire to be seen to promote the general good; the quest for truth; the yearning for recognition; the love of money and titles; competitive rivalry; and sheer, untrammeled curiosity—all of these impulses and others typically shuffled around in the background of whatever it was that Leibniz said he was doing at any one point in time. Behind some of his apparently selfish motives one may often discover some public-spirited ones; and the inverse, unfortunately, is also true. And yet, as one peels back each layer of purposivity to arrive at the next, the suspicion grows that the process will never end—that there is no self-consistent package of intentions that explains the complex totality of Leibniz's behavior. The truly disconcerting prospect is that, at the end of the day, one will find not a "mean" spirit, but no spirit at all.

The alarming fact about Leibniz is not that he did not always tell the truth, but that he was, in a certain sense, constitutionally—or perhaps metaphysically—incapable of telling the truth. In his handling of his first contact with Spinoza, to cite the most pressing example, what we observe is not straightforward duplicity, but a much more complex phenomenon that deserves the name "multiplicity"—that is, showing a variety of related but mutually incompatible faces, none of which seems to enjoy the privilege of being entirely "true" or entirely "false." From Leibniz's multidirectional correspondence on the subject of Spinoza, we may conclude neither that he was an anti-Spinozist intending to lure the sage of The Hague into a trap, nor that he was a crypto-Spinozist who concealed his true identity from his orthodox colleagues. Rather, he was—always to some degree, depending on the listener, the context, and the particular purposes in play—a subtle and indeterminate mixture of both. As Lewis White Beck has said, he was "all things to all men"; but the price paid for such omnidexterity was that he was no one thing to everybody.

Leibniz's apparent corelessness stands for a fundamental philosophical problem, a quandary that reaches to the foundations of his system of philosophy. In the metaphysics he later presented to the world, Leibniz claimed that the one thing of which we can all be certain is the unity, permanence, immateriality, and absolute immunity to outside influence of the individual mind. In identifying the mind as a "monad"—the Greek word for "unity"—he positioned himself in direct opposition to Spinoza, whose allegedly materialist philosophy of mind he adamantly rejected. And yet, the philosopher who made the unity of the individual the fundamental principle of the universe was himself incomparably fragmented, multiplicitous, exposed to the influence of others, and impossible to pin down. How could a monad be so multifarious, not to say nefarious?

AT THE SAME time that he was juggling his many perspectives on the Spinoza affair, the multitasking Leibniz was also energetically pushing the Egypt Plan toward its logical conclusion. On January 20, 1672, Baron von Boineburg sent a letter to Arnauld's nephew Pomponne, the French foreign minister, expressing his desire to consult with Louis XIV in person concerning a secret proposal of gravest consequence. The real author of the letter, of course, was Leibniz. Taking care not to reveal his mysterious plan, the writer teases the French sovereign with a list of twenty-two incredible advantages that he would gain from said plan. (For example: the plan will make Louis the "master of the seas"; and it will please both churches and all nations in Europe, with the notable exception of the abominable Dutch.)

On February 12, the bemused Pomponne sent back an equally vague expression of possible interest in whatever it was that was preoccupying the Germans.

No more encouragement was required. On March 4, Boineburg let the Elector of Mainz know that he was sending Leibniz to Paris. Boineburg himself would stay behind to attend to some other matters. The youthful privy counselor of justice immediately made preparations for his top secret mission to the French capital.

On the morning of March 19, having dispatched the last of his initial flurry of letters on the Spinoza affair just eleven days previously, Leibniz hastened for the waiting carriage. The preparations for the journey were made in such secrecy that his friends and family were left uninformed of his plans to leave. Only courtiers of the highest rank knew of the official purpose of his mission. And even they might have been surprised to learn of his unofficial agenda: to storm the citadel of the republic of letters.

Just before leaving, Leibniz had the chance the read the last letter from his sister, Anna Catharina, who had died only weeks previously. In this note, she warned her brother that unsavory rumors about him were circulating in Leipzig. People were saying that he was planning some kind of treachery against the Lutherans. Or maybe he was a spy in the employ of some foreign king. Dark actors in Mainz were on to him, the rumormongers whispered. From the other side of the grave, Anna Catharina fretted that his enemies were plotting to get her brother out of the way with poison.

None of it had any basis in fact, of course—at least, so far as we know. But it is perhaps less surprising than one might have hoped that, as his carriage lurched down the road to Paris, the young man from Leipzig should have been trailing the cloud of suspicions that seemed to follow him wherever he went.

8

Friends of Friends

The air was sweeter in The Hague than in Amsterdam, or so Spinoza maintained. Dominated by the Royal Palace that still occupies its center, the nominal capital of the United Provinces of the Netherlands was a small, wealthy, and sophisticated town of 30,000 inhabitants who, then as today, were better known for their political, military, and bureaucratic connections than their commercial acumen. The English traveler Edward Browne ranked it as "one of the two greatest villages, or unwalled places, in Europe." Samuel Pepys, who picked up a number of paintings at discount Dutch prices on his visit in 1660, remarked that "this is a most neat place in all respects." The ladies dressed especially well, he noted with pleasure, and just about everybody spoke French.

Spinoza lived in The Hague for the final six years of his life, laboring over his *Ethics*, tending to the lung complaint that was in all likelihood aggravated by the glass dust billowing from his lens-grinding lathe, and fending off the threats that inevitably came the way of a rebel living in plain view. Spinoza's newfound notoriety brought about some somber realignments in the circle of his friendships. A number of his old friends deserted him or were killed in action—

casualties in one way or another of the revolution being fought around the author of the *Tractatus*. New friends came his way, some of whom soon showed that were not entirely deserving of his trust. Among the new companions were the two individuals who ultimately engineered his encounter with Leibniz in 1676.

IF SPINOZA CHERISHED any hopes for increased toleration in the United Provinces as a result of the publication of his treatise on the liberty of philosophizing, those hopes were soon crushed by Louis XIV's armies. The French invasion of Holland in 1672 was a typically gory affair, spreading death and starvation across the Low Countries (not to mention large volumes of muddy seawater, thanks to the use of dikes as defense).

In the face of the French onslaught, the Dutch managed to keep their country; but they were not so fortunate with respect to their republic. The multitudes placed the blame for Louis XIV's heinous act of war on the leaders of the Republic, Johann de Witt, and his brother Cornelis, whom they accused (quite unjustly) of conspiring with the French in the plunder of their land. On an August afternoon in 1672, a surly mob cornered the brothers in the fortress in the center of The Hague. The rabble shot the door down, dragged the de Witts into the street, stripped them naked, clubbed, stabbed, and bit them, hung their (by now hopefully dead) bodies upside down, and hacked them into "two-penny pieces," according to the report of a visiting English sailor. Some of the bits of flesh were roasted and served as a treat for the rebellious populace; others were sold as souvenirs. William of Orange—the leader of the royal house that had waited in limbo during the years of the Republic—assumed the powers of a true monarch, and the Dutch golden age began its inevitable slide into the history books.

The event almost cost Spinoza his life, too, if Leibniz is to be believed. In one of the precious few comments he later made concerning their meeting in The Hague, Leibniz preserves the story: "He told me that on the day of the de Witt massacre, he was moved to go out in the night and put up a paper somewhere near the site of the murders saying: *ultimi barbarorum* [the last of the barbarians]. But his landlord locked him in the house to prevent him from leaving, for otherwise he would have risked being ripped to shreds." The implication that Spinoza believed that he (or at least his Latin placards) had a concrete role to play in the political affairs of the day seems to be confirmed by his decision to accept the invitation of Le Grand Condé, Prince Louis II of Bourbon, the leader of the French expeditionary force, to visit him at his temporary headquarters in Utrecht in 1673.

Notwithstanding the fact that he was spending most of his time crushing unarmed peasant villages, the great Condé was apparently rather liberal on philosophical matters. Unfortunately, by the time Spinoza arrived in Utrecht, the general had been called away on business, so the philosopher whiled away three weeks in the company of some of his advisers and other intellectuals of the town. Among those he met was Professor Johann Georg Graevius—the same man who, two years earlier, had denounced the *Tractatus* to Leibniz as "a most pestilent book." Graevius apparently got along quite well with the atheist Jew, and indeed Spinoza's extant correspondence includes a brief letter in which the philosopher reminds his newfound friend to return a borrowed Cartesian manuscript. Yet, only a few more years would pass before Graevius would denounce Spinoza to Leibniz in still more vicious terms.

In Utrecht the visiting heretic was also seen chatting amiably with the Condé's aide Colonel Stouppe. Yet this same Stouppe had just published *The Religion of the Dutch*, a book in which he laments the decline of religious observance in the Netherlands and cites as a particular outrage the fact that the Dutch have tolerated the existence of one Spinoza—"a very bad Jew and hardly a better Christian" whose work "destroys the foundations of all religions."

It is with friends such as Graevius and Stouppe in mind, presumably, that Lucas writes: "since there is nothing so deceitful as the heart of man, it appeared subsequently that most of these friendships were feigned, those who were most indebted to him having treated him ... in the most ungrateful manner that one can imagine." Spinoza clearly had a talent for attracting false friends along with true ones—a fact that surely testifies to a certain naïveté or ingenuousness on his part.

Upon Spinoza's return to The Hague, an angry mob gathered outside his lodgings on the Paviljoensgracht. The vigilantes—presumably the same group responsible for the grisly de Witt barbecue—clamored that Spinoza was guilty of treachery in his efforts to meet with the French general.

"Fear nothing on my account," the unruffled philosopher reportedly told his fretful landlord. "There are people enough, and even some of the most considerable persons of state, who know very well why I went to Utrecht." Unfortunately, the persons in question left no record on the matter, and so we have no very clear idea why the philosopher went to Utrecht in the first place. In any case, Spinoza was spared a popular grilling, and the affair ended well enough.

Even as he acquired false friends, Spinoza lost a true one. In 1674 news arrived from Paris of the tragic end of his first mentor, Frans van den Enden. Three years earlier, the philosopher's former schoolmaster had moved to the French capital, claiming, quite improbably, that he had been offered a position as medical counselor to Louis XIV. In fact, once in Paris, van den Enden had joined in a conspiracy to incite a rebellion in the northern regions of France, in hopes of establishing a democratic republic there with liberty, justice, and free education for all. The notorious advocate of free love had decided to put his (and in some sense Spinoza's) radical political theory into practice. The Chevalier de Rohan—a nobleman and war veteran with a confusing record of alternately opposing and supporting Louis XIV—assumed the leadership of the rebellion, and van den Enden became its chief ideologist.

On the evening of September 17, 1674, Frans arrived back in Paris from a covert journey to Brussels, where he had attempted to secure Spanish support for the uprising. He was just sitting down to dinner when he was told that the plot had been discovered. The Chevalier de Rohan had been arrested in Versailles six days previously, in the middle of a church service. It seems that one of van den Enden's Latin students, having noticed strange comings and goings from the schoolmaster's offices, had alerted the government to the conspiracy. Leaving his hot dinner on the table, Frans rushed off into the night, one step ahead of the king's police. The next morning, however, the police caught up with him on the outskirts of Paris and hauled him off to the Bastille.

The conspirators were allowed to stand trial, but the verdict was a foregone conclusion. Louis XIV himself oversaw the investigation, in which few techniques of interrogation were left untried. At four o'clock in the afternoon of a November day in 1674, in the inner courtyard of the Bastille, a crowd watched with quiet satisfaction as a gang of noble men and women were beheaded, one after the other. The last in line was Frans van den Enden. As a foreigner and a commoner, he was deemed unfit for the ax. So he was hanged.

Among those who followed the van den Enden case was Leibniz. Even as he was plotting against the state, as it happens, the radical schoolmaster had taken to running a salon of sorts on behalf of the chattering classes. One of his intellectual guests, surprisingly, was the theologian Antoine Arnauld; another, perhaps less surprisingly, was the omnipresent Leibniz, who expressed some resentment at Frans's unwonted success in attracting attention from the great Arnauld. In his later *Theodicy*, the German philosopher seems to greet the news of Frans's end with a knowing shrug.

The tragic fate of van den Enden cannot but have reinforced the message conveyed by the mob that greeted Spinoza on his return from Utrecht in the previous year: that he should exercise extreme caution in all of his dealings with France. And this, in turn, may further help to explain the nature of the reception he gave Leibniz when the latter attempted to renew from Paris the exchange that began in 1671. Indeed, it seems unlikely that Spinoza would ever have opened his doors for Leibniz, had it not been for the acquisition of a new friend.

Tall, aristocratic, arrogant, willful, and prickly, Walther Ehrenfried von Tschirnhaus was a brilliant mathematician with a talent for freewheeling metaphysical speculation and a desire to stay away from home for as long as possible. The son of a count, Walther manifested his intellectual skills and taste for adventure early in life, and so in 1668, at the age of seventeen, he was sent to Holland to study at the renowned University of Leiden. When Louis XIV launched his invasion of Holland in 1672, the young German enlisted with the Dutch in their fight for liberation. He rose rapidly in the ranks and distinguished himself in battle. When the hostilities ceased two years later, he returned to the university, where he studied mathematics, developed a fascination with Descartes and his philosophy, and formed an association with Georg Hermann Schuller, a young medical student.

Little is known about Schuller, and almost none of it is good. He called himself a doctor, though there is no evidence that he completed his studies. From the surviving correspondence it seems that he was a jack of several languages and the master of none; and he proved to be skilled chiefly in the art of spending other people's money, usually in pursuit of ill-advised alchemical schemes. Pieter van Gent, a scholar who shared his lodgings with Schuller for a time, described him to Tschirnhaus as a "good-for-nothing." "If only he had not deceived his girlfriend so shamefully!" van Gent added, regretfully failing to provide us with further detail. One of Leibniz's friends in Germany advised the courtier: "Above all, confide nothing in Dr. Schuller. . . . He cannot keep his mouth shut. With his prattle he has brought me to the brink of the greatest misfortune." Another complained that Schuller "was quite a nuisance to me and to others, with his false processes." The "false processes" in question, of course, were alchemical ones. Leibniz, however, failed to heed the advice of his friends. He took up a bizarre correspondence with Schuller, totaling sixty-six letters, many of which concerned money that the philosopher unwisely invested in the good doctor's surefire ideas for making gold.

But the important fact for the moment is that Schuller was an enthusiastic—if not particularly capable or scrupulous—admirer of Spinoza. Through Schuller, Tschirnhaus fell under the spell of the philosopher of The Hague. He studied Spinoza's available writings and wrote to the philosopher himself with penetrating questions on the finer points of his doctrines. By most scholars' accounts, their exchanges are some of the most fruitful in Spinoza's extant correspondence. In late 1674, Tschirnhaus traveled to The Hague and met with the master in person. The meeting was evidently a great success, for, in a sure sign of trust and respect, Spinoza rewarded his youthful acolyte with manuscript copies of some of his unpublished writings—including at least an extract of the *Ethics*. However, Spinoza requested that Tschirnhaus promise to reveal the secret writings to no one without his express consent.

That Tschirnhaus was a seeker of truth with genuine talent in his own right is clear; whether he was a man of his word, on the other hand, is rather more debatable. The major work of philosophy he produced in later life, *Medicina Mentis et Corporis*, betrays a considerable influence from Spinoza; but the author nowhere acknowledges the debt. When Christian Thomasius, the son of Leibniz's university mentor, leveled the heinous charge of Spinozism against him, Tschirnhaus went so far as to claim that he had never met Spinoza—a fact that, unfortunately, was directly contradicted by the letters published in Spinoza's posthumous works. To this deceit the wayward count added what must count as an exquisitely awful defense: "Even if I were the follower of a philosopher who is Jewish, that is of no importance, since almost all the Scholastics were committed to Aristotle, who certainly was not a Christian." As in his mathematics, where he tended to favor proof through the brute power of algebraic computation, Tschirnhaus was somewhat lacking in the remarkable talent for generalization, synthesis, and, above all, finesse with which Leibniz was so amply endowed.

In early 1675, with Spinoza's thoughts in his head and Spinoza's manuscripts in his valise, Tschirnhaus left Holland on a voyage of discovery that would last many years and take him through England, France, and Italy. He longed to see the world; and he was determined to avoid returning to Germany, where he feared that his father would force him to marry and settle down into the dreary life of a country squire.

His first stop was London. Presumably on Spinoza's advice, and possibly with his letter of recommendation, he called on Henry Oldenburg. When Tschirnhaus sat down with Spinoza's old friend in the dowdy offices in Gresham College, however, he discovered to his dismay that the secretary of the Royal Society had formed a "queer impression" of Spinoza's character. Having spent a few months in the Tower of London for political offenses in 1667, it seems, Oldenburg was a frightened man. With his natural conservatism stiffened by application of the rod, he now viewed Spinoza as possibly evil and in any event dangerous to know.

With all the enthusiasm of a true believer, Tschirnhaus brought Oldenburg around. He not only succeeding in dispelling the secretary's dire thoughts about Spinoza, but he even induced him "to return to a most trustworthy and favorable opinion of you, and also to hold in high esteem the *Tractatus Theologico-Politicus*," as he reported to Spinoza via Schuller. After relating the joyful news of the rehabilitation passed on from Tschirnhaus, Schuller injected a curious comment of his own: "In view of your directions, I did not venture to inform you of this." The implication is that Spinoza instructed Tschirnhaus not to discuss his person or his work with Oldenburg (or anybody else either, presumably). Tschirnhaus, perhaps ominously, broke his promise—though with apparently happy results in this case.

At Tschirnhaus's urging, Oldenburg picked up his plume and dashed out a note to his estranged friend in The Hague. He confessed to Spinoza that, previously, he had taken a dim view of the *Tractatus:* "At the time some things seemed to tend to me to the endangerment of religion." Now, he says, he thinks his earlier judgment was "premature." He understands that "far from intending any harm to true religion, on the contrary, you are endeavoring to commend and establish the true purpose of the Christian religion, together with the divine sublimity and excellence of a fruitful philosophy." He asks Spinoza to let him know, in strict confidence, what his future plans are for promoting his philosophical form of the Christian religion.

Spinoza embraced the renewal of amicable relations, and wrote to Oldenburg to say that he intended now to publish a five-part treatise—the long awaited *Ethics*—which he hoped to be able to forward to him soon. Clearly, the furor over the *Tractatus* and the fate of van den Enden had not dissuaded the philosopher from continuing to promulgate his explosive views.

But it soon became apparent that this wasn't the same old Oldenburg. Ten years earlier the secretary beseeched Spinoza in the name of humanity to publish his works. Now he implores him not to publish "anything that may seem in any way to undermine the practice of religious virtue." As for Spinoza's offer to send him copies of his new book, Oldenburg says cagily, "I shall not decline to receive some copies of the said Treatise"; but he insists that they be sent to him under cover to a third party. "There would be no need to mention the fact that the particular books have been forwarded to me," he adds, to drive home the point.

In late July 1675 Spinoza traveled to Amsterdam with the intention of overseeing the publication of his *Ethics*. In his next letter to Oldenburg, he tells the story best himself:

> While I was engaged in this business, a rumor became widespread that a certain book of mine about God was in the press, and in it I endeavor to show that there is no God. This rumor found credence with many. So, certain theologians, who may have started this rumor, seized the opportunity to complain of me before the Prince and the Magistrates. Moreover, the stupid Cartesians, in order to remove this suspicion from themselves because they are thought to be on my side, ceased not to denounce everywhere my opinions and my writings, and still continue to do so. Having gathered this from several trustworthy men who also declared that the theologians were everywhere plotting against me, I decided to postpone the publication until I should see how matters would turn out, intending to let you know what course I would then pursue. But the situation seems to worsen day by day, and I am not sure what to do about it.

Spinoza's concerns, as it happens, were well founded. Church records in The Hague from the summer of 1675 indicate that the local minister was under orders to "work to discover exactly as possible the state of affairs regarding [Spinoza], his teaching and its propagation." One theologian of the time sent a letter to one of his colleagues, warning that Spinoza intended to publish another book "even more dangerous than the first" and urging that they take steps "to make sure this book does not get published."

While in Amsterdam, Spinoza joined some friends for a private dinner party. Among the guests was an acquaintance of an acquaintance named Philip Limborch, a scholar and a theologian. Limborch had many friends among the enlightened folk of the city, but he was himself congenitally pious and conservative in his politics. Ominously, he was already on record identifying Spinoza as the spawn of Satan.

Limborch was shocked to find himself seated across the table from the great unbeliever. During the benediction before the meal, he later recounted with horror, Spinoza "showed his irreligious character by summoning gestures by which he apparently wished to demonstrate to those of us who were praying to God the stupidity of what we were doing."

What gestures did Spinoza make? Did he roll his eyes during prayer? Or did Limborch concoct the event out of his own anxieties, reading sacrilege into an absentminded yawn or naturally drooping eyelids?

In any case, two things are certain. First, this was one dinner invitation Spinoza should never have accepted. Evidently, he misjudged the nature of his mealtime companions, just as he had misjudged Stouppe, Graevius, the grain merchant Blijenburgh, and others before. Second, the event, whether real or imagined, left a permanent dent in Limborch's mind. The scandalized prelate told the story here six years after the dinner party from hell, and then he repeated it to a visitor twenty-eight years on. Once again, Spinoza's expression (or possibly his mere existence) touched off an avalanche of hatred.

Spinoza's relationship with Oldenburg, too, was now headed for a moment of truth. In the same letter in which he related the story of his misadventures in trying to publish the *Ethics*, Spinoza thanked Oldenburg for his "friendly warning" not to publish anything outré and asked him to name which of his doctrines offend against the practice of religious virtue. He also invited his correspondent to iden-tify any particularly obnoxious passages in the *Tractatus*. It is almost incredible that Spinoza should have been unclear about the matter: a ravenous pack of theologians, after all, had just finished telling him what they thought was wrong with his work. Nonetheless, Olden-burg obliged. The worst passages, he replied, are those where Spinoza seems to confuse God with Nature.

"I see at last what it was that you urged me not to publish," Spin-oza responds, as though just having experienced a revelation. How-ever, he observes, "this is the principal basis of all of the contents of the treatise which I had intended to issue." It is now December 1675—fourteen years and twice as many letters after they first met in the garden of the cottage in Rijnsburg. Spinoza at last sees that Oldenburg never properly understood the implications of the central doctrine of his philosophical system, and that now that he does so, he is utterly appalled—in short, that Oldenburg is not exactly a "man of reason."

All that remains is for the two old friends to get clear about the fact that Spinoza, for his part, isn't much of a Christian, which they do. Oldenburg asks for clarification of Spinoza's views on the Resurrection. Spinoza, in his final letter to Oldenburg, replies: "the death and burial of Christ I accept literally, but his resurrection I understand in an allegorical sense." Oldenburg almost shrieks back with alarm: "To seek to turn all this into an allegory is the same as if one were to set about destroying the entire truth of Gospel history." Oldenburg finally gets the picture, too.

There the surviving correspondence ends. It reads, with hindsight, as something of an inversion of Spinoza's ideals concerning friendship among men of reason. For it is clear that the two men developed an intimate bond; but this bond was an emotional and imaginative one, based on a radical misperception of each other's character and motives rather than on a shared philosophy of reason. And yet the glue of friendship had still not come unstuck. One more letter was to issue from Oldenburg's plume. But he would make the mistake of entrusting it to Leibniz for personal delivery.

While Spinoza's bond with Oldenburg approached its poignant denouement, the ever loyal Tschirnhaus was packing his bags to leave London for Paris, the next stop on his voyage of discovery. He had apparently created a highly favorable impression with Oldenburg and friends at the Royal Society. As the promising mathematician was getting ready to depart, Oldenburg approached him and told him of another young German now residing in Paris, an able geometer and a fellow member of the Royal Society, with whom perhaps Tschirnhaus would have much to discuss. So Tschirnhaus sailed across the Channel, bearing Spinoza's secret manuscripts in one hand and a letter of introduction to Leibniz in the other.

9

Leibniz in Love

At about the same age in which Spinoza entered the darkest part of his dark period, Leibniz arrived in the City of Light. After a bumpy, twelve-day ride across the French countryside, he stepped out of his carriage and fell in love at first sight—with Paris. The four years he resided on the banks of the Seine were his glory years, the time in which he made his most lasting mathematical and philosophical discoveries. In the gilded salons of the French capital he found his fashion sense and developed his signature personal style, to which he would cling long after it had fallen out of favor. The story of Leibniz in Paris offers the vicarious thrill of seeing one dazzled by life and desperately in love with the future; but it strikes a melancholy note, too, as it inevitably comes to an end, leaving the jilted lover always wanting more.

Paris came of age in the seventeenth century. After stagnating through the Middle Ages, the city tripled in land area and doubled in population to half a million during the course of the Grand Siècle. Most of the growth took place in the second half of the century, after Louis XIV ascended the throne. Paris under the Sun King had the spirit of a boomtown: "Everything here is going from good to better, regardless of where one turns; Paris was never so fine or stately as today," gushed one of Leibniz's correspondents, the famous theater critic Samuel Chappuzeau. Dr. Martin Lister, an English traveler, said in 1698 that Paris was "a new City within this forty years." Voltaire later remarked "there is little that was not either re-established or created in [Louis XIV's] time."

"Vanity," "opulence," and "elegance" are the words that recur most frequently in seventeenth-century travelers' descriptions of the French capital. Dr. Lister—his awe overwhelming any moral reservations—called Paris a "whirlpool of luxury." Aside from the new mansions, palaces, gardens, and plazas, visitors could feast their eyes on a flock of white swans, imported at considerable expense by Louis himself in order to bring grace and beauty to the slimy banks of the Seine.

Among the most visible (and audible) signs of the new wealth were the carriages. In 1594, there were eight carriages in all Paris, according to one count. By the end of the seventeenth century, there were as many as twenty thousand. The new vehicles were icons of progress not just in number but in quality. Voltaire enthused that the glass windows and new suspension systems of modern carriages rendered the earlier models obsolete. Among "people of quality," the right kind of carriage became a coveted status symbol. The new test of eligibility for a marriageable male was: What kind of carriage does he drive?

While the King thought of improving the city by means of swans, monuments, and other gestures redolent of the Middle Ages, his more forward-thinking deputies, led by Jean-Baptiste Colbert, began to look at the challenges of urban planning in a modern way. They doubled the number of public water fountains and refurbished the ailing sewers. To improve circulation on the city's congested streets, they invested heavily in pavement, and on the newly hardened thoroughfares they inaugurated a novel form of public transport: the public carriage, or omnibus. In the year before Leibniz's arrival, the municipal authorities also began installing street lamps, bringing light and security into the night. For perhaps the first time in the modern era, a cadre of professionals took a comprehensive approach to the matters of sanitation, water supply, transportation, security, health, education, and aesthetics. The historian Pierre Lavedan dates the start of the urban sciences from seventeenth-century Paris.

Despite the signs of progress, there was no tidy escape from the Middle Ages. Henri Sauval, a chronicler of the times, said that, although no city was better paved than Paris, none was muddier. This was no ordinary mud: it was "black, stinking, of an intolerable odor to strangers," and easily detectible at a distance of ten miles. After every rain—and often, inexplicably, without any aid from the heavens at all—the malodorous mire would ooze up from the gutters and claim the city streets, paralyzing carriages and pedestrians alike. "It clings like the mud of Paris," was the common way of describing anything that frustrated all efforts at eradication.

Paris stank, too, and not just on account of the high sulfur content of its inescapable mud. The pig farms, slaughterhouses, starch factories, and even ill-tended graveyards in the city center all contributed to the fumes. It cannot have helped that many Parisians were in the habit of emptying their chamber pots out the window—a practice as illegal as it was universal, for, as one police source complained, it occurred mainly at night "at a time when one cannot readily see from whence came the contravention."

In the tumultuous streets of Paris in 1672, an omniscient historical observer might well have detected the silent forces at work that were setting the stage for a tremendous clash between the medieval world and the modern world, a conflict that would radically transform the context within which human experience would take place. Such forces, however, were not always in the forefront of consciousness at the time, not even among the new breed of itinerant diplomat-philosophers, who nonetheless must be numbered among the most important agents of change.

Leibniz settled on the Left Bank, in the Faubourg St. Germain, home to the hard core of Paris's new class of theatergoers. During his four years in Paris, he lived in guesthouses of the sort patronized mainly by young men from abroad—businessmen, diplomats, students, and other people of quality in search of favor and fortune. The Hôtel des Romains on the rue Ste. Margarite, the philosopher's residence for about two years, had a reputation as a German colony.

In his valise the twenty-six-year-old privy counselor of Mainz brought with him the ultraconfidential Egypt Plan. There, alas, the vaunted plan remained. Perhaps because he never received Leibniz's epic paper, Louis XIV had already opted to invade nearby Holland rather than faraway Egypt, having secured an alliance with the English monarch for the purpose. But Boineburg and Leibniz were not going to let such a dramatic change in political circumstances get in the way of their manifest destiny. The philosopher revised his paper so as to present the conquest of Egypt not as an alternative to the invasion of Holland, but as the logical next step: Holland was just the appetizer, Leibniz now claimed; only Egypt could satisfy the imperial hunger of France.

For six months Leibniz banged on doors at the Foreign Ministry, hoping to state the case for a crusade against the infidel; but he was rebuffed on all approaches. Determined to get their message to its intended recipient, Leibniz and Boineburg persuaded the Elector of Mainz to intervene with a direct appeal to the French monarch. Louis's response suggests that his claim to the title of Sun King was not entirely without merit: "As to the project of Holy War, I have nothing to say. You know that since the days of Louis the Pious, such expeditions have gone out of fashion." Louis the Pious, incidentally, reigned in the ninth century.

Loath to give the last word to the absolute monarch, the philosopher wrote to the Duke of Hanover to enlist his support in making yet another effort to present the plan. In a perhaps typical example of the philosopher's agility in managing the facts, he neglected to mention to the Duke that the proposal had already been quashed twice. The ever obliging duke expressed some interest, but the French remained unmoved, and, for the time being, Egypt was spared. The whole affair was conducted in such secrecy that neither the plan nor Leibniz's involvement in it became public knowledge until Napoleon invaded Egypt, 130 years later, and some agents of the British royal family opened the dusty files of Hanover to investigate the rumors that it was someone there who first gave the feisty Frenchman the idea.

With the collapse of the Egypt Plan, Leibniz's official rationale for remaining in Paris crumbled, too. Instead of returning to Mainz, however, the young diplomat immediately began to cast around for other reasons to justify his stay in the capital of the republic of letters. "I believe I will always be an amphibian," he explained to a colleague, meaning that he hoped to split his time between France and Germany. But, in fact, the young courtier had already decided that he much preferred the fluid terrain on the banks of the Seine to the barren soil of his homeland.

IT WAS ONE of those ages in which the men dressed far better than the women. Men of quality sported feathered hats, long jackets, silk cravats, ornamented vests, culottes or breeches ending at the knee and tied by a ribbon, silk stockings, leather boots, liberal doses of perfume, and elaborate gauntlets truly worthy of being thrown down. In the early 1670s, just as Louis XIV began to lose his hair, wigs came into high fashion, and soon no head of any standing was complete without false curls extending to the shoulders or below. Leibniz delighted in the whole costume. He became recognizable for the exceptionally long, black wig that always warmed his prematurely bald dome.

In the beguiling but treacherous salons of the city, the young German also learned his manners. Superficiality was prized, lightness in tone was *de rigueur*, and passionate disputes were taken as a sure mark of inferiority. Leibniz even adopted a characteristically Parisian tenor in his French. "I speak in Parisian, as you can see," he jokes with one correspondent.

The philosopher's sparkling exterior, sadly, could not entirely mask the fact that his body fell somewhat short of the Olympian ideal. His limbs, we know from Eckhart, gyrated awkwardly whenever he moved. He had a protrusion on his head about the size of a quail's egg, and it may well be that he took to the luxurious coif as a means of hiding this deformity. Baron von Boineburg, who tended to be blunt at times, felt compelled to introduce his protégé to the French foreign minister in somewhat apologetic terms: "He is a man who, despite his insignificant outward appearance, is in a position to perform what he promises." Leibniz himself liked to tell a story about the time he visited a Paris bookshop and was received in a hostile way by the shop clerks, who judged from his appearance that he was unworthy of their attentions. Then, a well-known publisher and acquaintance walked in, greeted him, and spoke most favorably to the store owner of his intellectual prowess. The snooty clerks suddenly became very helpful, and the philosopher was left to ponder the fact that human beings attach such inordinate importance to the merely physical properties of individuals.

From the only early portrait (made in 1680, when he was thirty-four) it seems that in this part of his life, at least, the smallish Leibniz was well fed. His second chin spreads generously under and around the first and joins seamlessly with the ruddy cheeks. The rest of his portraits, all dating from his late fifties on, however, indicate a thinning out with age—perhaps the consequence of later digestive troubles that reduced his diet chiefly to milk. Eckhart, who knew him in his last two decades, calls him "more lean than fat."

Aside from noting its effect on others, Leibniz demonstrated remarkably little interest in his own corporeality. To judge from his writings, purely private sensations concerned him very little. He abhorred physical exertion and led a sedentary life. "He never sweats," he once wrote proudly of himself in the third person, blissfully unaware of the price he would have to pay in later years for such neglect. He was content to eat porridge. He took his meals at odd hours and often had them served at his desk among papers and books. He generally avoided wine, but perhaps he had a sweet tooth, for on the rare occasions that he did indulge, he preferred sweet vintages, diluted with water and extra sugar. In Leibniz's mind, it seems, the body was not much more than a rack on which to hang some beautiful clothes; he was always more interested in creating a sensation than in having one.

Leibniz was a hedonist of sorts—a hedonist not of the body, but of the mind. He once described his past reading habits as "being impelled by the instinct of *delectatio* [delectation]." The same instinct guided his sampling of the delights offered by the City of Light. At the time, Corneille and Racine ruled the stage. Molière died in 1673, but Leibniz managed to take in at least one of the great comedian's final performances. He later said he greatly enjoyed the *Ombre de Molière*, a posthumous commemoration, and he once described a promising German actor as "a second Molière." The new Paris opera house opened in 1672, to the delight of Leibniz and to the horror of a number of churchmen with whom he would later correspond. The philosopher maintained that the opera was a fine and morally edifying entertainment, provided, of course, the stories did not trespass on the limits of common decency.

Leibniz was so enchanted with public entertainments, in fact, that he at one point proposed to establish a society to amuse and edify the masses with a new kind of spectacle—something like a combination of magic show, science fair, and comic opera. In a very strange piece he wrote in Paris, he justifies the project with a perhaps all too revealing maxim: "It is necessary to snare the world in the trap, to take advantage of its weakness, and to deceive it in order to heal it."

Given Leibniz's efforts to make himself attractive, as well as his attraction to his adopted city, one is entitled to wonder whether perhaps it was some sort of carnal love that tied him to the French capital. In Paris under Louis XIV, after all, the bodices were made to be ripped, Molière could provoke laughter by describing a married woman who had no suitors, and the new carriages often doubled as traveling love nests, especially on excursions to the conveniently situated Bois de Boulogne.

Disappointingly, there is no convincing evidence that Leibniz ever shared his bed with any other human being. Among the fifteen thousand epistles in his surviving correspondence, there is not one that would qualify as a love letter. When he was fifty years old, the philosopher reportedly issued a formal and tepid marriage proposal. The recipient requested some time to ponder the offer, however, which gave the suitor's feet more than enough time to freeze over. Later writings suggest that one aspect of Paris life of which Leibniz did not approve was its sexual license. During the crisis of the Spanish Succession, in warning the Iberians of the evils that would follow should they accept a Bourbon on the throne, Leibniz said: "There is in France a great freedom, particularly in respect to sex, and it is to be feared that they will bring this with them to the prejudice of good morals."

There was, however, the strange case of Wilhelm Dillinger. In his last decade of life, Leibniz took on as secretary this young painter, who apparently became quite a favorite of the courtier. The two were seen together at all times, and the younger man entertained hopes of inheriting his master's fortune. But they had a falling-out, and Dillinger left on bad terms, never to speak to Leibniz again. A number of contemporaries remarked that the two men bore an extraordinary resemblance, and in 1730 one writer alleged that Wilhelm was Leibniz's illegitimate son. In 1789, a destitute descendant made a claim on the Leibniz family fortune on grounds that this was in fact the case. However, Wilhelm was born in Saarmund, Germany, in 1686, which places his mother 160 miles from Leibniz (then in Hanover) at least at the time she gave birth. It cannot be ruled out that Wilhelm may instead have been Leibniz's lover. Such a theory of the courtier's sexual orientation might explain something of his secretiveness and perhaps the permanent sense of loneliness that lurked behind the sociable face he showed the world. However, in the absence of other evidence, further speculation would be baseless.

All the sightseeing notwithstanding, Leibniz in Paris was a man dedicated above all to his studies. He often toiled late into the night and then fell asleep in his chair. One secret of his success was that, like many hyperachievers, he needed little sleep—four to six hours a night were sufficient. He continued the habit formed in his youth of reading and writing while riding in carriages or sitting at inn tables, for he was a man of little inclination to routine. Even the spectacles and delectations around town were really a part of this brainy project: they were his way of both stimulating the mind and securing the recognition and status he would require in order to carry on with his studies.

It may be said that Leibniz in Paris, no less than Spinoza in Rijns-burg, led a life of the mind. Yet their respective ways of being could hardly have been more different. Spinoza recommended a reasonable degree of sensual activity (which in any case it is not clear that he achieved) as a means to nourish the body, so that it in turn might provide a healthy home for the mind. His life of the mind was defined not at all in opposition to a life of the body, but in opposition to the life of *other people*—the dissembling, conventional life dedicated to the pursuit of riches and fame. Leibniz's life of the mind, on the other hand, was indeed somewhat at odds with the life of the body, which in his case always seemed to exhibit a certain degree of unreality. Most important, Leibniz's intellectual life was *all* about other people. It was by definition a life of spectacles and delectation, of seeing and being seen. Consequently, it was indeed a respectable subspecies of the pursuit of money and fame. And, when the need arose, it was not at all incompatible with a certain element of dissembling—of deceiving the world "in order to heal it."

THE OTHER PEOPLE with whom Leibniz was most concerned were a very special breed. His connections with German aristocrats opened the doors to Paris's finest houses, and the well-coiffed courtier did not hesitate to walk through those alluring portals. He formed an association with the Duke of Chevreuse, the son-in-law of Colbert, who in turn gave him access to the palace of the second most powerful man in France. Through Colbert he met still more dignitaries, including the famous scholar Abbé Gallois and Pierre-Daniel Huet, the future Bishop of Avranches—a man of such erudition, it was said, that his Paris apartment collapsed one day under the weight of all his books. Leibniz also exchanged philosophical arguments with the great Cartesian Nicolas Malebranche and, of course, his idol Antoine Arnauld, who in turn introduced him to still more of the leading lights of Paris. The list of people Leibniz met in the French capital further includes a famous doctor, a celebrated architect, an astronomer, a philologist, a publisher, several mathematicians, and several librarians.

One of Leibniz's most important contacts in his first year in Paris was Christiaan Huygens. The scion of a noble family from The Hague, Huygens was the leader of the prestigious Royal Academy of Sciences. By grace of the King himself, he resided in a splendid garden apartment at the Royal Library. At the time that Leibniz came to call on him, Huygens was in his forties, a little too plump, quite weak in the chin, and already suffering from respiratory ailments that would force him to retreat from Paris to the family castle in The Hague. Leibniz presented Huygens with his design for an arithmetical calculating machine, which he was just then in the process of building. He also described some of his recent work in mathematics.

Huygens was impressed. He sensed that, despite the lack of formal training, his youthful visitor was an exceptional talent. He suggested avenues of research that later proved quite fruitful for Leibniz. He might very well have had a few words to say on the subject of Spinoza, too. Though he tended to refer to the philosopher dismissively as "our Jew," Huygens had read the *Tractatus Theologico-Politicus* and reportedly thought highly of it.

In early 1673, Melchior von Schönborn, Boineburg's son-in-law and the heir to the Elector of Mainz, invited Leibniz to join him on a diplomatic mission to the court of Charles II. Eager to expand his network in London, the other great capital of European letters, Leibniz seized the opportunity. In his bags he packed his arithmetical calculating machine, which now existed in the form of a prototype.

After a stormy crossing of the Channel, Leibniz raced to Gresham College and the door of Spinoza's old friend, Henry Oldenburg, with whom he had been in correspondence for three years. Oldenburg welcomed his younger compatriot warmly and arranged for him to present his calculating machine to the members of the Royal Society. A few days later, the representatives of the Royal Society assembled to view the machine and meet the inventor. According to Leibniz's report to the Duke of Hanover, the panel of Britain's most celebrated scientists greeted him with "great applause" and acknowledged the calculating device as "one of the most considerable inventions of the time."

The records of the Royal Society, on the other hand, paint a somewhat different picture of the event. The machine was not yet finished and suffered from mechanical breakdowns. Robert Hooke was openly contemptuous of the device, and even more unpleasant in his comments about the young German behind his back. At the end of the show, Oldenburg secured a promise from Leibniz that he would make good on the defects of the machine by sending a finished version within the year.

On his return to Paris, Leibniz received notice from Oldenburg that his application for membership in the Royal Society had been accepted on the strength of that promise to supply a finished version of the calculating machine. In an effort to reassure his new associate, Oldenburg pointed out that Hooke was just as nasty with everyone else. (In fact, Oldenburg and Hooke were at each other's throats at the time.) Leibniz, apparently unaware that, according to Society custom, the invitation to membership called for a ceremonial reply detailing his scientific aims, sent back a perfunctory thank-you letter. Irked by this breach in protocol, Oldenburg prodded his new associate to produce a more substantial acceptance letter, which Leibniz, somewhat grudgingly, soon did.

Both Leibniz and Spinoza were about the same age when they first met Oldenburg in person: Spinoza was twenty-eight, Leibniz twenty-six. But Oldenburg's communications with Leibniz seem intended for a much younger man. In his letters to his fellow German, Oldenburg adopts a fatherly tone, sometimes encouraging the young scholar, sometimes scolding him. He seems to have taken an interest in Leibniz partly in the spirit of national solidarity. There is no sign of the intimacy, awe, or incomprehension with which he beheld Spinoza, nor is there any indication that he expected great things from Leibniz until the matter of calculus came up. There is, however, some sign of irritation. When, more than a year after his visit to London, Leibniz had still failed to send an improved version of the calculating machine, Oldenburg could not disguise his exasperation:

> Please allow me to advise you that you are obligated to send to the Royal Society your arithmetical machine as I promised on your behalf. I certainly wish that you, as a German and member of the Society, would keep your word, the sooner the better to relieve me of this anxiety for the reputation of a fellow-citizen, which has caused me no little distress. For the rest, farewell, and pardon my taking this liberty.

Another two years passed before Leibniz presented his machine to the members of the Royal Society, however, and even then the device remained unfinished.

Leibniz had a way with people. Like Spinoza, he made friends easily, and indeed the two philosophers shared many of the same friends. Leibniz, too, believed that nothing is so useful to the human being as another human being—that "man is a God to man," as Spinoza said. But Leibniz manifestly did not believe, as Spinoza did, that one's friends had to be "men of reason." On the contrary, Leibniz expected his friends to be able to *do* something for the world (and perhaps for himself, too). Power—whether the brute political power of the many dukes and princes with whom he mingled, or the intellectual power of his friends in the academies and churches—was the attribute most likely to win Leibniz's affection.

For the sake of humanity, in fact, it could have been no other way. Leibniz explains why to his beloved Duke of Hanover: "As it is from grand princes that one may await remedies to public evils and as they are the most powerful instruments of divine benevolence, they are necessarily loved by all those who have disinterested sentiments, who do not look for their own happiness but in the public."

The name best suited for the kind of people Leibniz wished to meet is the one he gave them himself: "excellent people." Excellent people included those who are made so by birth and those who become so in virtue of their gifts and accomplishments. The most excellent of all, in Leibniz's eyes, tended to be those who combined a noble pedigree with a great intellect—men such as Antoine Arnauld, Christiaan Huygens, and, soon, Walther Ehrenfried von Tschirnhaus.

BY HIS OWN account, Leibniz's performance in Paris was outstanding. "Never has a foreigner . . . had a more favorable reception from the people of merit," he says of himself. In a letter of January 1675 to the Duke of Hanover, he provides a characteristically ecstatic self-assessment:

> Paris is a place where it is difficult to distinguish oneself. One finds here the most able men of the time, in all the sciences, and much work as well as a certain solidity is required in order to establish a reputation. In sum, I don't know how it is that I managed to succeed and to be recognized as one who is capable of doing something extraordinary.

Leibniz needed no excuses to blow his own horn; but in this case, as always with the amply endowed Johann Friedrich, he had an agenda. He wanted financial support for continuing his life in Paris. His awe-inspiring reception notwithstanding, Leibniz's struggle to remain in the most learned and powerful city in the universe was not going well.

During his first year in Paris, Leibniz had the good fortune to have at his back Baron von Boineburg, a man who understood him well and shared his interests. Boineburg assigned his protégé to pursue the matter of his endangered real estate interests, and so gave Leibniz ample cover for remaining in Paris. The baron, however, died in late 1672, leaving the philosopher bereft of one of his greatest patrons. As something of a parting gift, the dying Boineburg sent Leibniz his sixteen-year-old son as a pupil.

Leibniz seized upon his pedagogical mission, devising a vigorous schedule of learning that would keep the distinguished teenager occupied from 6:00 A.M. to 10:00 P.M. every day and insisting that they live under the same roof. The younger Boineburg, unfortunately, soon rebelled against his tutor's extreme demands, preferring instead to cultivate his manhood in the company of his peers on nights out in the city. The aristocratic pupil and his hard-driving teacher grew to detest each other. The boy's mother protested on her son's behalf. Leibniz responded by complaining that he had not received proper compensation from the House of Boineburg for past and present work. After a long, cold war involving little instruction and no money, Frau von Boineburg fired the family tutor in the fall of 1674.

On his return from London, Leibniz had also pleaded with the Elector of Mainz to allow him to remain in Paris while still drawing his salary from Mainz. The Elector granted permission for him to "stay awhile" in France, but he declined to pay Leibniz for the favor. The Elector simply had no use for a mathematical diplomat in a foreign city, and, as his son eventually had to explain to Leibniz, "the liberality of princes does not extend so far as the ruin of their states."

Leibniz next turned his hand to jurisprudence. The nature of his law practice is evident in the example set by his most important client, the powerful Duke of Mecklenburg-Schwerin. Some fifteen years previously, the Duke had married one of his cousins—principally in order to add her lands to his realm. There was little love in the Duke's heart, however, and he began to beat his wife. She fled the country, and, when his subjects rebelled against his misrule, he in turn took refuge in the court of Louis XIV. From the safety of his apartments at Versailles, the Duke converted to Catholicism and eloped with a French lady. This time it was love—or else she was very persuasive—for, after his first wife died, the Duke took the trouble to remarry his French consort in a more formal way. But when the bloom of love faded from his French rose, this miniature Henry VIII decided to divorce her, too. Concerned to ensure the legality of the proceeding, he hired Leibniz to research the relevant church and state laws.

The able young jurist proved that the Duke's marriage to his first wife had never been properly ended in divorce; thus the second marriage was not valid, and so could be annulled without divorce. Things were looking good for the Duke when it was pointed out that Leibniz's impeccable logic, lamentably, applied only to the *first* wedding to the second wife, not to the second one that took place after the first wife's death. Leibniz declared himself satisfied with the result, but the Duke was most displeased, for he was now apparently saddled with his French wife for life. The Duke, presumably figuring that his lawyer was only half right, paid him only half the agreed-upon fee, whereupon Leibniz protested indignantly but without effect.

Still short of spending money, Leibniz now counted on his calculating machine to solve his material problems. By 1675, he was in possession of an improved, though not yet complete version of the device. However, rather than send it to the Royal Society, as he had promised Oldenburg he would, he chose to send it to Colbert, in hopes of making a sale. The first minister, who was at the time trying to balance Louis XIV's horrendous spending on Versailles with plans to reform the Paris government, clearly needed any help he could get in his accounting department. He made available to Leibniz the services of some of his craftsmen. Unfortunately, although the statesman very much approved of the idea behind the invention, he gathered that its physical embodiment was not quite ready to perform useful work, and so he declined to purchase it.

Leibniz entrusted his fondest hopes for career security with Paris's

Royal Academy of Sciences. The Academy was the seventeenth century's version of intellectual nirvana. Its sixteen members enjoyed
lifelong pensions, no teaching responsibilities whatsoever, and the satisfaction of knowing that there was no more prestigious institution of
learning in the world. Leibniz's prospects for achieving such a blissful
state of being brightened considerably at the end of 1675, when one
of the illustrious academicians expired. Things looked even better
when his candidacy received the endorsement of his friend the Abbé
Gallois. But then, in another one of those inexplicable outbursts of
hostility that would suddenly intrude on Leibniz's life, Gallois loudly
dropped his support, and the application was rejected.

The philosopher later suggested that the Academy denied him a
position because its members felt that, with the Dutchman Huygens
and the Italian astronomer Jean-Dominique Cassini already signed
up, there were already too many immigrants on the roster. Another
story, however, has it that Gallois was getting even. Apparently, when
the Abbé presented a scholarly discourse one day, Leibniz couldn't
help let slip a smile. The hypersensitive Gallois saw it as a smirk and
decided to exact the appropriate level of vengeance.

Leibniz's desperation to achieve material security is evident in the
euphoria with which he entertained what must count as the least
likely of his financial schemes. In a letter of October 1675 to his relatives in Germany, he asks for money for a once-in-a-lifetime investment opportunity:

> Having by my labor and the grace of God amassed some little
> money, I have found an opportunity to invest it so as to yield a
> certain and permanent income. . . . Several distinguished persons
> of rank, who are especially favorably disposed toward me, have
> proposed to me to purchase a certain office, or charge, the pro-
> ceeds of which would, in the course of time, suffice to discharge
> the small debt necessary to be contracted at the outset. These
> persons, on whom the matter depends in part, retain the office
> for me, and prevent others, who are willing to give a larger sum
> for it, from anticipating me. . . . For myself, I cannot but think
> that the circumstances are a divine dispensation and calling from
> God, who makes all things so wonderfully harmonize together.

The get-rich-quick office God so thoughtfully reserved for Leibniz must have been essentially a tax-collecting position, possibly of the sort that Louis XIV was in the habit of selling to aspiring members of the bourgeoisie as a means of raising funds for his costly military adventures. It would have entitled Leibniz to receive, by his own estimates, 800 thalers per year in the first years, rising to 1,000 thalers, and "even this sum may be increased."

The 1,000 or so thalers annually that Leibniz anticipated from his ideal job in Paris turns out to be about half the level of income he ultimately achieved in Hanover after strenuous efforts to improve his financial condition. According to the currency exchange rates of the time, 2,000 thalers was equivalent to approximately 3,300 Dutch guilders. Spinoza, by way of contrast, was content to live on roughly 300 guilders per year (in Holland, one might add, where prices were significantly higher than elsewhere on the continent). If we define a Philosopher's Unit as the amount a given philosopher feels is required to sustain himself in good philosophical spirits, then we may deduce:

$$\text{1 Leibniz Unit} = \text{11 Spinoza Units}$$

That is, you could feed, house, and clothe roughly eleven Spinozas for the price of one Leibniz.

It is also interesting to note that Leibniz indicates in the letter to his relatives that he has already "amassed some little money." His savings fell short of the amount required for his investment, but were not so small as to be irrelevant. It seems likely therefore that the young courtier was already in the possession of several hundred thalers—or several Spinoza Units. In other words, had he been content to live in the manner to which Spinoza was accustomed—say, renting a cottage on the outskirts of Paris, eating raisins for lunch and milk gruel for dinner, and dressing like the local pharmacist—Leibniz very likely already had the means to stay in Paris. But such an option was clearly unthinkable. Leibniz took for granted that the life of the mind is a life of status, too. He intended to leave his mark not in some future community of reason, but in the glittering society of the actual world, with its scarce supply of honors, offices, and riches.

God's plan for Leibniz's financial well-being, however, turns out to

have been different from what the philosopher anticipated. His relatives, not having heard from Gottfried for some time, and still in the
dark about the plans that brought him to Paris in the first place,
declined to participate in the office-investment scheme. Instead, they
dusted up the usual cloud of suspicions about his patriotism, his religion, and his personal behavior.

In his none too subtle message of 1675 to the Duke of Hanover,
Leibniz sighs: "A man like me has no choice but to seek a Grand
Prince." He yearns for the day "when I shall have at length brought
my ship into port, and be no longer compelled to run after people."
He is certain that a modest sum of money and a title appropriate to
his worth are all he requires in order to fulfill his destiny: "For experience has taught me that one will be first eagerly sought after by the
world, when one no longer needs to seek after it."

But enough was never enough. Leibniz's ship never came into
port. Even as he accumulated offices, titles, and savings enough to
count as a very wealthy man, he never stopped running after people
in search of still more money and more security. Life with Leibniz
was a constant struggle against the depredations of the material
world, a never-ending complaint against the precariousness of existence itself—a fact that stands in curious juxtaposition to the opti-
mistic metaphysics he later revealed to the public, according to which
all things happen for the best and the immaterial soul remains
immune to all outside forces.

Leibniz never saw it as greed; he saw it as part of his plan to
advance the sciences and serve God. Over and over, as he wrangled
with one employer after another to claim monies he believed he was
owed, he evinced genuine dismay, as though witnessing not merely
an injury to himself but an injustice to humanity, which would suffer needlessly should one of its best philosophers fail to secure the
funds he required to free himself from material worries. Among his
contemporaries, however, there seems to have been little doubt about
the matter. The generally upbeat Eckhart says: "Leibniz had a love for
money that was almost sordid."

For most of his stay in Paris, in any case, Leibniz had a fall-back
plan, though the prospect of falling back on it gave him no pleasure.

As early as 1673, the Duke of Hanover had offered him a post in his court—in Hanover. The proposal hung over Leibniz's future with all the gloom of a dark home to which a child knows he must return sometime before nightfall. For three years, Leibniz finessed the offer, striving to keep it alive without accepting it. His letter of 1675 to the Duke would prove to be his last, valiant effort to keep the game going for a while longer.

THE POINT OF the struggle, of course, was work. Notwithstanding the financial worries and other distractions, Leibniz in his Paris years pursued scientific knowledge with the vigor of an entire university. He was a learning machine. His capacity for study and writing would seem terrifying were it not so spectacular. The 150,000 sheets of writing in his archives must surely put him at or very near the top of the list of history's most productive intellectuals, whether measured in terms of wpm (words per minute of life), imp (ideas per minute), or any other metric.

On the surface, Leibniz's investigations in Paris show all the telltale signs of the omnimania that characterized his earlier activities in Germany. To the list of brilliant ideas he mentioned to the Duke of Hanover in 1671 must now be added a design for a new kind of watch, new insights into a variety of historical questions, and a project to translate certain ancient texts. He took particular interest in the mechanical arts. He visited many craftsmen in their workshops, noting that "there is here [in Paris] an infinity of curiosities, in goldsmithy, enameling, glass-making, watch-making, tannery, and the manufacture of pewter."

He also had an irrepressible fascination with believe-it-or-not-type mysteries. His far-flung network of intelligence operatives kept him informed of the latest oddities, such as a man who could eat fire (apparently by coating his tongue with some kind of resin); a seven-foot-tall giant; various inexplicable natural disasters, such as a mountain that mysteriously collapsed on itself; and, of course, the latest advances in alchemy. Once, later in life, hearing about a talking dog, he made a special journey to visit the supernatural beast. (He came away impressed, but not convinced that the case warranted any change in his philosophical views concerning the souls of animals.) Not surprisingly, Leibniz frequently complained that he had no time to get anything done.

Yet, in his Paris years Leibniz exhibited a degree of concentration in his studies that was exceptional in his long career. The focus of his intellectual passion now was mathematics. Despite the inadequate training he had received in Germany, the audacious autodidact soon caught up with the leading mathematicians of Paris and began making seminal contributions in his own right.

Leibniz's mathematical investigations initially centered on the summation of infinite series. The concern with indivisibility and the infinitely small was linked in his mind to some fundamental, metaphysical truths about the nature of substance, matter, and mind. His intuition told him that the problem of how to make sense of the infinity of points on a line was an instance of the problem of how to make sense of the relation between indivisible, pointlike souls and the continuum of the material world. For roughly the same reason that no number of points could ever be strung together to make up a line, he believed that purely physical or material principles could not account for everything in the material world, and that therefore an incorporeal or "mental" principle—"substance"—was required to explain the unity and activity of phenomena. He called this complex of ideas "the labyrinth of the continuum." Pursuing these premises through one end of the labyrinth, he would discover calculus; off in the opposite direction, he would envision a world comprised of nothing but an infinite number of pointlike, immortal souls. All of Leibniz's mathematical achievements in later life, and much of his metaphysics as well, had their origin in the ideas conceived in Paris before he turned thirty.

IF THE QUADRENNIUM in Paris was his time of glory, then Leibniz's thirtieth year and his last in the City of Light was his *annus mirabilis*. This was the year he invented calculus and this was the year in which his philosophical ideas were in their most fluid and chaotically productive state. It was also the year he faced Spinoza, first as an idea, then in person. If ever the errant courtier had an opportunity to make the case that his frantic efforts to find a secure position in life were in fact in the general interest of humankind, then this was that moment.

The year of miracles began in late August 1675 with the arrival of Walther Ehrenfried von Tschirnhaus. Fresh from his sojourn in London, Tschirnhaus appeared at Leibniz's door in the Hôtel des Romains with a letter of introduction from Henry Oldenburg. The two young Germans abroad became instant best friends, achieving a degree of intimacy rarely matched in the course of Leibniz's life. Leibniz was so pleased with his new friend that he immediately wrote back to Oldenburg: "Sending Tschirnhaus to us was a true act of friendship. I take great delight in his company, and I recognize in him excellent abilities, notwithstanding his youth." (At the time of writing, Tschirnhaus was twenty-five years old, and Leibniz was twenty-nine.)

In a fictional dialogue written the following year, Leibniz gives Tschirnhaus a starring role in the semi-anagrammatic character of Charinus. "There arrived a young man from a distinguished family," he writes, "who was nonetheless inquisitive and keen to learn, who had enlisted in the army at a tender age, and had become famous for his outstanding successes." (In that dialogue, to be sure, Charinus has much to learn from the wise Pacidius, Leibniz's Peacemaking alter ego.) Their friendship was close enough that it admitted quarrels, too. Walther has a "habit of stealing things," Gottfried fumed some years later in connection with the calculus dispute, and the two refused to speak to each other for many years before finally making peace.

In the Hôtel des Romains, the two expatriates promptly engaged in heated mathematical parleys. Their exchanges reached such a pitch that the papers preserved in Leibniz's files are crisscrossed with the scribbled handwriting of both men. It was around this time that Leibniz passed the threshold of the calculus. In a note from October 29, 1675, two months after Tschirnhaus's arrival, Leibniz for the first time used the symbol $\int$ to stand for integration, replacing the earlier "omn" (for "omnes"). Two weeks later, on November 11, he used dx for the first time to represent the "differential of x." Leibniz now believed himself to be in sole possession of the general method we call calculus. At some point he shuffled his new equations over to Tschirnhaus. But the youthful warrior—ultimately no match for the eagle-eyed man on the other side of the table—dismissed it all as mere playing with symbols.

Through the autumn of 1675, the winter, and into the spring of 1676 Leibniz organized his thoughts on the calculus. Not until he had it all down on paper would he learn through Oldenburg that a reclusive Cambridge don named Isaac Newton had arrived at sub-stantially the same discovery ten years earlier.

But more than just mathematics filled the chambers of the Hôtel des Romains in those crucial days in which Leibniz discovered the calculus. Tschirnhaus could hardly avoid raising the specter of his favorite living philosopher: Spinoza. Shortly after Tschirnhaus arrived in Paris, Leibniz dove back into the *Tractatus Theologico-Politicus*. His notebooks suddenly teem with excerpts from the notorious atheist's book—sixteen pages' worth, followed by brief annotations that, on the whole, add to rather than subtract from the author's claims. Spin-oza's criticisms of the scriptures—just as one might have expected—meet little resistance from the young German. One of Leibniz's Paris notes on the *Tractatus*, however, cautions against any direct rapproche-ment. Where Spinoza hints at his doctrine that God is Nature, Leib-niz writes bluntly: "I do not agree with this."

The tête-à-têtes with Tschirnhaus and the renewed readings of the *Tractatus* reawoke Leibniz's urge to make personal contact with the great thinker of The Hague. In the same week in November in which he put the *dx* in calculus, Leibniz reinitiated, in strangely indi-rect form, the exchange with Spinoza that had begun in 1671.

On November 18, 1675, Georg Hermann Schuller posted a letter to Spinoza, purportedly on behalf of his friend Tschirnhaus in Paris. Schuller starts by passing on Tschirnhaus's thanks for providing him with an introduction to Christiaan Huygens, who has proved quite helpful in finding him a job as tutor to the son of Colbert. After dis-cussion of a philosophical difficulty occasioned mainly by a flaw in Tschirnhaus's copy of the propositions of the *Ethics*, Schuller turns to the main purpose of the letter. He relates that in Paris Tschirnhaus has met a man named Leibniz and "established a close friendship with him."

He goes on to describe this new acquaintance in terms bound to appeal to Spinoza. According to Tschirnhaus, says Schuller, Leibniz is a man

> of remarkable learning, most skilled in the various sciences and free from the common theological prejudices. . . . In Ethics . . . Leibniz is most practiced, and speaks solely from the dictates of reason. . . . [I]n physics and especially in metaphysical studies of God and the Soul he is most skilled. . . . This same Leibniz thinks highly of the *Tractatus Theologico-Politicus*, on which subject he once wrote you a letter, if you remember.

Leibniz, then, is a Spinozist in embryo. And he "thinks highly" of the work he described to Antoine Arnauld as "horrible" and "terrifying." Next comes the point of all these good words: Tschirnhaus believes that Leibniz is "ready to receive" Spinoza's writings. Schuller hastens to add that if Spinoza should decline to allow Tschirnhaus to share the secret gospel, the philosopher should have no doubt that Tschirnhaus would "honorably keep them secret in accordance with his promise, just as in fact he has not made the slightest mention of them."

What Tschirnhaus may have understood by "slightest mention" here is open to question. Schuller's reference to an earlier letter from Leibniz to Spinoza strongly suggests that Leibniz himself was involved in drafting this communication with Spinoza. How else would Schuller and Tschirnhaus have known about a letter that Leibniz sent to Spinoza several years before either had met Spinoza? And if Leibniz was involved in this particular exercise in persuasion, then he must have had some inkling about the hidden treasure in Tschirnhaus's possession. In fact, it was widely known that Spinoza had produced a comprehensive statement of his philosophy: Oldenburg was in the know, as were many of Spinoza's other friends, not to mention some extremely irate Dutch theologians. The most likely scenario is that Leibniz was well aware of the existence of Tschirnhaus's stash of secret wisdom, and that he was frantic to get his hands on it. Schuller's communication from Tschirnhaus was, in effect, a plea from Leibniz to Spinoza.

Spinoza evidently considered the request a very important matter, for he replied on the same day that he received Schuller's letter. But the answer must have landed with a humiliating thud in Paris:

> I believe I know Leibniz, of whom he writes, through correspondence, but I do not understand why he, a Counselor of Frankfurt, has gone to France. As far as I can judge from his letters, he seemed to me a person of liberal mind and well versed in every science. Still, I think it imprudent to entrust my writings to him so hastily. I should first like to know what he is doing in France, and to hear our friend Tschirnhaus's opinion of him after a longer acquaintance and a closer knowledge of his character.

Why did Spinoza spurn the overture from Leibniz? Most likely, as we know, recent developments—van den Enden's execution in Paris and the threat of mob violence against Spinoza in The Hague—made him exceptionally wary of contacts with Paris. His question for Tschirnhaus was, in effect: Is Leibniz a spy?

While Leibniz struggled to penetrate Spinoza's defenses, he suffered a grievous blow to his plans to remain in Paris. On January 11, 1676, at the very moment he was composing his customary New Year's greeting for Johann Friedrich, he received a formal notification of his appointment as librarian at the Duke's court. The meaning was clear: take it or leave it. With no other honorable occupation in sight, Leibniz concluded his New Year's salutation to the Duke by saying he was overjoyed to accept the position. On the very same day, evidently dreading the prospect of returning to the hinterlands, he sent off a letter to Jean-Baptiste Colbert, pleading one more time for help in getting a position in the French Academy. There followed another flurry of letters to other notables of Paris, all asking for help in securing a position that might save him from the horror of life in Hanover.

Even as he juggled his job prospects and the calculus, however, Leibniz did not relent in his pursuit of the truth about Spinoza. The rejection of his request for admission into the Spinoza fan club, it seems, did little to diminish his desire to uncover the secret wisdom of the mysterious philosopher to the north. There is no record that Spinoza ever gave express consent to Tschirnhaus's request to share his writings with Leibniz. Possibly, the Schuller/Tschirnhaus/Leibniz trio rushed another plea to the philosopher of The Hague over the winter holidays, received a prompt and favorable response, and then destroyed the evidence. But that doesn't seem likely. There is a clear record, however, that, some weeks after being denied permission to do so, Tschirnhaus did indeed share with Leibniz what he knew about the contents of Spinoza's masterwork.

On a piece of notepaper that dates from early February 1676, Leibniz wrote the first words in the story that came to dominate the rest of his life: "Tschirnhaus has told me many things about the book of M. de Spinosa."

10

A Secret Philosophy of
the Whole of Things

"Spinosa's book will be about God, the mind, and blessedness, or the idea of the perfect man," Leibniz announces in his notes on his discussion with Tschirnhaus. He then attributes to Spinoza a series of claims that must seem opaque to the uninitiated: "God alone is substance"; "all creatures are nothing but modes"; "mind is the very idea of the body"; and "man is in no way free—even if he participates in freedom more than other bodies do." Within the confines of a single sheet of paper, as it turns out, Leibniz traces the signature doctrines of Spinoza's philosophy.

It is a rare event in the history of philosophy when an abstruse system of metaphysics manages to summarize everything that matters about an age; and rarer still when it portends a worldwide revolution. Such was the nature of the system that Leibniz now beheld, and whose implications he was, arguably, the first to understand.

"The vulgar begin philosophy with created things, Descartes began with the mind, [Spinoza] begins with God," Leibniz continues. No truer statement about Spinoza's philosophy can be made—save possibly the claim that "Spinoza begins *and ends* with God." Part I of the *Ethics* is titled "Of God"; but in fact all of Spinoza's philosophy is all about God, the subject to which we now turn.

God

God became the name of a problem in the seventeenth century. No doubt many historical factors contributed to this unexpected development. The bewildering diversity of religious faiths arising out of the Reformation, for example, produced a crowd of new conceptions of the deity, none of which seemed to get along particularly well with the others; and this fact in turn stimulated much theorizing concerning their similarities and differences. The increasingly secular tone of public and economic life, too, eroded some of the evidence on which belief naturally rested. Among a small elite of educated Europeans, however, it was modern science that threw the most troubling spotlight on the Almighty. Learned individuals could not overlook the fact that recent advances in human knowledge rendered the biblically sanctioned stories on the genesis and structure of the cosmos untenable. *Eppur si muove*—"and yet it moves"—Galileo's alleged words concerning the earth after his trial—had become the secret rallying cry of humankind's newest pioneers.

In retrospect, of course, we know that science still had a long way to go. But even at the time, at least two farsighted philosophers could see where it was headed. The scientific investigation of nature, our heroes suspected, might one day unravel the mysteries of the world into a series of efficient causes. Miracles would dissolve into ignorance, and the cosmos in all its splendor would stand revealed as a grand but ultimately self-sufficient machine. In that event, what would be left for God to do? In more recent times, the physicist Richard Feynman has framed the problem in a laconic way: when you understand the laws of physics, he pointed out, "the theory that it is all arranged as a stage for God to watch man's struggle for good and evil seems inadequate." Or, as the physicist Steven Weinberg put it: the more we know about the origins of the universe, the more pointless it seems.

The question for seventeenth-century philosophers was not yet about the *existence* of God—for no writer of the time, not even Spinoza, explicitly doubted that—but rather about the *function* of God. If science did eventually manage to explain all of nature in terms of mechanical principles, it seemed, then the providential, miracle-working God of old would be out of a job. Science and religion—or God and Nature—seemed locked in irreconcilable conflict, or so the seventeenth-century philosophers sensed.

In his *Ethics* Spinoza presents his bold solution to the apparent conflict between God and Nature, a solution whose essentials had been undoubtedly already clear in his mind when he faced expulsion from the Jewish community in his twenty-fourth year. In Spinoza's view, to put it simply, God and Nature are not and never will be in conflict for the simple reason that God *is* Nature. "I do not differentiate between God and Nature in the way that all those known to me have done," Spinoza explains to Oldenburg. In Part IV of the *Ethics* he tosses off an enigmatic phrase that has since come to stand for the whole of his philosophy: "God, or Nature"—which really means: "God, or what amounts to the same thing, Nature." On the basis of this daring intuition, Spinoza constructs something that looks very much like a new form of religion—what should perhaps count as the first religion of the modern era (although it would also be true to say that in some sense it was the revival of an ancient and long forgotten one).

The "Nature" in question here is not of the blooming and buzzing kind (though it would include that, too). It is closer to the "nature" in "the nature of light" or "the nature of man"—that is, the "nature" that is the subject of rational inquiry. Inasmuch as Spinoza speaks of "Nature" with a capital N, he refers to a generalization over all these other "natures." It is the "Nature" of everything, or that which makes all the other natures what they are. One may also think of "nature" as an "essence"; Nature, in this sense, is the essence of the world, or that which makes the world what it is.

The most important feature of Spinoza's Nature—and, in a sense, the very point of his philosophy—is that it is in principle intelligible or comprehensible. His philosophy is at a deep level a declaration of confidence that there is nothing ultimately mysterious in the world; there are no inscrutable deities making arbitrary decisions, and no phenomena that will not submit to reasoned inquiry—even if that inquiry is inherently without end; in short, that there is nothing that cannot be known—even if we do not necessarily know everything.

Spinoza's concept of God, or Nature has this in common with the more pedestrian notions of divinity: God is the cause of all things. However, Spinoza hastens to add, God "is the immanent cause of things, and not the transitive cause." A "transitive" cause lies "outside" its effect. A watchmaker, for example, is the transitive cause of his watch. An "immanent" cause is in some sense "inside" or "together with" that which it causes. The nature of a circle, for example, is the immanent cause of its roundness. Spinoza's claim is that God does not stand outside the world and create it; rather, God exists *in* the world and subsists together with what it creates: "All things, I say, are in God and move in God." In simple code: Spinoza's God is an *immanent* one.

Spinoza also refers to his "God, or Nature" as "Substance." Substance is, very generally speaking, that stuff in which "attributes"—the properties that make something what it is—inhere. By way of skirting the arcana of Aristotelian and medieval metaphysics, one may think of substance as that which is "really real," or the ultimate constituent(s) of reality. The most important thing about substance is that no substance can be reduced to the attribute of some other substance (which would then, of course, constitute the "real" substance). Substance is where the digging stops—where all investigations come to an end.

Before Spinoza, it was generally taken for granted that there are many such substances in the world. With a chain of definitions, axioms, and proofs, however, Spinoza claims to demonstrate once and for all that there can in fact be only one Substance in the world. This one Substance has "infinite attributes" and is, as a matter of fact, God. Leibniz accurately sums it up: According to Spinoza, he notes, "God alone is substance, or a being subsisting through itself, or, that which can be conceived through itself."

According to Spinoza, furthermore, everything in the world is merely a "mode" of an attribute of this Substance, or God. "Mode" is just Latin for "way," and the modes of God are simply the ways in which Substance (i.e., God, or Nature) manifests its eternal essence. Leibniz once again hits the nail on the head in his note on the discussion with Tschirnhaus: "All creatures are nothing but modes."

At this point it would be quite normal to experience some difficulty in breathing, and not just on account of the high level of abstraction in Spinoza's thought. The philosopher's rather unsettling message is that everything in the world—every human being, every thought or idea, every historical event, the planet earth, the stars, the galaxies, all the spaces between them, yesterday's breakfast, and even this book—it is all in some sense just another word for God. Being itself, in a sense, is the new divinity. Little wonder, then, that the German writer Novalis branded Spinoza as "that God-intoxicated man." Hegel—who was fond of both his tipple and bibulous metaphors—claimed that in order to philosophize "one must first drink from the ether of this one substance." Perhaps Nietzsche came closest to the spirit of Spinoza when he said that the philosopher "deified the All and Life in order to find peace and happiness in the face of it."

Spinoza deduces many things from his concept of God, but one in particular deserves mention for its central role in subsequent controversies. In Spinoza's world, everything that happens, happens necessarily. One of the most notorious propositions of the *Ethics* is: "Things could not have been produced by God in any manner or in any order different from that which in fact exists." This is a logical inference from the proposition that the relation of God to the world is something like that of an essence to its properties: God cannot one day decide to do things differently any more than a circle can choose not to be round, or a mountain can forswear the valley that forms on its side. The view that there is a "necessary" aspect of things may be referred to by the sometimes inappropriate name of "determinism."

Of course, Spinoza acknowledges, in the world we see around us, many things seem to be *contingent*—or merely possible, and not necessary. That is, it seems that things don't have to be the way that they are: the earth might never have formed; this book might never have been published; and so on. In fact, Spinoza goes on to say, *every* particular thing in the world is contingent when considered solely with respect to its own nature. In technical terms, he says that "existence" pertains to the essence of nothing—save God. Thus, at some level, Spinoza stands for the opposite of the usual caricature of the determinist as reductivist, for, according to his line of thinking, we humans are never in a position to understand the complete and specific chain of causality that gives any individual thing its necessary character; consequently, we will never be in a position to reduce all phenomena to a finite set of intelligible causes, and all things must always appear to us to be at some level radically free. (In this sense, incidentally, he should count as a radical empiricist.) In somewhat less technical terms, we could say that, from a human point of view, everything must always seem contingent; even though from a divine or philosophical point of view, everything is nonetheless necessary. From the philosophical point of view—and only from the philosophical point of view—the distinction between possibility and actuality vanishes: if something may be, it is; if it may not be, it is not.

Spinoza takes pains to show that his determinism does not restrict God's freedom. To be free, as he defines it, is to be able to act in accordance with one's own nature (as opposed to someone else's nature). In other words, Spinoza supposes that the opposite of freedom is not necessity, but compulsion or constraint. Since God—and God alone —acts purely from the necessity of its own Nature, God is absolutely free. Leibniz assimilates this point quite well, too: "[Spinoza] thinks freedom consists in this, that an action or determination results not from an extrinsic impulse, but solely from the nature of the agent. In this sense he is right to say that God alone is free."

If the heady notions still leave one guessing just a little about what Spinoza thinks God is, there can be little doubt about what he thinks God is *not*. (And the intuition that Spinoza's God is more comprehensible in the negative, as we shall see, turns out to have crucial implications.) Spinoza's God is not the God of Sunday school and Bible readings. It is not the kind of supernatural being who wakes up one morning, decides to create a world, and then stands back at the end of the week to admire his achievement. In fact, God has no "personality" at all: it isn't male or female; it has no hair, no likes or dislikes, is not right- or left-handed; it does not sleep, dream, love, hate,

decide, or judge; it has no "will" or "intellect" in the way we understand those terms.

It also makes no sense to say that God is "good," according to Spinoza. Inasmuch as everything in the world follows of necessity from
God's eternal essence, in fact, then we must infer that all those things
we call "evil" are *in* God just as much as that which we call "good."
But, Spinoza elaborates, there is no good or evil in any absolute sense.
Good and evil are relative notions—relative to us and our particular
interests and uses. Spinoza's God—or Nature, or Substance—may be
perfect, but it isn't good.

Spinoza's God does not intervene in the course of events—for that
would be to countermand itself—nor does it produce miracles—for
that would be to contradict itself. Above all, God does not judge individuals and send them to heaven or hell: "God gives no laws to
mankind so as to reward them when they fulfill them and to punish
them when they transgress them; or, to state it more clearly, God's
laws are not of such a nature that they could be transgressed."

All of the traditional notions of a bearded deity blowing hot and
cold from the heavens, in Spinoza's view, are contemptible instances
of the human fondness for anthropomorphism. Besotted with our
unruly imaginations, we humans often attribute to God whatever is
desirable in a man. But, "to ascribe to God those attributes which
make a man perfect would be as wrong as to ascribe to a man the
attributes that make perfect an elephant or an ass," as Spinoza scoffs
to Blijenburgh. "If a triangle could speak," he adds, "it would say that
God is eminently triangular."

In Spinoza's adamant rejection of the anthropomorphic conception of God we may glimpse a very deep link between his metaphysics and his politics. According to the political analysis first laid
out in the *Tractatus*, the orthodox idea of God is one of the mainstays
of tyranny. The theologians, Spinoza suggests, promote the belief in a
fearsome, judgmental, and punishing God in order to extract obei-
sance from the superstitious masses. A people living under Spinoza's
God, on the other hand, could easily dispense with theocratic oppression. The most they might require is a few scientists and philosophers.

Spinoza's concept of divinity is so clearly drawn as the antithesis of the theocratic one, in fact, that the question naturally arises whether he invented his new God in order to save himself or in order to destroy the reigning political order. Inasmuch as Spinoza's God is easier to understand in the negative—that is, in terms of what it is *not*: a personal, providential, creator deity—than in the positive—what it *is*—then to that extent his political commitments would seem to be prior to his philosophy. That is, his metaphysics would be intelligible principally as the expression of his political project, to overthrow theocracy.

There are many more subtleties to Spinoza's bracing concept of God, and the philosopher draws out many more implications than those listed here. His *Ethics* is at first glance a thorny thicket of archaic terms and forbidding abstractions; but the rewards for penetrating the verbal barriers are great. Not the least attraction is the aesthetic experience, for the intricate web of definitions, axioms, and propositions is in some ways a prose poem, a dazzling intellectual sculpture. But the final point to consider here is just the method Spinoza claims to follow in his exposition of the nature of God.

Embodied in that method is Spinoza's most ambitious claim. His concept of God is not an intuition or a revelation or a preference, he maintains; rather, it follows with rigorous necessity from the guidance of reason. He avows that he can see God just as clearly as he can see the results of a proof in geometry: "I know it in the same way that the three angles of a triangle are equal to two right angles," as he famously says. He also maintains that any other reasonable person will see the same God, too.

Mind

If to be God was a problem in the seventeenth century, to be human smacked of outright error. In that crucial age, European humankind suffered some of the heaviest blows to its collective self-esteem. Hitherto, it had been understood as self-evident that the earth was the center of the cosmos, that Christian Europe was the source of civilization, and that the human being was the purpose of all creation. Copernicus and Galileo did away with the first of these truths;

Columbus and the Chinese, among others, conspired to eliminate the second; and so the third was left dangling quite uncomfortably in midair. To be sure, Darwin wasn't yet even a dream, and the moral majority had few doubts about the unique status of humankind among God's creations. But farsighted philosophers could glimpse the ancient questions looming with new menace on the horizon: What is it to be human? What, if anything, makes us special?

Descartes presented an answer that worked for many of the intellectuals of the time (and that still wields considerable influence). There are two radically distinct classes of entity in the world, Descartes said. On the one hand, there are minds. Minds think, exercise free will, and live forever. On the other hand, there are bodies. Bodies bounce around in space according to fixed, mechanical principles (which Descartes thoughtfully supplied). Human beings are special because we alone have minds. We alone are empowered to say: I think therefore I am. The rest of the world—rocks, stars, cats, dogs, and so on—is a giant machine, grinding through a series of states with the iron necessity that characterizes the laws of nature.

In the most widely accepted narratives of the history of thought, Descartes's so-called dualism is often taken to represent a fundamental revolution in ideas and the starting point of modern philosophy. In style and method Cartesian philosophy did indeed mark an important, hugely influential breakthrough in European letters; but in substance his work is perhaps better understood as an attempt to conserve the old truths in the face of new threats. His dualism was in essence an armistice of sorts between the established religion and the emerging science of his time. By isolating the mind from the physical world, the philosopher ensured that many of the central doctrines of orthodoxy—immortality of the soul, the freedom of the will, and, in general, the "special" status of humankind—were rendered immune to any possible contravention by the scientific investigation of the physical world. Conversely, the complete self-sufficiency of the machine-like material world guaranteed that physical science could proceed without fear of contradiction from revealed religion.

Not everyone was happy with Descartes's solution. In the eyes of many of his critics, the great philosopher appeared to solve one problem only to create another, namely: How is it possible for minds and bodies to interact at all? That they interact is obvious every time we lift an arm, eat breakfast, or go to sleep, not to mention when we are born and die. Yet, according to the Cartesian conception, it would seem to be impossible to explain how a mind can intervene in the material world without violating the mechanical principles that govern that world—or else submitting itself to those same laws and thereby reducing itself to matter. Furthermore, if such causal links between the mind-world and the machine-world were to be discovered, then that would open the door to the scientific investigation of the mind, which would in turn imperil the religious truths that the Cartesian dualism was designed to protect.

The mind-body problem manifested itself in other ways that kept seventeenth-century thinkers awake at night. The strict Cartesian dualism left animals, for example, impaled on the horns of dilemma: Do dogs, say, have minds like us or are they machines? To endow a dog with a mind, according to Cartesian logic, was tantamount to giving it a place in heaven; so the Cartesians stuck to the less theologically risky position that animals are indeed machines. Their critics forced them to concede that this implied that beating a dog and thus causing it to bark, for example, is equivalent to beating a bagpipe and causing it to squeal—a philosophical howler that seemed then, as now, both repellent and obviously untrue.

Babies, sleepers, and dreamers all presented similar forms of the mind-body problem. Since babies cannot say "I think therefore I am," do they lack minds? Do they acquire them later—say, on the thirteenth birthday? When we sleep, do our minds go on holiday? Can a dreamer say "I think therefore I am"? And if we should at long last fall into a very deep sleep, *sans* dreams, do we cease to be human for the duration?

The best indication of the vexation caused by the mind-body problem among seventeenth-century observers is the extremity of the solutions it called forth. Descartes himself sometimes said that the interaction between mind and body was so complex that only God could understand it. Many critics simply took this as a restatement of the problem—for how does God accomplish that which is inconceivable? At other times Descartes proposed that the mind is located in the pituitary gland, an organ of unique sensitivity and motility whose rapid and intense gyrations serve to convey the mind's desires to all the other parts of the body through complex mechanical pathways. This theory, however, had no basis whatsoever in the evidence; it failed even to address the mind-body problem it purported to solve (how does the mind move the pituitary?); and it was, frankly speaking, ludicrous. "Such is the view of this illustrious man, a view I would scarce have credited had it not been so ingenious," Spinoza says with undisguised contempt.

The work of the theologian Malebranche provides the best illustration of the lengths to which Cartesians felt compelled to go in order to patch up the embarrassing hole in their master's philosophy. Malebranche favored the view that every time a mind interacts with the material world, God intervenes on that "occasion" and brings about the desired change. When the mind "wills" to fry an egg, for example, God promptly reaches into the physical world and puts a pan on the stove. The theory was soon dignified with the name of "occasionalism." Even in the credulous seventeenth century, however, all but the most besotted Cartesians could see that occasionalism was just a kind of *deus ex machina* on a grand scale—which is to say, it simply used the name of God as a cover for ignorance.

The solutions were so desperate, of course, because the stakes were so high. In the strident world of seventeenth-century philosophy, the mind-body problem was not a word puzzle that could be safely relegated to undergraduate classes. For men such as Descartes, Malebranche, and Leibniz, solving the mind-body problem was vital to preserving the theological and political order inherited from the Middle Ages and, more generally, to protecting human self-esteem in the face of an increasingly truculent universe. For Spinoza, it was a means of destroying that same order and discovering a new foundation for human worth.

As a general rule, philosophers deal with their "problems" in one of two ways. Either they construct a theory to "solve" the problem such as it is; or they pull the rug right out from under the problem—in effect, they deny that it is a problem. Malebranche offers a good example of the first approach with his occasionalist response to the Cartesian mind-body problem. Spinoza exemplifies the second approach in his response to the same. Spinoza's answer to the mind-body problem marks a radical break in the history of thought—the kind that happen only every millennium or two.

The crucial premise of the Cartesian version of the mind-body problem is that the mind is something very distinct from the body, or, in more general terms, that man occupies a very special place in nature. This idea, of course, belonged not to Descartes alone, but to all of his theological predecessors as well. Spinoza expresses this premise in an elegant formula:

> They appear to go so far as to conceive of man in Nature as a kingdom within a kingdom.

It is because the Cartesians (and others) conceive of mind as something utterly incompatible with body that they encounter a "problem" in attempting to explain how mind and body may interact at all—i.e., how one kingdom may communicate with the other.

Spinoza flatly rejects the premise. The mind, he says, is not exempt from the laws of nature. In *The Short Treatise on God, Man, and His Well-Being*, which dates from around the end of his dark period, he announces his core conviction:

> Man is a part of Nature and must follow its laws, and this alone is true worship.

There is only one kingdom in Spinoza's world, the kingdom of God, or Nature; and human beings belong to this kingdom in the same way that stones, trees, and cats do. With this simple proposition, Spinoza drives a stake through the heart of two millennia of religion and philosophy, which in almost all of its forms had taken as its most basic premise that human existence is special and sets man apart from the rest of nature.

Leibniz had an inkling of Spinoza's thesis here, though some time elapsed before he assimilated its horrifying consequences. In his notes on the discussion with Tschirnhaus, he observes: "Mind, according to [Spinoza], is in a way a part of God."

Although he insists that the mind is a part of the same Nature as the body, Spinoza does not deny that there are mental phenomena—ideas, decisions, even "minds," in a sense. So, having pulled the premise out from under the Cartesian mind-body problem, he now faces an inverted version of the same problem. Instead of having to explain how it is that two classes of entity that are so different could possibly interact with each other, he must explain how it is that one kind of entity could manifest itself in two very different ways—first in the form of mental phenomena, then in the form of physical objects.

Spinoza's answer, in somewhat technical terms, is to say that two of the infinite attributes of Substance—and, in fact, the only two of which we have any knowledge—are "Thought" and "Extension." When we consider Substance under the attribute of Thought, he says, we see minds, ideas, and decisions; when we consider the same Substance under the attribute of Extension, we see physical bodies in motion. As he puts it:

> Thinking substance and extended substance are one and the same, comprehended now under this attribute, now under that.

In more concrete terms, this implies that every mental act has a correlative in some physical process, with which it is in fact identical. The point becomes clear in this passage:

> Mental decision on the one hand, and the appetite and physical state of the body on the other hand, are simultaneous in nature; or rather, they are one and the same thing which, when considered under the attribute of Thought and explicated through Thought, we call decision, and when considered under the attribute of Extension and deduced from the laws of motion-and-rest, we call a physical state.

The view Spinoza articulates here was later given the name "parallelism," for it suggests that the mental and the physical worlds operate in parallel. The most succinct and famous expression of parallelism is to be found in Proposition 7 of Part II of the *Ethics*: "The order and connection of ideas is the same as the order and connection of things."

Perhaps the most remarkable feature of Spinoza's answer to the mind-body problem is the unprecedented demands it makes on the body. If, as Spinoza says, mental decisions are nothing more than the appetites themselves, varying according to the disposition of the body, then it follows that the body is an extraordinarily complex device, capable of "embodying" (literally) any mental act conceivable. Anticipating the most common objection to his theory—that it is inconceivable that a lump of inanimate matter should be able to write poems, build temples, and experience love, and that therefore the body cannot produce the mind—Spinoza writes:

> Nobody as yet has learned from experience what the body can and cannot do . . . solely from the laws of its nature insofar as it is considered corporeal. For nobody as yet knows the structure of the body so accurately as to explain all its functions, not to mention that in the animal world we find much that surpasses human sagacity, and that sleepwalkers do many things in their sleep that they would not dare when awake . . . [the human body] surpasses in ingenuity all the constructions of human skill.

Written three centuries before the neurosciences began to reveal something of the extraordinary capabilities of the human brain, Spinoza's words here can only give courage to philosophers in doubt about the power of reason alone to overcome common prejudice.

In jettisoning the premise that the mind is radically distinct from the body, Spinoza dissolves many of the paradoxes of Cartesianism. For example, he does away with the dilemmas concerning borderline cases such as animals, babies, sleepers, and dreamers. "In proportion as a body is more apt than other bodies to act or be acted upon simultaneously in many ways," he says, "so is its mind more apt than other minds to perceive many things simultaneously." In other words, there is a continuum of sorts in mental capacity, in the same way that there is a continuum in the complexity of bodies. Thus, Spinoza has no difficulty in assimilating what experience tells us every day: that some minds are superior to others; that the same individual may think better at some times than at others depending on, say, whether one has had one's morning coffee; that damage to the brain can result in the impairment or loss of mental functions; that animals exhibit some degree of thinking; and that people who are in deep sleep, unconscious, dead, or unborn may not be thinking at all.

Spinoza's philosophy of mind, like his concept of God, is in some ways easier to understand in the negative—that is, in terms of the theories it rejects—than in the positive. Indeed, when considered as positive doctrine, his philosophy may give rise to a number of perplexities. One could argue, for example, that the division of Substance into the two attributes of Thought and Extension amounts only to an assertion *that* mind and body are the same thing, not an explanation of *how* the identity of these two very different kinds of phenomena comes about. In other words, Spinoza's theory, when considered as positive doctrine, may simply be kicking the mind-body problem upstairs, from humankind to God. It also seems odd—as Tschirnhaus, for one, points out in one of his letters—that Spinoza happens to name only these two of God's purportedly infinite attributes. One may even doubt that these two in fact count as attributes of equal status. For, if an attribute is, according to Spinoza's definition, that which "the intellect perceives as constituting the essence of substance," then one might conclude that the Extension is perceived through Thought, and so cannot count as being in the same relation to Substance as Thought.

But no such quibbles trouble our understanding of what Spinoza means to oppose with his theory of mind. The largest part of philosophy since Plato has stood for the belief that mind is a special kind of thing, endowed with free will and immortality, whose possession grants humankind an exemption from the order of nature. And this is the creed that Spinoza sets about to destroy. In fact, Spinoza's philosophy, if true, pulverizes not just the theories of his philosophical predecessors, but also many of the religious doctrines they sought to protect—not to mention common intuitions about mental life that prevail even today. And Spinoza is not shy to draw out these heretical and counterintuitive implications.

For one thing, it follows from Spinoza's position that human beings have no free will in an absolute sense. Our experience of freedom, says Spinoza, consists only in this: that we are conscious of our desires but ignorant of the causes that determine them. If a stone tossed in the air suddenly acquired consciousness, he argues in one notorious passage, it would imagine that it was flying freely. Leibniz clearly picks up the point: "Man is free to the extent that he is not determined by anything external. But since this is not the case in any of his acts, man is in no way free—even if he participates in freedom more than other bodies do."

Not satisfied with obliterating the idea of free will, Spinoza goes on to suggest that there is no will at all, in a certain sense. That is to say, we have particular volitions but there is no faculty of willing that exists independent of these particular volitions. What we call the will is "only an idea of our willing this or that and therefore is only a mode of thought, a thing of reason, and not a real thing; nothing can be caused by it."

Not only is there no will, according to Spinoza; there is also no mind at all, in the usual, Cartesian sense of that word. That is, there is no entity in which thoughts and desires inhere that exists before or apart from those same thoughts and desires. For Spinoza, the mind—like the will—is just an abstraction over a collection of mental events. It is an idea, not a thing. Specifically, Spinoza proposes, the mind is the idea of a particular, existing body. Thus it is the body—that is, the fact that a collection of thoughts and desires pertain to a particular body—which supplies the unity and the identity of the mind, such as it is. Leibniz once again gathers the essentials: "[Spinoza] thinks mind is the very idea of the body."

Of course, the implication of the claim that the mind is the idea of the body is that the mind does not in fact possess unity or self-identity in any absolute sense. The mind does not know itself, Spinoza reasons, except insofar as it perceives the ideas of the modifications of the body; but the idea of each modification of the body does not involve an adequate knowledge of the body itself; therefore, "the human mind . . . has not an adequate but only a confused and fragmentary knowledge of itself, of its own body, and of external bodies."That is to say, in Spinoza's world, our knowledge of ourselves, just like our knowledge of particular things in general, is mediated through the body itself, and is therefore always imperfect or fallible and open to revision.Thus, minds are every bit as complex and multifarious as the bodies of which they are the ideas. (It is worth noting that Spinoza's position is quite close to that which the historians of philosophy ascribe to radical empiricists, such as David Hume, and not at all consistent with the "rationalism" with which he is often incorrectly identified.)

One could point out that Spinoza here originates the idea of the unconscious, although this may be to give a bad theory a better pedigree than it deserves. Spinoza does not suggest that there is a mysterious, second mind buried underneath the conscious one and endowed with a will and desires of its own; rather, he contends that any mind is only partially conscious of itself. The place to look for the unconscious part of the mind, then, is not in a fictional, hidden mind, but in the gap between the idea of the body that constitutes the mind and the body itself.

A final (and for his contemporaries, dreadful) consequence of Spinoza's theory of the mind is that there is no personal immortality. For, to the extent that mental acts always have a correlate in physical states, then when the physical states turn to dust, so, too, does the mind. In other words, inasmuch as the mind is the idea of the body, then when a particular body ceases to exist, so, too, does its mind.

The ruthless quashing of personal immortality reveals again the extent to which Spinoza's metaphysics is linked to his radical politics. The theologians, says Spinoza, shamelessly use the prospect of eternal reward and damnation to cow the masses. If Spinoza is right, then philosophy since Plato is not just wrong, but an abomination, a fraud of global dimensions intended to excuse oppression in this world with the empty promise of justice in the afterlife. In fact, inasmuch as Spinoza's "negative" theory of mind remains easier to grasp than his "positive" one, then to that extent his political commitments once again seem prior to his philosophical ones.

In sum: To the fundamental question—what makes us special?—Spinoza offers a clear and devastating answer: nothing. And yet, there can be little doubt that for Spinoza there *is* something special about the human being. Or perhaps more accurately, there is some way in which the human being can *become* special. This is what he declared in his very manner of living, through his unwavering commitment to a "life of the mind." And, as happens only with the most acute philosophers, it is also what he declares in his writings. Spinoza's assault on the mind-body problem isn't just about developing a more convincing hypothesis to explain some puzzling observations about thoughts and brains; it is, as he says in his *Short Treatise*, about "true worship," or the path to salvation.

Salvation

Happiness, too, became a problem in the seventeenth century. Much of the blame for this development, as usual, should go to the Reformation of the previous century. So long as there was a single, "catholic" church, the question of how to achieve blessedness remained in the hands of the appropriate ecclesiastical authorities. Once that church lost its universality, however, the question of happiness fell out of the hands of God and landed in the lap of individual conscience. The success of so many new varieties of religious practice, ironically, made plain the individual character of faith.

Spinoza himself makes the point: "You will not be able to deny that in every church there are very many honorable men who worship God with justice and charity," he tells one correspondent. "For we have known many such men among the Lutherans, the Reformed Church, the Mennonites, and the Enthusiasts, to say nothing of others. . . . You must therefore grant that holiness of life is . . . common to all." Spinoza politely neglects to include in the list his own confessional status, that of an apostate Jew—itself perhaps the most glaring evidence for the existence of a purely personal path to salvation.

At the very time that happiness became a personal matter, it also seemed to become much harder to achieve. In a world where God was increasingly remote and indifferent, where humankind's privilege in the order of things seemed under threat, and where no rational individual could accept the cosmogonies handed down by the theological traditions, assurances of salvation were not easy to come by. No one, of course, believed God to be more indifferent, or humanity's privilege less sure, than Spinoza himself. Happiness was therefore his biggest problem. That is, the greatest challenge Spinoza faced was to explain how to be happy—and how to be moral, which in his view was the same thing—in a world that is thoroughly secular. In his *Treatise on the Emendation of the Intellect*, as we know, Spinoza announced that the sole aim of his philosophy is to acquire "supreme, continuous, and everlasting happiness." In the *Ethics* he claims he has done just that.

Happiness is freedom, says Spinoza. It follows when we act in accordance with our own deepest nature—when we "realize ourselves," as it were. Unfortunately, we humans rarely have the privilege of acting according to our deepest nature, for in our ignorance of ourselves and of the world we submit ourselves to the guidance of forces beyond our control. Humankind is battered about on a sea of emotions, the philosopher thunders; we are tossed about in a chaos of hope and fear, joy and despair, love and hate, impelled along a random course whose only certain destination is eventual unhappiness. Most people most of the time, concludes Spinoza, are passive. But the point of life is to be active.

Spinoza's first step toward freedom is to haul the emotions before the bar of reason. "I shall consider human actions and desires," he writes, "as though I were concerned with lines, planes and solids." In the *Ethics* he presents a theory according to which all the emotions we experience—love and hate, self-content and humility, wonder and consternation, and so on—may be analyzed in terms of three basic concepts: pleasure, pain, and the *conatus*. The *conatus* is a drive or desire—in essence, the desire to persist in one's own being. Every person—and, indeed, every rock, tree, and thing in the world—has a *conatus* to act, live, preserve itself, and realize itself by pursuing its own interest (or "advantage"). "Pleasure" is the state that results from anything that contributes to the project of this *conatus*, that is, anything that increases a thing's power or level of "perfection"; and "pain" is the state that results from anything that does the opposite, that diminishes the power of a thing.

On the basis of these three concepts, Spinoza builds a rich theory of the emotions. A number of his definitions are perhaps a little too obvious; others are uncannily apt and pithy. Some examples: Love, he says, is pleasure accompanied by the idea of an external object as its cause. Self-content (or self-love) is pleasure arising from the contemplation of one's own power of action. And pride is thinking too highly of oneself on account of self-love. The important general point is that all the emotions have their foundation in the *conatus* of the individual: "desire is the essence of man," as Spinoza puts it. To be clear: this desire is fundamentally self-centered.

There is nothing wrong with the emotions *per se*, in Spinoza's view, nor with this unending and apparently selfish desire called the *conatus*. Quite to the contrary, he maintains, pleasure—or the maximization of the *conatus*—is the source of all good. Indeed, Spinoza pauses long enough to take another swipe at the theocratic order of the day: "Nothing but grim and gloomy superstition forbids enjoyment," he says, alluding to the ascetic ideal of the reigning church. "[N]o deity, nor anyone else but the envious, takes pleasure in my weakness and misfortune, nor does he take to be a virtue our tears, sobs, fearfulness, and other such things that are the mark of a weak spirit."

The problem with the emotions is rather that they often fail to set the *conatus* on the true course to happiness. Emotions generally arise at the call of external forces and are therefore not self-centered in a perspicuous way. Owing to human ignorance, we fear things that don't exist (such as a personal God who might judge us); we allow present experiences to distract us from the value of future goods; we let pride go to our heads; and we otherwise add every day in the usual ways to the limitless catalogue of human folly. Most emotions, concludes Spinoza, are based on inadequate conceptions of things. They are "passive"—which is why we call them "passions," after all.

The first contribution of reason is to bring order to the emotions, so that we may understand how to guide them under the rubric of our true self-interest. Reason teaches us, for example, to value future goods in direct proportion to present goods; that excessive pride is a bad thing; that humility is no good either (or, at least, so says Spinoza); and so on. The resulting, orderly state of the emotions Spinoza names "virtue." In a neat reversal of the traditional understanding of the term—which is usually freighted with forbidding connotations of self-denial and abstemiousness—Spinoza insists that the more we seek our own interest, the more we are endowed with virtue. He goes out of his way to reject explicitly the orthodox notion of virtue: "Hence we clearly understand how far astray from the true estimation of virtue are those who, failing to understand that virtue itself and the worship of God are happiness itself and utmost freedom, expect God to bestow on them the highest rewards in return for their virtue and meritorious actions as if in return for the basest slavery."

Although virtue has its feet planted firmly in self-interest (or, better, self-realization), Spinoza maintains that virtue in fact leads to very unselfish social behavior. As noted above in connection with his political philosophy, he argues that men who live under the guidance of reason invariably treat others with respect, they repay hate with love, and in general behave like model citizens and "good Christians."

Nevertheless, Spinoza acknowledges, seeking one's best interest and getting it are two different things. He emphasizes that human beings are extremely weak in the face of the external forces arrayed against them, and that even the most reasonable men will find that the objects of hope and fear lie mostly outside their control. The second contribution of the guidance of reason is to teach us to understand the inner necessity of things, and therefore not to find unhappiness in the vast part of human experience over which we have no control. When he writes, "Insofar as we understand, we can desire nothing but that which must be, nor can we find contentment in anything but the truth," Spinoza expresses the classic sentiment of acquiescence that has been associated with the very name of philosophy at least since the time of the ancient Stoics. In describing the proper philosophical attitude toward events beyond our control, however, he does not employ terms like "resignation" or "indifference" but rather "desire" and "contentment." The stance he adopts is not "fatalism," but something more like what Nietzsche describes as "*amor fati*"—the love of fate.

Of course, the love of fate is not for the faint of heart. Human beings are weak not just with respect to outside forces, Spinoza cautions, but also with respect to the demons within. The passions are so strong that they can overrule the mind with ease and lead us "to fol-low the worse course even when we know the better." The only way to overcome the emotions, he says, is with a higher kind of emotion: you have to fight fire with fire. Spinoza thus distinguishes himself from the Stoics, who argued that the only thing to do with the surly crowd of human emotions is to have them all shot, as it were. And this brings us to the ultimate contribution of the guidance of reason in the quest for happiness. For, reason supplies us with an emotion of its own, a stronger and more durable emotion than all the others put together. It is an active emotion, unlike the passions, because it is based on an adequate idea rather than an inadequate one. Spinoza calls it "the intellectual love of God."

The intellectual love of God is the same thing as the knowledge of God contained in the first part of the *Ethics*. Spinoza identifies it as "the third kind of knowledge," or "intuition," in order to distinguish it from sense experience ("the first kind") and the reflective knowl-edge that arises from the analysis of experience ("the second kind"). To know his God in the third way, Spinoza claims, is the same thing as to love God. Furthermore, this love is greater than any other pos-sible love, and can never waiver. Since the individual is just a mode of God, the intellectual love of God is God's way of loving itself.

At this point, where we reach the long sought union of man and God (or Nature), Spinoza goes on to say, we achieve a kind of immortality. Contrary to what he seems to imply in his philosophy of mind, Spinoza now contends that "the human mind cannot be absolutely destroyed with the body." The eternal part of the mind, it turns out, is the "intellect"—the faculty with which we grasp the eternal truths of philosophy. The immortality Spinoza offers here, however, is not of the kind that would provide much solace for the superstitious: we take with us no personal memories of who we were or what we did in our journey to the eternal ideas, and we receive no rewards other than those that come from having such beautiful thoughts in the first place. In fact, Spinoza's immortality doesn't really occur "after" life; it is something more like an escape from time alto-gether. By immortality Spinoza means something like the union of the mind with ideas that are themselves timeless.

The end point of Spinoza's philosophy—the intellectual love of

God, or blessedness—transfigures all that precedes it. It can sometimes sound paradoxical and more than a little mystical. It is the
union of the individual and the cosmos, of freedom and necessity, of
activity and passivity, of mind and body, of self-interest and charity, of
virtue and knowledge, and of happiness and virtue. It is the place
where all that which was previously relativized in Spinoza—the
good, which was relative to our desires; freedom, which was relative
to our ignorance; self-knowledge, which was relative to our imperfect perceptions of the body—suddenly reappears in the form of
absolutes: absolute good, absolute freedom, and absolute knowledge.

It cannot be overlooked that Spinoza assigns a stupefying onus to
the faculty of reason. It is one thing to say that reason can help bring
order and acceptance to our emotional lives; it is quite another to say
that it may lead us to supreme, continuous, and everlasting happiness
in an eternal union with God. Spinoza's ambition for philosophy was,
by any measure, extreme.

That overweening ambition returns us to the paradox that first
emerged in the consideration of the young Bento's unusual behavior
in the context of his expulsion from the Jewish community. On the
one hand, Spinoza's philosophy clearly represents a "transvaluation"
of traditional values, to use a Nietzschean phrase. The dominant religion of Spinoza's time—and perhaps most religion, viewed in a general way—promises happiness in *exchange* for an unhappy virtue. But
Spinoza says that happiness *is* virtue. Religion generally makes charity the highest good. But Spinoza names self-interest as the sole
source of value, and reduces charity to one of its incidental consequences. Religion tends to reserve its most lavish praise for those
who deny themselves the pleasures of the body. But Spinoza says that
the more (true) pleasure we have, the more perfect we are. Religion
tells us that happiness results from submission to an external authority—if not God, then his representatives on earth. Spinoza stakes his
life on the claim that happiness is freedom.

On the other hand, there is clearly more than a little piety in the
iconoclastic spiritual journey recorded in the *Ethics*. The longing to
transcend the limits of the human condition and the ultimate arrival
at a kind of immortality and a union with God—these are the staples

of religious narratives throughout history. Many commentators, beginning in the seventeenth century, have gone so far as to interpret Spinoza's work as the expression of a characteristically Jewish theological position. His monism, they say, may be traced to Deuteronomy ("the Lord our God is One"); and his seemingly mystical tendencies link him to the Kabbalah.

If indeed it is a religion—a very problematic possibility—then Spinoza's philosophy is in any case one of those religions that offers itself only to an elect few. The philosopher's last words on the highway to salvation are "all things excellent are as difficult as they are rare." Part of the rarity of his way, no doubt, stems from the fact that it is very difficult to read tracts like his, written in the geometrical style and stuffed with medieval barbarisms like "substance" and "attributes." But there is another sense in which salvation is no easy task.

Spinoza's God is a tremendous thing (actually, it is every thing), and it is bound to inspire awe, wonder, and perhaps for some even love. But it is not the kind of thing that will love you back.

> It cannot be said that God loves mankind, much less that he should love them because they love him, or hate them because they hate him.

> He who loves God cannot endeavor that God should love him in return.

Spinoza's God, in other words, will make no exception to its natural laws on your account; it will work no miracles for you; it will tender no affection, show no sign of concern about your well-being; in short, it will give you nothing that you do not already have. Spinoza's God is so indifferent, in fact, that one may even ask whether it is *reasonable* to love it. For, if love is pleasure accompanied by the idea of an external object as its cause, as Spinoza says, then of what pleasure can such an unhelpful God be said to be the cause? Spinoza, to be sure, devotes a number of his intricate and arduous proofs to the proposition that loving God is the finest expression of reason. But his many beautiful words on the subject do not necessarily close a gap that some would say can be crossed only with a leap of faith. In any case, there can be little doubt that the road he traveled was difficult and rare.

Spinoza and Modernity

"Gradually it has become clear to me what every great philosophy is," says Nietzsche, "namely, a personal confession of its creator and a kind of involuntary and unperceived memoir." No finer evidence for such a claim may be found than in the pages of the *Ethics*, which expresses with luxurious abandon the character of its creator. The modesty that beguiled Rabbi Morteira, Henry Oldenburg, and so many others presents itself in a vision in which human individuals vanish to mere ephemera in the vast workings of nature. The self-confidence that allowed him to take extraordinary risks throughout his career manifests itself in his declaration that the world, or Nature, is intelligible, and that the truths established by reason and observation can never be bad. The eerie self-sufficiency that made him serene in the face of the wrath of his community emboldens the mature philosopher's confrontation with the value system of an entire civilization. The halo of piety that hovered strangely over the young apostate's head, too, shines in the God-drenched paeans to virtue and salvation that round off his masterpiece.

Great philosophy is also, as Hegel once said, its own time apprehended in thought. Like the owl of Minerva, it arises at dusk and sees all that has come before. The age that Spinoza surveyed with his large and pitiless eyes was one of momentous transition, a world in flux between the medieval and the modern. With an acuity that must have been in part native and in part the consequence of his unusual circumstances in life, Spinoza perceived the fragility of the self, the precariousness of freedom, and the irreducible diversity in the new society emerging around him. He saw that the advance of science was in the process of rendering the God of revelation obsolete; that it had already undermined the special place of the human individual in nature; and that the problem of happiness was now a matter for individual conscience. He understood all this because these same developments determined the nature of his own existence as a double exile in the golden age of the Dutch Republic.

Because he rose so high above history in some sense, too, Spinoza foresaw its general direction with an often uncanny prescience. He described a secular, liberal, democratic order a full century before the world provided any durable examples of the same. Two centuries before Darwin proposed a theory to explain how the grand design of nature evolves through natural processes, without need of a designer, he effectively announced that such an explanation was inevitable. In an age when the brain was generally thought to be about as complex as a bowl of custard, he anticipated insights from the neurosciences that would be three centuries in coming. The world he describes is in many ways the modern one within which we live.

The defining gesture of Spinoza's philosophy is to embrace this new reality. His work is an attempt to make the new world he saw emerging around him the foundation of a new form of worship—to realize a new and distinctly modern kind of self. To borrow from his own vocabulary, his philosophy may be usefully described as an *active* form of modernity. That is, it is an attempt to identify that which it holds to be the new truths of the world around us with the source of all that is valuable in life.

SOMEWHERE ON THE left bank of the Seine, another individual was beginning to trace the contours of the new world. In light of the new ideas radiating from The Hague, a keen, scrutinizing, and very different set of eyes began to take in the challenges of modernity. Here was a mind that longed to see God as clearly as one could see a triangle, too, that grasped the general direction of history, and that sought a response to the problems of the modern condition. But it was a mind with tastes and proclivities very much its own. And so it began to fumble with the questions that must inevitably arise from any serious contemplation of Spinoza's thought.

Does Spinoza manage to construct a new theory of the human being, or does he simply destroy the old one? Does he demonstrate that there is only one Substance—or that the very idea of substance is incoherent? Is his form of exposition really a method, or is it just a style? Is the "intellectual love" of his Nature-God in fact *reasonable*?

The questions all circle back to the point where Spinoza's philosophy begins and ends: God. Spinoza claims to find divinity in nature. He avows that God is in all things—in the here and now. But, in all of human history, God has always been understood as something *super*natural—as a being outside of all things, residing in the "before and beyond." Does Spinoza's God really deserve the name of God? That is, does the philosopher succeed in his project of deifying Nature? Or does he merely naturalize—and thereby destroy—God?

These were the questions that first met modern eyes when Leibniz sat down in the Hôtel des Romains in the winter of 1676; and these were the questions whose answers the tireless, reckless courtier sought when he journeyed to The Hague in November of that year.

11

Approaching Spinoza

In a note dated February 11, 1676—quite possibly, the very same day Tschirnhaus first revealed to him the secrets of Spinoza—Leibniz declares his ambition to write a grand statement of his own philosophy of everything. This note and those that follow in the weeks and months ahead take on a loose, personal, experimental, speculative, and highly incoherent character that distinguishes them from his other writings, both before and after. The fragments do not in fact come close to a comprehensive philosophy of everything, nor do they even admit of any single, unambiguous interpretation; what they reveal most clearly is Leibniz's extraordinary ambition to develop a philosophical system of his own that would resolve all the timeless questions about God, humankind, and salvation.

Spinoza's sway is already evident in the title Leibniz now gives to his unwritten masterpiece: *The Elements of a Secret Philosophy of the Whole of Things, Geometrically Demonstrated.* This is precisely the title one would have expected Leibniz to give to Spinoza's (as yet unpublished) *Ethics.* That Spinoza's work is a "secret philosophy" goes without saying, as does the fact that it is "geometrically demonstrated." The most interesting coincidence, though, has to do with the phrase "of the whole of things." In some passages, Leibniz uses the phrase "*de summa rerum*" to refer to "the totality of things" or "the universe." In other places, however, he uses it to mean "the highest of things," or simply "God." "Meditations on [God]," he writes, "could be titled *On the Secrets of the Sublime* or *De Summa Rerum.*" In other words, God and the universe are at least lexically indistinguishable. The demonstration that God and the universe are metaphysically indistinguishable, of course, is the principal point of Spinoza's *Ethics*.

The alternative title of Leibniz's prospective book, *On the Secrets of the Sublime*, lends his project a surprisingly underground sensibility. In the letter he sent to Thomasius seven years earlier, Leibniz excoriates a book by Bodin under precisely that title. The author of that book, he says at the time, is "a professed enemy of the Christian religion" and a crypto-atheist. Yet Bodin's title now stands at the head of his own "secret" philosophy.

In the same pages of notes from February 11, Leibniz comes close to making his philosophical debt to Spinoza explicit: "There seems to be . . . some kind of most perfect mind, or God. This mind exists as a whole soul in the whole body of the world; to this mind the existence of things is also due. . . . The reason for things is the aggregate of all the requisites of things. The reason for God is God. An infinite whole is one." The Spinozism here is blatant. The identification of God as "a whole soul in the whole body of the world" is, if anything, a caricature of Spinozism. (Spinoza nowhere uses the rather archaic concept of a "world-soul," though he would have affirmed that the "body of the world" is in God.) More subtle is the implicit identification of "the aggregate of the requisites of all things" with "God": this is a version of Spinoza's doctrine that God is the immanent cause of all things. Leibniz's formula that "the reason for God is God" nimbly captures the essence of that which distinguishes Spinoza's God from "do-gooder" conceptions of God—namely, that God is absolutely self-sufficient and answers to no external principle, such as the principle of "doing good." "An infinite whole is one" is an apt, poetic rendition of Spinoza's concept of a Substance that expresses itself through infinite attributes and modes.

But a few paragraphs down on the same scrap of notepaper, Leibniz suddenly recants: "God is not something metaphysical, imaginary, incapable of thought, will, or action, as some represent him, so that it would be the same if you were to say that God is nature, fate, fortune, necessity, the world. Rather, God is a certain substance, a person, a mind." The intended target of this tirade is unambiguously Spinoza—or perhaps Leibniz's own lapse into Spinozism just moments before. Leibniz at this point senses that great danger lies ahead; but he only feels the padded contours of the threat, and he does not have his defenses at the ready.

As if to guard himself against further possible lapses, Leibniz sets himself a task: "It must be shown that God is a person, i.e., an intelligent substance." Here and for the rest of his career, Leibniz clings tightly to the notion that God must be an agent, a decision maker who faces options and makes choices. The phrase "it must be shown," too, captures something of the essence of Leibniz's enduring philosophical disposition. The moral imperative to produce the "correct" philosophy is paramount. Behind the "it must be shown" lies a characteristically Leibnizian anxiety—an unspoken "or else." . . . Or else what? What if he should fail to prove that God is a person, and not "something metaphysical"?

On February 24, Leibniz and Tschirnhaus went on a hunt through the bookshops of Paris for Cartesian manuscripts, perhaps hoping to answer the questions about Spinoza with the help of his illustrious predecessor. In the dusty back room of one shop, they hit pay dirt: several unpublished works by Descartes. The two Germans sat down and copied out as much as they could in the course of a long afternoon.

Buried in his metaphysical investigations, Leibniz apparently forgot about his appointment in the court of Hanover. Six weeks had passed since he had accepted the Duke's offer, and heads were being scratched vigorously in Germany. In a letter of February 28, the Duke's secretary, deftly combining carrot and stick, promises the new hire that he will be placed on the payroll retroactively as of the beginning of the year. Leibniz responds with a gracious note to the Duke, in which he affirms that "all my ambition is but to find a grand Prince" and that "I have always believed that there is nothing so beautiful in human affairs as great wisdom joined with power," but in which he delicately avoids providing a date when he plans to leave Paris for Hanover. On March 19, the Duke's secretary, exasperated, gives him "fourteen days or at most three weeks" to settle his affairs in Paris and get on the carriage home.

But March turns to April, and Leibniz remains transfixed in the City of Light. His diary entries are those of a man still riding the carousel of Parisian intellectual life. He jots down some wry observations about some new acquaintances; he takes notes on some alchemical secrets passed on by a mysterious Italian; he comments on news from Tschirnhaus concerning the incredible microscope work of a man from Delft (clearly, Antoni von Leeuwenhoek). Mainly, though, he forges ahead with his dizzying metaphysical and mathematical speculations.

In his notes from April, Leibniz once again rebels against Spinoza's teachings. "Is the mind the idea of the body?" he asks himself, clearly referring to Spinoza's doctrine. "That cannot be." If the mind is the idea of the body, he reasons, then it must perish with the body; and this contradicts the doctrine of personal immortality. He also returns to the idea of a world-soul—the idea he seems to have endorsed in February—and explicitly rejects it. There can be no world-soul, he concludes, because souls cannot form a "continuum"—which is another way of saying that the concept of a world-soul appears to be incompatible with the existence of individual, immortal souls. Leibniz is becoming clearer on the fact that Spinoza's concept of God is inextricably linked to his theory of mind, which in turn seems to undermine the orthodox idea of the soul—and orthodoxy in general.

Yet the attraction remains. In the same set of April notes, Leibniz dallies with formulations such as "It seems to me that the origin of things from God is of the same kind as the origin of properties from an essence"—an idea that is impossible to square with Leibniz's earlier insistence that God is a person. If things originate from God in the same way that properties originate from an essence, it follows that God no more wills the existence of particular things than a circle wills to be round; that all things have a necessary character; that the distinction between God and things is merely apparent or perspectival; and that God, in sum, is the sole substance or essence of the world. It also follows that individual *souls* originate from God like properties from an essence—and are therefore, it would seem, merely properties of a thing and not things themselves. The logical destination of Leibniz's ideas about an essencelike God is Spinozism, or so it would appear.

In April 1676, Leibniz's interest in Spinoza began to take on the character of an obsession. Through his liaison with Schuller, he managed to get his hands on a thirteen-year-old letter from Spinoza to his friend Lodewijk Meyer concerning the nature of the infinite and other topics. Leibniz copied out the letter—which extends for half a dozen pages—then added marginal notes of his own as lengthy as the original text.

Not surprisingly, April brought Leibniz no closer to Hanover. One can only presume that he found Paris in the springtime irresistible. With the three-week deadline now a matter of history, the Duke of Hanover's secretary grudgingly granted an extension. The absent courtier now had until May 24 to pack his bags.

Leibniz once again felt the urge to make direct contact with Spinoza himself. On May 2 a missive sailed out of Paris under Tschirnhaus's name. The letter queries the philosopher of The Hague on two points. First, it asks him to comment on whether it is possible to deduce "figure and motion" from "extension, taken in an absolute sense." From Leibniz's writings in the early 1670s as well as his Paris notes, we know that the impossibility of deriving motion from the concept of extension was very dear to his heart, for he believed that it justified a number of metaphysical conclusions pertaining to the nature of the soul. The letter next asks Spinoza to clarify a somewhat obscure point he makes in his letter concerning infinity. Leibniz had raised the same question, almost word for word, in his marginal notes on Schuller's letter. The letter to Spinoza from Tschirnhaus, in sum, is actually a letter from Leibniz.

In the final paragraph of the letter, Tschirnhaus (or Leibniz) writes: "Further, I have learned from Mr. Leibniz that the tutor to the Dauphin of France, by name Huet, a man of outstanding learning, is going to write about the truth of human religion, and to refute your

Tractatus Theologico-Politicus. Farewell." Leibniz's association with Huet was an important one for his career: Huet had arranged to give Leibniz translation work, and, as tutor to the Dauphin, he was well placed to influence many matters in French intellectual life—not least, the selection of members of the Royal Academy of Sciences. But Huet, as Leibniz well knew, believed that Spinoza deserved to be "covered in chains and whipped with a rod." Astonishingly, Leibniz was apparently willing to double-cross his ally Huet in order to forewarn Spinoza about a possible danger.

The editors of Spinoza's posthumous works—who included Leibniz's gopher Schuller—evidently believed that there was something sensitive here for, in the Latin edition of 1677, the final paragraph of Tschirnhaus's letter is absent. In the Dutch version of Spinoza's works, however, the paragraph slips back in—perhaps because Huet would not have been expected to read Dutch, or more likely through an oversight.

In July, six months after he was initially expected in Hanover, Leibniz was inexplicably still in Paris. The secretary to the Duke was now flatly mystified and openly wondered whether the new appointee intended to perform the duties required of the position for which he was already being paid. The secretary's suspicions were well founded. Just a week previously, Leibniz had begged his friend Huygens one more time to help him secure a position in the Royal Academy.

Later that same month, the Hanoverian ambassador to Paris implored Leibniz to leave "immediately" and report to the Duke "as speedily as you can." But the hot summer months rolled past, and Leibniz, still clinging to the hope of rescue from the French Academy, did not budge.

On September 26, the Hanoverian ambassador in Paris wrote Leibniz one last time to warn him that the Duke was "impatient" and to urge him to leave "immediately." Leibniz had run out of excuses.

On Sunday morning, October 4, 1676, the philosopher finally shook the mud of Paris off his boots and boarded the mail-carriage for Calais. He arrived in Calais six days later, then waited five miserable days in an inn there while a storm cleared. He caught the first boat across the Channel, stayed overnight in Dover, and reached London on the evening of October 18.

The first order of business, naturally, was to call on Henry Olden-burg. In the offices of the Royal Society at Gresham College on the morning of October 19, Leibniz presented his compatriot with a new and improved—though still unfinished—calculating machine. Old-enburg rewarded him by allowing him to make excerpts from one of Newton's papers—a fact that would later be used against him (base-lessly) in the dispute over the calculus.

The subject of conversation swiftly turned to Leibniz's reigning obsession. The courtier divulged his plan to visit Spinoza in person on his way through Holland. Nearly two years had passed since that other young German, Tschirnhaus, had come to London exuding a similar enthusiasm for Spinoza, and nearly one year had passed since Oldenburg's correspondence with the sage of The Hague had bro-ken down in fear and misunderstanding. Yet, evidently, the embers of friendship still glowed in Henry's heart. He penned one more letter to Spinoza, and entrusted it to Leibniz for personal delivery.

While the older German scribbled out his missive, Leibniz copied out three of Spinoza's letters to Oldenburg, which the latter allowed him to view. As was his custom, the young philosopher soon added marginal notes lengthier than the originals.

Later in the week, Leibniz called on resident German diplomats and aristocrats, including Prince Ruprecht von der Pfalz, a cousin of the Duchess of Orléans. The Prince mentioned that he was sending his yacht back to the continent to fetch some of his favorite vin-tages, and Leibniz seized on the opportunity to secure free passage to Holland.

On October 29 Leibniz boarded Prince Ruprecht's yacht. Two days later, under the command of Captain Thomas Allen, the bark sailed down the Thames estuary to Gravesend, arriving that same evening. For four days, the sailors loaded cargo. Then they tacked up to the English port of Sheerness—the scene of a stunning Dutch vic-tory over the Royal Navy some years earlier. In Sheerness a strong headwind pinned the vessel in port for six tedious days.

Unable to move, the restless philosopher composed a dialogue on motion—the one featuring his alter ego Pacidius and an eager pupil named Charinus. In the dialogue, Leibniz returns to one of his favorite themes, neatly encapsulated in the claim that "certain metaphysical mysteries of a truly spiritual nature may be found in [motion]." The mysteries of motion, as we know, were intimately connected in Leibniz's mind with his ideas about the unique meta-physical status of the individual, the immateriality of the mind, and the doctrine of personal immortality. On the eve of his voyage to The Hague, it would appear, the young philosopher was committed as ever to theological doctrines to which Spinoza was unstintingly opposed.

With no one aboard with whom he could converse (save, presumably, the mariners), the temporarily silenced philosopher also turned his attention to "my old design of a rational writing or language" that would permit one "to grasp not words, but thoughts."

On November 11, the weather at last eased, and the crew weighed anchor. With the winds still gusting strongly, the crossing took a mere twenty-four hours. The yacht docked in Rotterdam, where Leibniz remained for the night. The next morning, he scurried to catch a canal-boat up to Amsterdam.

In the most beautiful city in the world, the canals were thick with Spinozists. Leibniz promptly met all the important ones. He called on Georg Hermann Schuller, his chief liaison with Spinoza; Johannes Hudde, a local politician and mathematician who had corresponded with Spinoza on important philosophical matters; Lodewijk Meyer, a doctor, thespian, philosopher, and editor of Spinoza's book on Descartes; and Jarig Jelles, retired merchant, future editor of Spin-oza's posthumous works, and Spinoza's oldest friend. From his new acquaintances in Amsterdam Leibniz gathered up and copied out still more of Spinoza's correspondence. Possibly, the purpose of his excursion to Amsterdam was to secure the letters of introduction he might have required to persuade the ever cautious sage of The Hague to open his door for him. In any case, he acquired personal news and gossip that would doubtlessly serve to smooth the path to friendly exchange.

On or around November 16 Leibniz returned south; over the next ten days he cruised the canals of South Holland aboard an inland boat, which he used as a floating hotel. His first stops were Haarlem, Leiden, and the tile-making capital of Delft. In the last he spent some hours with Antoni von Leeuwenhoek, whose microscopic investigations greatly inspired the philosopher and later served him as evidence of a sort in support of his metaphysical theories.

SOMEWHERE IN THE course of his travels, perhaps while he was aboard Prince Ruprecht's yacht, if not a canal boat, Leibniz composed a draft of the argument he would soon make *viva voce* to Spinoza. Its title: "That a Most Perfect Being Exists."

"I seem to have discovered a demonstration that a most perfect being . . . is possible," Leibniz begins. By "most perfect being," of course, he means God, whom he further defines as "one that contains all essence, or that has all qualities, or all affirmative attributes."

Whose God is this? The answer seems to come from Leibniz's earlier note on his discussion with Tschirnhaus: "[Spinoza] defines God as . . . a being that contains all perfections, i.e., affirmations, or realities, or things that can be conceived." It seems, then, that Leibniz intends to prove to Spinoza that Spinoza's God is possible.

Leibniz next sets out to demonstrate that such a God, if possible, necessarily exists. His argument is that such a God, if it exists, must have a reason for existing, and this reason must come from either without or within God. But it cannot come from without, for he has just proved that anything that can be conceived must be conceived through God. Therefore, God's reason for existing must come from within God itself—or, as he writes in the note of February 11: "The reason for God is God."

The door to Spinozism is now wide open. While mulling this concept of an utterly self-sufficient God of reason, Leibniz writes:

> It can be easily demonstrated that all things are distinguished, not as substances, but as modes. [He then writes "radically" over "substances."] This can be demonstrated from the fact that things that are radically distinct can be understood without another. But in truth this is not the case in things; for since the ultimate reason of things is unique, and contains by itself the aggregate of all requisites of all things, it is manifest that the requisites of all things are the same. So also is their essence, given that an essence is the aggregate of all primary requisites. There-

fore, the essence of all things is the same, and things differ only modally, just as a town seen from a high point differs from a town seen from a plain.

The chain of logic here duplicates in abbreviated fashion the first, crucial propositions of Spinoza's *Ethics*: substances are radically distinct and can be understood without one another; but all things in the world are understood through the unique and ultimate reason for all things; therefore, there cannot be two or more substances in the world; therefore, there is only one substance, and all things are modes of this one substance. Since Leibniz's draft concerns the concept of a God who is the ultimate reason for all things, furthermore, it is evident that the one substance in question is just another word for God. In effect, Leibniz's argument begins with his irrevocable commitment to the principle of sufficient reason—that for every thing there must be a reason—and ends in a declaration of belief in the core doctrines of Spinoza. The passage is all the more remarkable because Leibniz says that all of this "can be easily demonstrated" and is "manifest."

In case we missed the point, Leibniz jumps straight to the conclusion that all things are one: "If only those things are really different which can be separated, or, of which one can be perfectly understood without the other, it follows that no thing really differs from another, but that all things are one, just as Plato argues in the *Parmenides*."

The only false note here is Leibniz's attribution of this doctrine to Plato. "Just as Spinoza argues in the *Ethics*" would have been more honest; for the train of thought here has the same destination as the boat on which Leibniz was sailing at around the time he wrote these lines: Spinoza.

Nor can there be any doubt that Leibniz knew very well in what direction he was heading. In his notes from the meeting with Tschirnhaus in February, he attributes to Spinoza the claims that "God alone is substance . . . and all creatures are nothing but modes." Even more telling is a note Leibniz made to himself on one of the letters to Oldenburg that he picked up in London. Where Spinoza says, "All things are in God and move in God," Leibniz writes: "One could say: all things are one, all things are in God in the way that an effect is entirely contained within its cause and properties of a subject are in the essence of the same subject." Leibniz here implicitly acknowledges that his own speculations—notably, his repeated suggestion that the things of the world are to God what properties are to an essence—are elaborations of the central doctrine of Spinoza's philosophy.

"An attribute is a predicate which is conceived through itself," Leibniz continues in his shipboard draft. (Spinoza himself says: "Each attribute . . . must be conceived through itself.") "An essence is . . ." Suddenly, the manuscript breaks off in midword, midsentence: *Essentia est pr . . .*

Something throws Leibniz off; his quill quivers; he stops to think about what he is doing. He retreats from philosophy to the "philosophy of philosophy." His next lines are perhaps the most revealing he ever committed to paper:

> A metaphysics should be written with accurate definitions and demonstrations. But nothing should be demonstrated in it apart from that which does not clash too much with received opinions. For in that way this metaphysics can be accepted; and once it has been approved then, if people examine it more deeply later, they themselves will draw the necessary consequences. Besides this, one can, as a separate undertaking, show these people later the way of reasoning about these things. In this metaphysics, it will be useful for there to be added here and there the authoritative utterances of great men, who have reasoned in a similar way. . . .

Coming as it does after what seems like a restatement of Spinoza's core doctrines, and scribbled quite possibly aboard a ship that was just then steering its way along the waterways of The Hague, this passage points to an inescapable conclusion: Leibniz was a Spinozist—at least at this moment—and he knew it. His strategy would be to conceal his true views wherever they offended the orthodox, to cite great thinkers like Plato and Parmenides as a diversion, and, in general, to work for the day when Spinozism might emerge out from under the false accusations of heresy and claim its rightful place in the sun. In the meantime, as this passage itself demonstrates by cutting off his preceding, Spinozistic reflections, Leibniz would censor himself. Even in the privacy of his shipboard cabin, he would not permit himself to express thoughts that the world was not ready to receive.

Thirty years after the event, in a writing he withheld from publication at the last moment, the aging philosopher seemed to confess to his lapse: "You know I went a little too far in another time and that I began to lean to the side of the Spinozists, who grant nothing but an infinite power to God."

And yet—only a few months had passed since he had written the notes in which he insists that "it must be shown" that God is not "nature," but a "person," and in which he rejects the doctrine that "the mind is the idea of the body"; and only days had elapsed since he composed his un-Spinozistic dialogue on the philosophy of motion. Nor was there at this time any sign of a letup in his political activities on behalf of the theocratic establishment, nor of any change in the courtly lifestyle so absurdly at odds with that of the man he was about to visit. As ever, the philosopher-diplomat blended in so well with his surroundings as he traversed the motley landscape of seventeenth-century thought that it was never very clear which color was truly his. And it is surely more than mere coincidence that the great chameleon happened to produce his most Spinozistic writings at around the same time that his boat was gliding through the canals of The Hague.

The only certainty, in fact, is that there were too many ideas in Leibniz's head for them all to add up in a single view of the world. One part of him believed in Spinoza's God of reason; another part of him believed in the providential deity of orthodox religion; and other parts, no doubt, adhered to a still wider variety of incompatible notions. Even as he closed in on the philosopher of The Hague, it seems, he held in reserve the commitments that would make true communion impossible. Leibniz came not just to agree with his host, but also—perhaps to his own surprise—to disagree.

On or around November 18, 1676, in any case, after painting himself in the hues of the local freethinker and then reminding himself not to express any ideas that might clash too much with received opinions, the thirty-year-old inventor of the calculus, the former privy counselor of Mainz, and newly appointed librarian to the Duke of Hanover stepped ashore, arms flapping, wig billowing, perfume dissipating in the autumn wind, and gamboled in his awkward way along the leaf-strewn canals toward the door of the house where Spinoza lived.

12

Point of Contact

A cloudy afternoon filters through rattling windowpanes. Outside, autumn leaves race past in their merciless assault on the civic order. From upstairs come the sounds of children squealing over creaky floorboards. The warm smell of chicken broth fills the air. In the front room of the house on the Paviljoensgracht, two men engage in earnest discussion over a small, wooden table. One is young, full of energy, and fashionably attired, the trademark wig looming over his forehead perhaps blown slightly off course by the November winds. The other is older, wears a simple shirt, and coughs too frequently into one of his five handkerchiefs (the checkered one). Such, presumably, was the scene when Leibniz and Spinoza met in The Hague in 1676.

The encounter between the two greatest philosophers of the seventeenth century in fact extended over several days. From a letter Leibniz posted to the Duke of Hanover's secretary from Holland, it is possible to infer that the courtier arrived in The Hague on or before November 18 and remained for at least three days and possibly as much as one week. Leibniz later told his Parisian friend Gallois that he had conversed with Spinoza "many times and at great length."

Sometime shortly after one of their engagements Leibniz scratched out a note to himself. "I spent several hours with Spinoza after dinner," he recorded. His host regaled him, he continued, with the story of his antics on the horrible night when the mob barbecued the de Witt brothers. Evidently, the suspicions with which Spinoza had first greeted Leibniz's overtures from Paris had dissipated. Leibniz, as we know from Eckhart, had the ability to get along with all sorts, and Spinoza, according to Lucas, could be a pleasing conversationalist. One may readily imagine then, that as the two men finished up their milk gruel and watery beer, or whatever was on the menu, they chatted about the miserable weather in the lowlands, the health of their mutual acquaintances across the continent, the fanatical hygiene of the housewives of The Hague, Louis XIV's pigheaded invasion of Holland, and other topics of the kind that serve to clear the table for amicable exchange.

The discussion soon turned to the eternal questions. In the same après-dinner note, Leibniz went on to remark: "Spinoza did not see well the faults in M. Descartes's rules of motion; he was surprised when I began to show him that they violated the equality of cause and effect." The critique of the Cartesian philosophy of motion, of course, was the subject of the dialogue Leibniz penned in Sheerness, while hemmed in at port by the winds. The suggestion that Leibniz felt he had discovered some holes in Spinoza's philosophical armor is intriguing, and would be greatly amplified in his later comments on his erstwhile host. But there is also a hint here that, on the topic of their great French predecessor, the two dinner companions may have been talking past each other. Leibniz's chief aim in undermining Cartesian physics, it should be remembered, was to make room for a principle of activity which he identified with mind. Spinoza never showed a lack of enthusiasm in criticizing Descartes, but his aim in doing so was ultimately to destroy the very idea of mind that Leibniz implicitly hoped to defend.

The physics of motion, in any case, was just one of a range of philosophical topics that the two men discussed. In his later letter to Gallois Leibniz indirectly concedes that Spinoza presented him a variety of "demonstrations in metaphysics." Indeed, it is difficult to imagine that two such men, their lives ruled by the passion for wisdom and their reputations based on their philosophical acumen, should have done anything but engage in metaphysical parleys. But, equally, it would be a mistake to imagine that everything that happened in those days in The Hague could be reduced to the exchange of abstruse arguments.

Already the crucial first impressions would have been formed. In Spinoza's case, of course, we have no direct testimony on his reaction to Leibniz. It is worth noting, however, that Spinoza had found Tschirnhaus to be a most worthy friend, that Tschirnhaus in turn viewed Leibniz as a man "most skilled in the various sciences and free from the common theological prejudices," and that between the two young German enthusiasts who came to call on the philosopher of The Hague there can be little doubt on whose side the advantage in talent and experience lay. None of Spinoza's previous visitors, for that matter, could match Leibniz in erudition and force of intellect.

For his part, Leibniz could not overlook the obvious: that Spinoza was a Jew. Much later, he recorded something of his first impression in a characteristically dismissive note: "The famous Jew Spinoza had an olive complexion and something Spanish in his face; for he was also from that country. He was a philosopher by profession and led a private and tranquil life, passing his time polishing glass in order to make lenses for magnifying glasses and microscopes." But there is every reason to think that Leibniz formed a much deeper impression of his host than the one he retailed here.

More than a Jew, Spinoza became, for the later Leibniz, "that discerning Jew." Seven years after their meeting, even after his attacks on Spinoza's doctrines had hardened into a metaphysical reflex, he allowed that his former host was the type of man who "says what he believes to be true" and who believes (however erroneously) "that he is serving all humankind in delivering it from ill-founded superstitions." Thirty years after the meeting Leibniz wrote, "I know that there are people of an excellent nature who would never be led by [their] doctrines to do anything unworthy of themselves." Leaving no doubt as to whom he had in mind, he immediately added: "It can be acknowledged that Epicurus and Spinoza, for example, led entirely exemplary lives." He then went on to say that Spinoza's ideas would one day soon set fire to the four corners of the earth. To the end of his life, Leibniz never shook the impression formed in that November that his great intellectual adversary—the philosopher on whose shoulders the blame for global calamity would eventually fall—was a man of unimpeachable virtue.

ONLY ONE PIECE of evidence survives directly from the encounter in The Hague. First published in 1890, the item in question consists of a single sheet of writing, in Leibniz's hand, titled "That a Most Perfect Being Exists." It offers a condensed version of the argument that Leibniz prepared in the days preceding the meeting, to the effect that a being with all perfections is possible, or conceivable, from which it follows that such a being necessarily exists. In a note at the bottom of the document, Leibniz explains its provenance: "I presented this argument to M. Spinosa when I was at The Hague, who thought it to be sound. Since at first he contradicted it, I wrote it down and read this paper to him." The remark is brief, and yet these few words express the essence of the two characters who met in The Hague and the philosophical dynamic between them.

The debate about God offered a perfect culmination for the encounter between the two philosophers. Leibniz and Spinoza were two men with God on the brain. But did they have the same God in mind? The central question Leibniz faced in his confrontation with Spinoza was whether Spinoza's "God, or Nature" was truly a God—whether a divinity stripped of anthropomorphic attributes and residing only in the here and now could be considered divine at all.

According to a literal reading of his proof, little separates that which Leibniz identifies as "the subject of all perfections" from that which Spinoza defines in the *Ethics* as "substance consisting of infinite attributes." A certain part of Leibniz believed in Spinoza's God of reason—a perfect, infinite being whose essence and existence would shine forth from philosophical proofs just as brilliantly as any theorem about the angles of a triangle. Yet, Leibniz arrived in The Hague with more than one idea about God in his head. It seems more than likely that with his tone of voice, his casual invocation of the customary pieties, and even with his clothes—the very costume of orthodoxy—he expressed his commitment to the providential deity of orthodox religion. He wore his faith on his sleeve.

From Leibniz's note, it is clear that the proceedings began at his initiative. In a voice clear and keen, in impeccable and extemporaneous (if well-rehearsed) Latin, the young German presented his subtle new argument. He was every inch the former childhood prodigy, the straight-A student and aspiring doctoral candidate who believes that he is saying exactly what his teachers want to hear. Now as ever, he had few doubts about the value of his work and his own importance.

Leibniz, it must be frankly acknowledged, was stupendously vain. In boastful letters to dukes, ecstatic assessments of his progress in Paris, and worshipful recollections of his own schoolboy triumphs, the young man from Leipzig rarely stinted in his praise of himself. In the philosophical system he unveiled to the world ten years after departing The Hague, he painted a picture of the universe and his place within it that glows with self-satisfaction—a world in which everything is for the best; in which individuals in the form of what he calls "monads" flourish in splendid isolation; and in which the philosopher himself receives thanks from God and humankind alike for having rendered these pleasing truths in living prose. Even Eckhart, the philosopher's loyal amanuensis in later life, had to admit that "his self-conceit, which would admit of no contradiction, even when he himself saw that he was in the wrong, was his greatest failing."

But Leibniz was no exception to the rule which says that the other side of self-love is a self desperately in need of love. In his ceaseless scramble for financial security, in his serial efforts to ingratiate himself with figures of authority, in his willingness to take punishment and keep coming back for more, and in his apparent inability to distinguish clearly his own opinions from those with whom he happened to be engaged at any one moment, he evinced a desperate anxiety to please, an insatiable longing to see his good deeds reflected back to him in the praise of others. And it was this second self—the picture on the other side of Leibniz's rapturous valentine to himself—that expressed itself most clearly in his mature philosophy, and that perhaps should be held primarily responsible for his behavior in

Spinoza's presence as he presented his proof of the existence of God. It would have been astonishing were it not so characteristic that Leibniz should have insisted on registering the approbation for his proof even of the philosopher whom he earlier called "intolerably impudent" and later blamed for the fall of western civilization.

Spinoza was on home ground. God was his territory, his corner in the philosophical marketplace. From Leibniz's note, it seems clear that the philosopher of The Hague promptly fell into a customary pose. Bento was a childhood prodigy, too, but of a very different kind. He was the rebel, the kind who picks his friends from the raffish margins of society as if to make a point. From an early age he immunized himself to the influence of others and staked his happiness on a supreme self-sufficiency. In the presence of Leibniz, as ever, he was the one who kept his own counsel. He was, we may be sure, both engagingly modest and insufferably arrogant, like an extraterrestrial come to sit in judgment on a wayward representative of the human imagination.

So, at first, according to Leibniz's note, Spinoza did not accept the argument. Did the older man glimpse the shadow of the providential deity of orthodoxy lurking behind his young visitor's proof? One is entitled to wonder if a certain expression passed over Spinoza's eyes, a look of the sort that infuriated his peers at the synagogue, that sent Blijenburgh off to write his five-hundred-page polemic, that remained stuck like a piece of gristle in Limborch's mouth nearly three decades after the dinner party from hell.

Leibniz's reaction is easy to imagine. He was uniquely unsuited to being contradicted; he could brook no condescension. The yellow bile inevitably erupted up from within. He cast aside the façade of pleasantries, furiously sharpened his metaphysical distinctions, and scribbled out his proof. Then he leapt out of his chair and articulated each word with violent precision. He demanded his listener's unconditional approval.

The moment is a perfect snapshot of the two philosophers in action: Spinoza sitting unmoved, deeply indifferent, perhaps silently contemptuous, the very incarnation of his own Nature-God; Leibniz pacing around the room, clinging to his proof, desperately shouting out his demands, the perfect representative of an ever needy human race.

In the event, all ended well for God and man, or so Leibniz triumphantly reported. Spinoza judged his proof to be "sound." Leibniz's note is the last word we have on the subject.

But did Spinoza in fact approve?

In the absence of any other evidence on the matter, and in view of the range of other sentiments that might very well have glimmered in the black opal eyes of the most ruthlessly frank philosopher of recent times, we should perhaps leave open for the time being the question as to whether or not this note, too, was less a statement of fact than an expression of its author's needs.

13

Surviving Spinoza

Hanover was not Paris. On its unpaved streets there were no bright lights; and, with a mere 10,000 inhabitants, it wasn't exactly a big city. The entire population of the surrounding province—150,000 people, mostly farming folk—was less than a third of that of the French capital. Even in downtown Hanover, the cows routinely outnumbered the pedestrians. There were plenty of drinking troughs for the town's four-legged visitors, but not a single coffeehouse for its lonely literati. The glory of the metropolis was an old cloister that the Duke's family had refurbished and claimed as their palace. In the oversized chapel where the nuns once prayed, the recently converted Johann Friedrich held elaborate, Romish ceremonies, much to the disgust of his predominantly Protestant subjects. On or around the afternoon of December 12, 1676, Leibniz stepped off his carriage onto the frozen earth outside the gates of the home that he would spend the remaining forty years of his life trying to leave.

The thirty-year-old junior courtier unpacked his trunks and tidied his new home in the former cloister's converted stables. There he had been assigned a bed, a desk, and the three thousand books that made up the ducal library. He was eager to begin serving God and duke. His first professional concern, however, was to renegotiate the terms according to which he would render such service.

In the short, cold days of January 1677, the new hire snowed his employer with a half-dozen missives on the subject of his station in life. He was not happy with the title of librarian, and wished for a promotion to privy counselor—the rank he had previously held in the court of Mainz. He also wanted to collect the salary promised him for the previous year—the year he spent in Paris desperately seeking other sources of employment—plus 200 thalers to cover the cost of his travels. ("Otherwise," he complains indignantly, "I will have made the trip at my own expense.") And he believed his efforts were worth at least 500 thalers per year, not the 400 to which he had previously agreed.

In his appeals for increased status and compensation, Leibniz did not stint on the bathos. The anxieties about his personal future that had driven him from the glittering salons of Paris to the glum safety of Hanover had evidently not abated upon his arrival in his homeland: "I may not now dream only of living, but must recover my losses and provide for the future, so as not to be crushed one day, after the flower of my youth has passed, should misfortunes, changes in circumstances, or illness keep me from working with the same success or deprive me of supporters and protectors." The campaign had its intended effect. The ever pliant Johann Friedrich, who evidently had a heart to match the size of his body, awarded Leibniz some back pay, a salary increase to 500 thalers, and a promotion to privy counselor. The new position brought with it onerous judicial and administrative duties, but, the philosopher told his friends, it was well worth it. To Tschirnhaus he confided that "it is a great advantage" to spend time near such a prince, "who has at his command an unbelievable mass and shows such good intentions toward me."

Soon, however, Leibniz discovered that his fellow privy counselors in Hanover received 600 thalers per year for their services, and he became unhappy all over again. After baring his wounded self-esteem in still more letters to the Duke, he received another 100 thaler raise.

As a measure of Leibniz's relative wealth and status among the

Hanoverians: the kitchen ladies in the Duke's cafeteria received 9 thalers per year and the rat catcher 11 thalers (along with all they could eat in both cases); the top courtier, on the other hand, received 2,000 thalers in salary, plus the opportunity to collect bribes worth many times as much.

With the matter of his personal circumstances settled (at least for the time being), Leibniz, true to form, immediately launched himself in several dozen directions. In his correspondence with the Duke concerning his compensation, he assigns himself an inhuman number of tasks, including: to catalogue all of the library's holdings; to acquire many more books for the library; to maintain learned correspondence with his many contacts throughout Europe (he lists over thirty by name—including Spinoza); to alert the Duke to new developments in the arts and sciences (examples: new medicines, iron-forging techniques, mining techniques, firefighting technology, and a mysterious invention for transporting heavy loads); to pursue his own inventions and ideas in the fields of natural theology, jurisprudence, physics, geometry, and mechanics; and to resume the project of church reunion that he began as a young courtier in Mainz.

Leibniz also had no shortage of ideas about how the Duke should spend *his* time. In a series of political memoranda, the junior courtier proposes a list of possible initiatives for local government, including: perform a comprehensive demographic and geographic survey of the principality in order to measure population by occupation, wealth, and income and to inventory assets such as woods, streams, and so forth; establish an Academy of Commerce and Languages, modeled on Italian trade associations (in effect, a Chamber of Commerce); create a *bureau d'addresse*, where people could find out what goods and services were available in the economy, how they could spend free time, and so on (i.e., something like a tourist information office combined with the yellow pages); build department stores that would sell all kinds of merchandise at low, low prices; fund an insurance scheme for widows and orphans; found a society called L'Ordre de la Charité, a quasi-religious order akin to the Society of Jesus, that would militate "against the atheists" by mastering "the remarkable work of God and nature"; establish a Ducal Archive for all government-related documents; appoint as director of said archive Leibniz himself; offer incentives for farmers to adopt the best agricultural techniques and practices; encourage the development of country music and dancing in order to make the farmers' workload feel "light"; introduce a "very good beer" to make it feel still lighter; and establish an Academy of the Sciences, modeled on the Royal Society of London and the Royal Academy of Sciences of Paris.

In Leibniz's mind, clearly, there was no end of good things that the state could do. In fact, according to his way of thinking, the state has a positive duty to institutionalize benevolence through rational planning. He was indeed the first apostle of the welfare state.

On the to-do list of good deeds for the Duke of Hanover, the one that was always dearest to Leibniz's heart—and the only one for which there is a clear record of implementation, albeit a quarter of a century later and not in Hanover—was the last: the Academy of the Sciences. Unfortunately, as Leibniz understood, the Duke of Hanover's generosity did not extend so far as to spend money he did not have on a group of scientists who for the most part did not yet exist. The philosopher therefore took it upon himself to raise funds for the project. From his berth in the old stables of Hanover he pursued a wide variety of business ventures: the manufacture of wool, silk, gold- and silver-embroidered textiles; the production of phosphorous; the distillation of brandy; trade in spices from the Far East; and many more schemes. None of these, sadly, turned a thaler for Leibniz or his prospective academy.

Even while still in Paris, the philosopher had beheld a fantastic vision of future material security, one that would enable him to fund his cherished academy and guarantee his own financial independence. The treasure that would at last put his world on solid foundations, he came to believe, lay buried in the misty, forest-covered hills of Lower Saxony—where Dr. Faustus, perhaps appropriately, made his pact with the devil. The Duke of Hanover, as it happens, owned controlling interests in a large silver-mining operation in the scenic Harz Mountains. Extracting silver ore was a difficult business, however, largely because the mines tended to flood. Leibniz's grand idea provided yet one more instance of the elegance and harmony of the world at work: he proposed to use the power of wind to pump water out of the earth and thus make accessible the silver below the surface.

Naturally, the endlessly inventive genius of Hanover could hardly settle for ordinary windmills and pumps. Instead, he designed a unique system that eliminated intermediary cogwheels, thereby reducing friction, and that was capable of pumping water from 1,000 feet underground (or so he maintained). If ever a mechanical invention deserved to be kept secret (on account of its miraculous, moneymaking properties), he assured the Duke, this was it.

Even as he juggled his many projects to improve the world, the Duchy of Hanover, the Harz mines, and himself, Leibniz continued to pursue an interest about which he was somewhat less than forthcoming with his employer.

THE FIRST SIGN that something went wrong appears in a note dated December 12, 1676. (Leibniz's earliest official communication to his fellow courtiers in Hanover dates from December 13, so the note in question must count as either the first thing he wrote on arrival or the last thing he jotted down in the carriage on the way back from Holland.) Leibniz writes: "If all possibles were to exist, there would be no need of a reason for existing, and mere possibility would be enough. So there would not be a God, except insofar as he is possible. But a God of the kind in which the pious believe would not be possible, if the opinion of those who believe that all possibles exist were true." "Those who believe that all possibles exist" is Leibniz's roundabout way of saying "Spinoza." If Spinoza is correct, Leibniz now concludes, then "a God of the kind in which the pious believe" does not exist. Days—or perhaps moments—after meeting with the philosopher of The Hague, Leibniz suddenly seems very clear on a matter about which he was previously in two minds: that Spinoza's God is incompatible with orthodox belief.

It may very well have been on the same, bumpy ride to Hanover that Leibniz picked up his copies of Spinoza's letters to Oldenburg and added some additional notes in the margins. In new handwriting, Leibniz registers an insight that seems to follow from the thought in his note of December 12. Where Spinoza writes "all things follow necessarily from God's nature," Leibniz comments: "If all things emanate of necessity from the divine nature, then all possible things exist, with equal ease unfortunately for the good and the bad. Therefore moral philosophy is destroyed." Leibniz's position, again, suddenly seems unequivocal. He is now clear that Spinoza's doctrine concerning the necessary origin of all things in God—the same doctrine that he had apparently endorsed just days previously while aboard Prince Ruprecht's yacht—takes down not just the God of orthodoxy, but also all of morality. A note of anxiety sounds in the background of his comments on Spinoza here—a cacophonous note that will grow in volume until it drowns out all the others in the Leibnizian symphony.

Notwithstanding the alarming epiphany about Spinoza's (and his own) heresies, Leibniz's obsession with his rival waxed unabated. On the same scrap of paper on which he presented to Spinoza his proof "That a Most Perfect Being Exists," Leibniz scrawled: "Propositions whose demonstration is desired." He then went on to list *by number* a half dozen of the most crucial propositions in Parts I and II of the *Ethics*. Leibniz evidently had in his possession a list of the principal propositions of at least the first two parts of Spinoza's as yet unpublished masterwork, and he was keen to lay hands on the missing pieces of the text. The propositions in whose proof he showed particular interest, not surprisingly, are those that are central to the proof that God alone is the substance from whose nature all things follow necessarily.

Within moments of his arrival in Hanover, Leibniz set about trying to acquire those desired demonstrations from Spinoza. In a letter since lost, he asked Schuller to supply the proof of Proposition 5 in Part I, that "there cannot be two or more substances in the world." In his reply of February 6, 1677, Schuller copied out the missing proof for Leibniz, referring to other propositions by number only. Clearly, Schuller was aware that Leibniz had in his possession a numbered outline of the *Ethics*.

At around the same time, Leibniz received an extremely irate letter from Henry Oldenburg. "Why you have not delivered my letter to Spinosa," the secretary of the Royal Society fumed, "I truly cannot fathom." Unfortunately, we are in no better position than Oldenburg to understand why Leibniz should have failed to give Spinoza the letter with which he had been entrusted in London. In any case, Oldenburg would not have long to harangue Leibniz on the subject; he would be dead before the end of the year.

In his next letter to Schuller—posted within days and also lost—Leibniz promptly offered Schuller a series of objections to the proof of Proposition 5, clearly with a view to eliciting a response from Spinoza. Leibniz, it seems, had undertaken a project to debate the contents of the *Ethics* piecemeal with its author via third-party correspondence. But in his letter of February 6, Schuller had already hinted at a development that would soon bring an end to Leibniz's plan for carrying on the exchange with Spinoza through back channels: "I fear that [Spinoza] will not be with us much longer, for his lung disease (which runs in his family) seems to be growing worse daily."

ACCORDING TO HIS second biographer, Colerus, Spinoza was in fine spirits on the day before his death. In the afternoon, he joined his landlord, Hendrik van der Spyck, in the parlor of the house on the Paviljoensgracht. He lit a pipe, as was his custom, and conversed with Hendrik for several hours about the most recent sermon of the local Reformist minister.

On the following morning, February 21, 1677, Colerus reports, the affable iconoclast had another chat with Hendrik and his wife, Ida Margarete. Spinoza informed the van der Spycks that he would be receiving a visit from a doctor on that day. The doctor, he said, had ordered him to eat broth made from a chicken. Ida Margarete obligingly plucked a bird and set it to boil with some onions and a pinch of salt. The van der Spycks then gathered their children and set off for the Sunday morning church service.

When they returned, they found Spinoza conversing with the doctor in the parlor. The philosopher was eating the broth with a hearty appetite.

At some point, Hendrik noted that Spinoza had absentmindedly left on the table a gold ducatoon, some small change, and a silver knife. Hendrik thought little of the matter, for the philosopher was often casual with his possessions in this way.

At two o'clock, the van der Spycks once again assembled their brood and set off for the second church service of the day, as was their custom.

At four o'clock, as they spilled out of the church doors, a neighbor rushed up to Hendrik and gave him the news.

Spinoza was dead.

He had died at three o'clock in the presence of the doctor from Amsterdam.

According to Colerus, the van der Spycks were stunned. They had no idea Spinoza's condition was so dire. He was only forty-four years old. They had not imagined that his illness would prove fatal so soon.

Back in the house on the canal, the van der Spycks found the doctor in the parlor with his bag packed. The philosopher's corpse lay in state on the small bed in the downstairs forechamber. Hendrik and the doctor agreed to go upstairs and perform an inventory of the dead man's possessions.

After hurriedly compiling a list of the philosopher's possessions, the doctor begged excuses and edged himself out the front door. He wanted to catch the evening boat back to Amsterdam. His hasty exit shocked Hendrik and Ida Margarete, for the philosopher's body had yet to receive proper care. But the doctor was gone before they could collect themselves to rebuke him.

On that same evening, as he glanced around the parlor, Hendrik noticed that the money and other items that Spinoza had left lying on the table in the morning had gone missing along with the young doctor from Amsterdam.

Hendrik assumed responsibility for the management of the funeral. Colerus reports that it was an impressive event. Six state carriages led the procession, and many persons of high social rank attended along with the philosopher's numerous admirers. Notwithstanding his solitary ways and international notoriety, it seems, the sage of The Hague had developed quite a following among his fellow citizens.

Spinoza left no will, but he had made an odd request some

weeks previously. He had asked that, in the event of his death, Hendrik should ship his writing desk to Rieuwertsz—his publisher in Amsterdam. He insisted that the crate be unmarked, its contents not declared to the customs authorities. Locked inside the desk was the manuscript of his *Ethics*, along with other manuscripts and his correspondence.

After the funeral, van der Spyck arranged to transport the desk—incognito—to Amsterdam. According to a letter from Rieuwertsz to van der Spyck sent a few weeks after the philosopher's death, the precious cargo made it safely to the publisher's offices. Spinoza's relatives went snooping around the wharves in hopes of locating the desk, Rieuwertsz added, for they were convinced that it contained great riches. Because van der Spyck had taken the precaution of not marking the crate, fortunately, its contents reached the publisher untouched. Van der Spyck auctioned off the philosopher's other worldly goods, which raised just enough money to cover funeral expenses and other debts.

The philosopher's death, no less than the life that preceded it, rapidly became the subject of rumor and controversy. Many among the orthodox claimed that in the midst of gruesome final agonies, the hateful heretic repented of his atheistic ways and pleaded mawkishly for absolution from a minister. Others said he had taken poison—opium, or "mandrake juice"—in order to hasten his miserable descent into hell. Still others claimed that he ended his days in an unlit prison cell in Paris. The possibility that Spinoza might have died as happy and unrepentant as any of the other good citizens of The Hague was just as vexing to the seventeenth-century mind as the claim that he had lived free of the usual vices.

Colerus was in a good position to set the record straight. He interviewed Hendrik van der Spyck and others who were around at the time. As a devout minister of the Reformed Church, furthermore, he could not be suspected of any bias in favor of the deceased. (In fact, he was convinced that his subject was roasting in hell at the moment of his writing.)

In his account, Colerus flatly rejects the rumors concerning Spinoza's final hours. Eyewitnesses confirmed unequivocally, he says, that there was no sign of undue suffering, no deathbed recantation, and no last-minute plea for benediction. Colerus also notes, after review-ing the yellowing bills from the local chemist that came due upon Spinoza's death, that there was no evidence of the use of opium or any other toxin.

On one matter, however, Colerus's account is demonstrably inac-curate. He identifies the doctor who attended Spinoza in his final moments only with the initials L.M. This is odd because the biogra-pher elsewhere does not hesitate to name names. Later commentators mostly assumed that L.M. stood for Lodewijk Meyer. Meyer would indeed have been a respectable choice for the part: he was an expe-rienced physician, a radical philosopher in his own right, and Spin-oza's trusted friend. Indeed, Meyer might have been *too* respectable for the part: from what is known of his writings and his character, it is difficult to picture him stealing Spinoza's spare change and running off leaving the corpse unattended.

In fact, the individual who attended Spinoza in his final moments was not Lodewijk Meyer, but Georg Hermann Schuller—Leibniz's bungling, two-timing, uncredentialed, alchemical friend. Schuller must also be counted as the only suspect in the theft of the gold ducatoon, small change, and silver knife that Spinoza had left lying on the table before his death.

On the inventory taken the day of Spinoza's death, next to the sig-nature of Hendrik van der Spyck, appear the Latin forenames—sub-sequently crossed out—of a witness to the proceedings: "Georgius Hermanius." In a later letter to Leibniz, Tschirnhaus reports that Schuller has written him to say that he was indeed present with "our friend in The Hague" on his last day. "After [Spinoza] gave orders concerning how his posthumous manuscripts should be handled" to Schuller, Tschirnhaus recounts, "he died." A subsequent letter from Schuller to Leibniz seems to confirm the story: "before and after [Spinoza's] death (for your ears only) I scrutinized all of his papers thoroughly one by one, and, at the bidding of his friends and himself (while he still lived), I removed any that smelled of erudition [*sic*] or oddity."

Schuller lived with a fellow Spinoza enthusiast, Pieter van Gent, who harbored a great dislike for his lodger, describing him as a good-for-nothing and scoundrel in his treatment of his fiancée. From Schuller, presumably, van Gent learned something about the circumstances surrounding Spinoza's death. He later wrote to his friend Tschirnhaus: "God willing, I shall give you an account in person of what happened when our friend [Spinoza] died, and then I shall tell you more that will astonish and dumbfound you." Unfortunately, van Gent's story never made it into any of the surviving correspondence.

Why did Spinoza call for Schuller? What exactly happened on the day that Spinoza died? Why did Schuller, along with perhaps Tschirnhaus, van Gent, Leibniz, and even Colerus, connive to cover up his role in the affair? The astonishing and dumbfounding questions that linger over Spinoza's death can only be the subject of speculation. Only two facts about the case seem certain and relevant for us: whatever it was that happened on the day that Spinoza died, Schuller was involved; and Leibniz was in the know.

LEIBNIZ GOT THE news within days. In a letter dated February 26, 1677, Schuller informs him of Spinoza's demise, adding: "It seems that death took him so much by surprise that he left no testament to indicate his last will." In his next breath, the Amsterdam doctor makes a startling proposal:

> The manuscript of the *Ethics*, in the author's hand—the same one you saw at his house—is being held at a friend's house. It is for sale, provided the price (150 guilders, I believe) corresponds with the dignity of the object. I thought that since no one knows better than you the significance of the work, perhaps you could persuade your prince to buy it at his cost.

Schuller does not explain how he came into control of the manuscript in question. It is impossible to know whether he refers to the papers locked in the desk van der Spyck was in the process of shipping to Rieuwertsz—which would imply that Spinoza's publisher was the "friend" hoping to cash in on the goods—or to a manuscript that he acquired by some other means.

If Leibniz had any scruples about the legality of Schuller's offer, he kept them well hidden. He was evidently more than keen to buy the precious document, whose significance, as Schuller rightly points out, he better than anyone understood. Naturally, he intended to take the money from the Duke of Hanover's library budget; but it seems that he preferred not to inform his patron about the potential acquisition for the time being.

Four weeks after making the offer, however, Schuller suddenly changed his tune:

> I am greatly relieved that you have said nothing to your prince about the purchase of the *Ethics*, for I have changed my mind entirely, and I do not want to be responsible for the exchange (even if the seller raised his price). The reason is that I have been able to arrange a consensus among his friends, who were in much disagreement, to publish for the public good not only the *Ethics*, but also all the manuscript fragments (the greatest part of which . . . in the author's hand has fallen into my hands).

Here Schuller takes credit for one of the greatest adventures in the history of publishing: the publication of Spinoza's posthumous works. Yet it is hard to escape the conclusion that he claims more credit than is properly his due. In the interval between Schuller's two letters to Leibniz, Rieuwertsz had received Spinoza's manuscripts in Amsterdam and posted a letter of acknowledgment to van der Spyck. A more likely story is that Schuller lost control of the publication process to Rieuwertsz, but preferred to represent the new development to Leibniz as the fruit of his own effort.

With Spinoza's papers out of his (and presumably Schuller's) hands, Leibniz now became greatly alarmed. In April 1677, Tschirnhaus relayed the news from Schuller that among the dead philosopher's papers was "a writing" from Leibniz. The "writing" in question was most likely one of the letters Leibniz had sent Spinoza. The horrifying prospect for Leibniz was that Spinoza's correspondence might now be published in full. Would the editors include his letters to the reviled atheist? Leibniz's career, if not more, hung in the balance.

• • •

WHILE KEEPING A nervous eye on developments in Amsterdam, Leibniz abruptly pulled the trigger on another intellectual front. In a letter that same month in which he introduces himself to a professor of philosophy in a nearby town, Leibniz suddenly steps outside the flow of the discussion in order to fire off a brutal fusillade against the late Descartes. The attack comes out of nowhere, and yet it slams its victim from all sides. Before, Leibniz had little but anodyne praise for the work of the great French philosopher; indeed, just one year previously, he had gone hunting for Cartesian manuscripts with his friend Tschirnhaus in the bookshops of Paris. Now, it seems, the Cartesian philosophy is a catalogue of outrageous errors. Leibniz himself characterizes his violent critique as the consequence of a revelation of sorts. "I was vexed to discover such things *chez* M. des Cartes," he says. "But I could see no way to excuse them."

Leibniz's criticisms of Descartes have a nasty, personal edge. Descartes has "a rather mean spirit," he sneers. He is unduly "arrogant" with respect to other philosophers. His ignorance in chemistry "causes pity"; and "one had best forget the beautiful novel of physics he has given us." His skills as a mathematician and geometer are nothing like what they are cracked up to be. And he fabricated his war record. Above all, says Leibniz, the philosophy Descartes propounded is "dangerous."

To readers of the time, the dawn raid on Descartes must have seemed reckless and inexplicable, as it in fact did to his first correspondent on the matter. "It seems that Mr. Leibnits wishes to establish his reputation on the ruins of that of Mr. Descartes," laments a horrified reviewer, after the dispute went public. In that initial declaration of war of April 1677, however, Leibniz offers us a very discreet clue as to the genesis of the conflict. In cataloguing some of Descartes's errors, he writes: "nor do I approve of his dangerous idea, that matter assumes all forms of which it is capable successively." A reader of the time, of course, would have had no way of knowing that the doctrine Leibniz here attributes to Descartes (that matter assumes all forms of which it is capable) looks suspiciously like the one he attributes to Spinoza (that all possible things exist) in both his personal note of December 12, 1676, and his marginalia on Spinoza's letter to Oldenburg.

WHILE LEIBNIZ WAS jousting with the strangely Spinozistic ghost of Descartes in Hanover, a scramble broke out along the canals of Amsterdam. Rieuwertsz, Jarig Jelles, Schuller himself, and a small band of unsung heroes of the early Enlightenment were making rapid progress in their clandestine effort to publish Spinoza's posthumous works. The material in the philosopher's unmarked crate had to be transcribed into fair copies for use by the printers. Spinoza's Latin required some correction—apparently, he sometimes slipped into Spanish or Portuguese constructions—and letters written in Dutch had to be translated into Latin. For the Dutch edition, conversely, all of the Latin material required translation. Along the way, crucial editorial decisions concerning what to include had to be made. Many of Spinoza's letters were deemed to be of merely personal interest, and, to the unheard groans of future historians, they were destroyed.

The editors carried out their feverish labors in the back rooms of private houses along the canals of Amsterdam. They were running from the law and they were running from God, too—or, at least, so the Vatican avowed. Shortly after Spinoza's death, the papal secretary of state, Cardinal Francesco Barberini, got wind of the publication effort and convened an emergency meeting in Rome. The Vatican committee resolved to spare no effort in suppressing the insurgency. They alerted the vicar of the Dutch Catholic Church, who assigned the case to a leading priest in Amsterdam, who in turn called on all the denominations to contribute fellow spiritual detectives to his squad. On the canals of Amsterdam at the time, it seems, a visitor might well have espied the proverbial boat with a rabbi, a Protestant minister, and a Catholic priest.

At the same time, in Hanover, it seems that Leibniz himself wanted to get in on the fray. With his friend Johann Daniel Crafft, he plotted a secret journey to Amsterdam, in hopes of reviewing Spinoza's posthumous manuscripts. No doubt the manuscripts that most interested him were the ones in his own handwriting. But his obligations in Hanover prevented him from making the trip, so Leibniz remained in his library, writing panicky letters to his man in Amsterdam, Georg Hermann Schuller.

Meanwhile, in Amsterdam, the priestly sleuths prowled the waterways, stopping in many of the city's hundreds of bookshops and printing houses. After some months without a break in the case, the rabbi picked up the first lead. Possibly tipped off by the philosopher's feckless sister Rebecca, the investigators turned up at Rieuwertsz's door.

But the poker-faced publisher professed to have no connection with the author after printing the *Tractatus* of 1670. He feigned surprise that Spinoza should have written any more works. Astonishingly, the ministers fell for it, and thereby lost the opportunity to prevent the publication of the work that one of their colleagues later deemed the vilest book written "since the beginning of the world."

In his infrequent comments on Spinoza to scattered correspondents at this time, Leibniz maintains an air of calm detachment. To his friend Gallois in Paris, for example, he writes:

> Spinoza died this winter. I saw him when passing through Holland, and I spoke with him many times and at great length. He has a strange metaphysics, full of paradoxes. . . . I noted that some of the pretended demonstrations that he showed me are not exact. It is not as easy as one thinks to give true demonstrations in metaphysics. Still, there are some, and quite beautiful ones, too.

For the benefit of the Duke of Hanover, Leibniz also took the time to analyze the exchange of letters between Spinoza and Albert Burgh, an estranged young friend who converted to Catholicism and accused the philosopher of being in league with the Prince of Darkness. Naturally, Leibniz rejects out of hand Spinoza's critique of revealed theology; but he adopts a surprisingly conciliatory stance with respect to the philosopher's commitment to the guidance of reason. "What Spinoza says about the certainty of philosophy and of demonstrations is good and incontestable," he tells the Duke.

Behind the scenes, however, Leibniz was anything but cool about the Spinoza affair. He could scarcely conceal his impatience to lay hands on Spinoza's writings. Above all, he agonized over the possible publication of his earlier correspondence. He obviously made his feelings clear to Schuller, for in a reply of November 1677, the latter takes pains to calm the sleepless philosopher, assuring him that on the day of Spinoza's death he personally cleaned his files of anything that might offend the living.

It is worth noting that Leibniz at this point was in a position to have put a stop to the publication effort. He knew who the renegade editors were, for he was in direct contact with one of them and had met the rest on his travels through Holland. Furthermore, he now worked alongside Nicholas Steno—one of Spinoza's epistolary antagonists and a zealous Catholic convert who had contacts at the highest levels in Rome. A word to Steno and Spinoza's writings—along with his editors—might very well have gone up in smoke, quite literally. But Leibniz remained silent.

In the final days of 1677, the *Opera Posthuma of BDS* at last careened forth from the secret presses of Amsterdam. The work immediately reignited the firestorm of denunciation and censorship that was left smoldering after the publication of *Tractatus* in 1670. It is "a book which . . . surpasses all others in godlessness and which endeavors to do away with all religion and set godlessness on the throne," said a typical reviewer of the time.

On January 25, 1678, Schuller hastily arranged to deliver a copy of the *Opera Posthuma* to Leibniz by means of secret courier, referred to only as "the Jew." Upon receipt of the unmarked package, Leibniz locked himself in the Duke's library and feverishly scanned the seven hundred pages of Spinoza's posthumous work.

He soon experienced the kind of anguish known only to those who have seen their own words in print in a most unbecoming context. There in black and off-white was his 1671 letter to the "celebrated and profound philosopher." Next to it was Spinoza's courteous reply, offering Leibniz a copy of his *Tractatus* and inviting clandestine correspondence. Flipping a few pages further, the horrified reader came upon Schuller's 1675 letter to Spinoza, in which Tschirnhaus describes Leibniz as "free from the usual theological prejudices" and "ready to receive" the rest of Spinoza's writings.

Leibniz was beside himself. He fired off a furious reprimand (since lost) to Schuller. The Amsterdam alchemist, true to character, groveled. In his reply, he pleads that he had no prior knowledge of the inclusion of Leibniz's first letter to Spinoza, and that in any case "the letter is no danger to you, for it concerns only mathematics." (Actually, as we know, it was about optics.) Schuller had a point, though: he knew that Leibniz had to count himself lucky that his other presumed letters, such as the one in which he reportedly praised the *Tractatus*, did not make it into the book.

By February 4—ten days after Schuller sent him his copy and presumably less than a week after having received it—Leibniz had devoured the *Opera Posthuma*. On that date, he offered his judgment to Henri Justel, a friend from Paris who had already made known his view that Spinoza was a diabolical atheist. With Justel, Leibniz is measured but firm in his verdict: "The Posthumous Works of the late M. Spinosa have at last been published. . . . I find there a number of beautiful thoughts in agreement with my own, as some of my friends who were also friends of Spinoza know. But there are also paradoxes that I find neither true nor even plausible." He goes on to list the principal doctrines with which he does not agree, including: that God alone is substance; that all creatures are but modes of substance; that God has no will or intellect; that immortality entails no personal memory; and that happiness is the patient acceptance of the inevitable. In other words, Spinoza is wrong on every point, beginning with the very notion that fifteen months earlier Leibniz had intimated was "easily demonstrated": that God alone is substance. In a contemporaneous letter to another correspondent, Leibniz repeats the same list of unacceptable doctrines and exclaims: "How much better and more true are the Christian ones?!" To Justel he concludes: "This book is dangerous for those who would take the trouble to read it profoundly. The rest will not be able to understand it at all."

To judge from the extensive notes he made on his personal copy of *Opera Posthuma,* Leibniz would have been compelled to number himself among those for whom the book was dangerous. His comments on the *Ethics* extend for fifteen pages. The largest share of his notes refers to Part I, "On God," where he registers his responses to almost every definition and proposition. But these are not the casual remarks of a curious reader; they are the notes of a man who is deter-mined to disagree with what he is reading.

The assault begins on the second line of Spinoza's text and does not let up through the entire first part of the *Ethics*. Leibniz takes no prisoners: Spinoza is wrong on just about every point. Although the criticisms range far and wide, Leibniz returns reliably to the claim that he first made on December 12, 1676: that Spinoza's belief that all possible things exist is incompatible with the existence of a God "of the kind in whom the pious believe."

Perhaps the most remarkable feature of Leibniz's commentary is its pointedly personal tone. He derides Spinoza's proof of Proposition 20 as an "empty, pretentious device to twist the whole into the form of a demonstration." On the next proposition, he scrawls: "He demon-strates this obscurely and at length, though it is easy." Then, on the subsequent proofs: "this demonstration is fallacious"; "this proof car-ries no weight"; "this demonstration is obscure and abrupt, being carried through by the abrupt, obscure, and questionable propositions that have preceded it"; "he proves this in an obscure, questionable, and devious way, as is his wont." By the time he reaches Proposition 30, Leibniz is fuming: "It seems that our author's mind was most tortu-ous: he rarely proceeds in a natural and clear way, but always advances in abrupt and circuitous steps." As these notes were never intended to be read by any one other than Leibniz himself, they must count as about as sincere as anything he ever wrote. And they make clear that the honeymoon, such as it was, is over.

Indeed, Leibniz's disagreements with Spinoza are by now so emphatic that one may even be inclined to doubt whether there ever had been a honeymoon. But, at around the same time that he recorded his reactions to the *Ethics*, Leibniz himself provided the evi-dence to remove any such doubts. In "On Freedom," an unpublished essay dating from 1678 or 1679, he confesses:

> When I considered that nothing occurs by chance . . . and that
> nothing exists unless certain conditions are fulfilled from all of
> which together its existence at once follows, I found myself very
> close to the opinions of those who hold everything to be

> absolutely necessary. . . . But I was pulled back from this
> precipice by considering those possible things which neither are
> nor will be nor have been.

"Those who hold everything to be absolutely necessary," of course, just means "Spinoza." Leibniz here confirms that his earlier rapprochement with Spinoza was quite real.

Perhaps most revealing is Leibniz's choice of metaphor to describe his earlier lapse into Spinozism. A "precipice" is the kind of peril that one may encounter unexpectedly in the midst of a journey and that may be averted in an instant, by simply pulling back. Most important, it evokes the fear of a "fall" in more than just a physical sense.

Not for another twenty-five years did Leibniz feel ready to make a similar confession about his youthful affair with Spinozism. Yet, crucially, in his famous comment in the unpublished *New Essays on Human Understanding*, he expresses almost exactly the same thought: that he had once "leaned to the side of the Spinozists," whom he specifically accuses of holding everything to be absolutely necessary. In that celebrated passage, he goes on to say that "these new lights have healed me, and since that time I have sometimes taken the name of Theophile." Clearly, the story of Leibniz's fateful bite of the Spinozist apple and his subsequent recovery from such a hideous lapse marks a pivotal moment in his own narrative of his life. The tone of both confessions is something like that of a repentant sinner or recovering alcoholic. If (*per impossibile*) there were more people like Leibniz in the world, one could imagine them circling together in a kind of Spinozists Anonymous to trade qualifications, share lessons about their illness, and discuss the twelve steps to healing.

Leibniz's claim that he settled on the name Theophile only after curing himself of the affliction of Spinozism is intriguing, and seems to refer to an important step on his road to recovery. Sure enough, a dialogue in his unpublished notes from 1678, the year in which he received Spinoza's posthumous works, features a fictional character bearing Leibniz's new pseudonym. (In the dialogue on motion he wrote just days before visiting Spinoza, incidentally, Leibniz also names one of the participants Theophile; but he does not in that instance identify himself with the character in question.) Theophile, says Leibniz now, "had a certain self-effacement and simplicity which gave ample evidence of great resources and an enlightened and tranquil soul." He is clearly everything Leibniz wants to be.

Theophile's debating partner is a man named Polidore, who is pretty much what Leibniz does not want to be. Polidore suffers from a kind of *vanitas* not at all unlike that of the author of *The Treatise on the Emendation of the Intellect*: "Now that I have attained the things I wanted," he says, "I have come to recognize their vanity." He dismisses the "presumptuous" doctrine of personal immortality, and he dabbles in the theory of a world-soul. God, he seems to think, is nothing but nature, and nature is cruel:

> A wretched sheep is torn apart by a wolf, a pigeon falls prey to some vulture, the poor flies are exposed to the malice of spiders, and men themselves—what a tyranny they exercise over other animals, and even among themselves . . . [we] must say that [God] cares not at all for what we call justice and that he takes pleasure in destruction. . . . Individuals must give way; there is room only for the species.

Polidore, in other words, is Spinoza without the aura of metaphysical enchantment.

Naturally, Theophile gets the better of the argument. He eventually brings Polidore around to the recognition that God has a will and intellect, that he actively plans everything for the best, that the individual soul is immortal, and that there is no such thing as a world-soul. In other words: that Spinoza is wrong about everything. The dialogue concludes with a spectacular passage in which Leibniz announces the creed that served to guide his entire life:

> I see that virtue and honor are not chimeras. I recognize that the general lament about the misery of life poisons our satisfaction and strangely deceives us. Instead we must remember that we are the most perfect and happiest of all known creatures, or at least that it takes only us to become so. Most blessed are those who

know their own good. Hereafter let us no longer complain of nature; let us love this God who so loved us, and know, once and for all, the knowledge of great truths, the exercise of divine love and charity, and the efforts which one can make for the general good—by assuaging the ills of men, contributing to the happiness of life, advancing the sciences and arts and everything that serves to acquire true glory and immortalize oneself through good deeds—all these are pathways to this felicity, which lead us as far as we are capable of going toward God and which we may take as a kind of apotheosis.

Among the thousands of pages that fill the Leibniz Archive, this one offers perhaps the most heartfelt declaration of the great philosopher's ambition to serve the human race principally in advancing the arts and sciences and always according to the maxim "Justice is the charity of the wise." According to the editors of this manuscript, his handwriting grows larger and rounder as the passage progresses, overflowing the margins of the paper. He was clearly in a state of deep exultation as he made this statement of what he took to be his most noble aspiration.

But it should not be overlooked that the character in whose voice this final, breathless profession of faith emerges is not the serene Theophile, but the recovering Spinozist Polidore. Leibniz, it seems, was the latter as much as he was the former. Theophile is perhaps best interpreted as Leibniz's *idea* of himself—the idea with which he was ever so much in love. But Polidore should be counted as his other, more real self—the multiplicitous one who desperately needed affirmation, who perhaps secretly still doubted that the world had enough love to go around.

In other writings from this time, Leibniz's assault on Descartes takes on a highly revealing character. Though the attack remains fierce and scattered, it is no longer inexplicable. Leibniz returns time and again to the critique of the "dangerous" Cartesian doctrine he first attacked in April 1677: the belief that "matter receives all forms possible successively." It is a curious nit to pick with Descartes, since other commentators would not necessarily have regarded this as one of the French philosopher's central doctrines. Why pick on this particular nit, then? By early 1680, Leibniz allows himself to be explicit:

> If matter assumes all forms possible successively, then it follows that one cannot imagine anything so absurd nor so bizarre nor contrary to that which we call justice, that has not happened or will not happen one day. These are precisely the thoughts that Spinoza explained more clearly, to know that justice, beauty, and order are naught but things that are relative to us, that the perfection of God consists in the amplitude of his work, that nothing is possible or conceivable that he does not actually produce. . . . This is, in my view, the *proton pseudos* [first lie] and foundation of the atheistic philosophy.

The problem with Descartes, in a word, is Spinoza. And the problem with Spinoza is that he is an atheist. Indeed, he is the world's first and foremost atheist, the one who best articulates the "first lie and foundation of the atheistic philosophy." Thus Leibniz announces his definitive response to the single most important question that can be raised about Spinoza's philosophy: Is his God really a God?

Leibniz's use of the term "atheism" here marks a pivotal moment in European culture. Unlike almost all his contemporaries, Leibniz did not use the label of atheism in order to suggest that Spinoza led a debauched life. Quite to the contrary, Leibniz would go out of his way to acknowledge that the philosopher of The Hague was irreproachable in his manner of living. Rather, perhaps for the first time, Leibniz understood that atheism stood for a new and very different kind of problem, a latent, philosophical potentiality of modernity, a condition afflicting especially those who, like Spinoza, did little but meditate on the existence and nature of God.

It is equally important to note that although Descartes preceded Spinoza, chronologically speaking, it is the later philosopher who has logical priority over the earlier one in Leibniz's mind. Descartes's theory of God, according to Leibniz, "is nothing but a chimera and consequently it would be necessary to conceive of God in the manner of Spinoza, as a being who has no intellect or will." And again:

"Descartes thinks in a whisper what Spinoza says at the top of his voice."

In fact, Leibniz is so sure that Descartes is just a feeble pseudonym for Spinoza that he goes ahead and criticizes the former for views that are more properly attributed to the latter. For example, he blasts Descartes for his concept of immortality—an "immortality without memory" that "cannot console us in any way" and that "destroys all reward and punishment." But the doctrine in question properly belongs to Spinoza; Descartes, in fact, explicitly rejects it.

It was far from the last time that Leibniz engaged in proxy warfare against Spinoza's stand-ins. But it was one of the last times he was so explicit about his aims. Descartes by now was the marquee name of a new brand of orthodoxy in the universities of Europe. As word of Leibniz's dawn raid spread, the Cartesians rounded on him for having dared to associate their master's good name with that of the apostate Jew. "One hopes that [Leibniz] will return to mathematics, in which he excels, and not get mixed up in philosophy, where he does not have the same advantage," mutters a seething Cartesian in the Parisian *Journal des Sçavans.* Chastised, Leibniz acknowledged his error. "I would never have mentioned Spinoza," he replies, "if I had thought that one would publish what I was writing."

LEIBNIZ HAD DISCOVERED what he was against, philosophically speaking. But he was not yet entirely clear on what he was for. While he labored on his own spectacular and inimitable response to the philosophical problems of his age and ours, the great courtier of Hanover went underground—quite literally.

In October 1679, Leibniz's lengthy negotiations with Duke Johann Friedrich concerning the Harz mines came to fruition in the form of a contract. The document specifies that if, after a one-year trial period, the windmill invention works as planned, Leibniz is to be paid an annual pension of 1,200 thalers for the rest of his life. Although the original rationale for the project had been to secure funding for a proposed Academy of the Sciences, the sole beneficiary of the new contract, it seems, was to be Leibniz himself. The philosopher was brimming with satisfaction: "I have the affair of the windmill at such a state of perfection that I am certain that it will please the world marvelously," he told the Duke.

One month after signing the contract, sadly, Leibniz's great champion, Duke Johann Friedrich, died. The new duke, Ernst August, shared few of the spiritual and cultural interests of his brother and predecessor. He was a trim figure, known among his peers chiefly for his skills as a huntsman. Although he appreciated Leibniz's unique intellectual gifts, he was less than inspired by the courtier's philosophical projects. Nonetheless, the two evidently were able to talk about money. The philosopher promised Ernst August that his mining project would generate 400,000 thalers of additional income for the duchy over ten years at almost no cost, and the Duke reaffirmed his predecessor's commitment to the venture.

The greatest German philosopher of the time promptly became something like a management consultant *avant la lettre*. From 1680 to 1686, he made thirty-one journeys to and spent half of his days and nights—a total of 165 weeks—in the Harz Mountains. Hundreds of pages of his collected works are taken up with correspondence on the subject of the Harz mines—far more than the number devoted to any of his philosophical or scientific projects during the period.

By 1683, the project was two years behind schedule and 800 percent over budget. There was no windmill, and among the locals in the Harz Mountains Leibniz was about as popular as black lung. The complaints of the mining engineers will sound eerily familiar to any who have had experience with management consultants in the present day. First, they said, their self-appointed adviser had little actual knowledge of the business in which they were engaged. Second, he seemed to suffer from the illusion "that in this business all mathematical speculations whatsoever can be applied in practice." Third, his compensation was entirely out of proportion to the service he supplied. Finally, not coincidentally, he sought only his "own interest, and not that of the mines" and he "cared only about making money for himself."

The surviving evidence suggests that the aggrieved miners may have had a point. Leibniz's plan, for example, involved the creation of ancillary structures to handle the new operations, and the required investment was great enough to call into question the commercial value of the windmill project as a whole. But the courtier argued, infuriatingly, that those expenses were not specified as part of his project in his contract with the Duke, and so were no concern of his.

Leibniz also failed conspicuously to win points with the miners for honesty. Although he presented the windmill plan as his own brainchild, in fact a version of the idea had first been suggested by a mining engineer who had died before the philosopher began the project. The deceased engineer had also proposed that the water pumped out by the windmills should be stored in reservoirs, to be run through water-powered pumps as the need arose. Earlier, when the engineer's plans were revived as an alternative to Leibniz's scheme, the philosopher scoffed, arguing that the other system would never work. As he became more familiar with the realities of mining life, however, Leibniz turned around and presented the dead man's scheme as his own. The miners, perhaps understandably, judged that the bewigged courtier from Hanover was "a dangerous man and evil to deal with."

AS HE BURROWED in search of silver in the Harz Mountains, Leibniz, true to his word, only rarely allowed the name of Spinoza to slip from his plume. And yet, even as his explicit references to his rival dwindled to almost nothing, they grew all the more revealing. A case in point is his letter to Count Ernst von Hessen-Rheinfels of August 14, 1683, which expresses in the clearest terms the extraordinary and complex transformation in Leibniz's attitude toward Spinoza that took place in the months and years immediately following his return from The Hague.

Ernst was a Catholic convert who was very keen on Leibniz's project of church reunion and even more enthusiastic about the prospect of winning Leibniz and his employers to the true faith. In his letter to the count of 1683, Leibniz turns to the subject of corporal punishment by religious authorities—a topic of considerable concern to Protestants, who had seen what the Catholic inquisitors were capable of doing with kindling wood and metal implements. Leibniz begins, mercifully, by taking a stand against the methods of "fire and iron." Corporal punishment, he says, should be reserved only for those heretics whose actions are themselves against natural right—e.g., those who attempt to foment insurrection or to poison a bishop.

But the philosopher–management consultant abruptly has a second thought. "As for those atheists who concern themselves with developing sect-followers like Vanini and Spinosa, there is a little more cause for doubt" about whether to refrain from corporal punishment, Leibniz says. "It's another thing; for, having no conscience, what need do they have to teach?" The Italian philosopher Lucilio Vanini, incidentally, was burned at the stake in 1619 in Toulouse for being an "atheist." A similar application of corrective justice, Leibniz seems to suggest, might not have been such a bad thing in the case of Spinoza.

Having built a figurative woodpile under the feet of the man he visited seven years earlier, Leibniz is suddenly not sure whether to throw the match. He has a third thought:

> Nonetheless, when I consider the natural right one has to say what one believes to be the truth, and that they [people like Spinoza] believe in the manner of Epicurus that they are providing a great service to the human race in delivering it from ill-founded superstitions, I do not yet dare to decide if one has the right to sentence them to the ultimate punishment.

Leibniz is now well and truly divided against himself. On the one hand, Spinoza has no conscience; he ought to burn. On the other hand, Spinoza says what he believes is true—that is, he does have a conscience—so perhaps he should be spared. Leibniz knows what he should do and he hardly doubts what the count wants him to do; but he cannot erase from his mind the image of the man he met in The Hague: a rare philosopher, sincere, honest, inspired by noble goals, and incapable of doing anything unworthy of himself.

But he steels himself for the inevitable. Perhaps striving to make a harsh verdict more bearable, he lashes out:

> Regarding Spinosa, whom M. Arnauld has called the most impious and most dangerous man of this century, he was truly Athe-

ist, which is to say, that he allowed absolutely no Providence dispensing rewards and punishments according to justice. . . . The God he puts on parade is not like ours; he has no intellect or will. He had a pleasant concept of immortality of the soul: he thought that the platonic idea of our being, which is without doubt as eternal as that of a circle or triangle, constituted our true immortality. . . . He fell well short of mastering the art of demonstration; and he had only a mediocre knowledge of analysis and geometry; what he knew best was to make lenses for microscopes. I conversed with him for a few hours while passing through The Hague, and I learned the rest from a few of his sect-followers, whom I happen to know familiarly. One assures me that also in 1672 when the French had taken Utrecht, some very considerable persons caused Spinoza to come visit them.

If we were to focus only on the literal meaning of Leibniz's words, we would naturally conclude that Spinoza at this point is of about as much philosophical interest to him as sawdust. Spinoza's God is just a charade, and his philosophy as a whole is so transparently bad as to be hardly worth refuting. Worse, he was a deviant—a political agitator bent on achieving a specious form of honor by cultivating a sect-following. To top it all, he was of mediocre intelligence. With his pretended proofs he demonstrated nothing more than his twisted will to power.

But the tone of Leibniz's comments seems to hint at a different story behind the dismissive arguments. The raillery ("the God he puts on parade"), the gratuitous sarcasm ("a pleasant concept of immortality"), the insults ("what he knew best was how to make lenses"), and the fact that the digression flares up in the context of an analysis of the merits of incinerating atheists—everything points to a very deep, personal, and abiding anxiety concerning his late colleague, an anxiety that expresses itself mostly in the form of loathing, sometimes as a grudging admiration, and always with a degree of obsession that may serve as a vital clue that the problem of Spinoza remains very much alive in Leibniz's mind.

The letter to Ernst also makes clear that Leibniz's continuing conflict with Spinoza will henceforth take place deep underground. The philosopher-courtier's strategy now goes beyond merely avoiding the mention of his rival's name. He intends to avoid the facts as well, at least insofar as they concern his own, earlier entanglements with Spinoza.

The visit with Spinoza, he now maintains, lasted merely "a few hours"—although in the earlier letter to Gallois he says that they met "many times and at great length." He happened to see his fellow philosopher "in passing," Leibniz now avers—although his hurried visits to London and Amsterdam, where he collected a fistful of Spinoza's correspondence, suggest that the primary purpose of his trip to Holland was in fact to call on its most famous philosopher. He "learned the rest" of Spinoza's philosophy from mutual friends, he claims—although, in fact, as we know, in the privacy of his library he had studied his rival's works assiduously. Leibniz's allusion to the fact that the great Condé invited Spinoza to Utrecht in 1673 is perhaps his most desperate attempt to minimize the significance of his own journey to The Hague: Even famous aristocrats, he means to say, occasionally take the time to chat with notorious atheists.

Leibniz was even less forthcoming about his other little secret concerning Spinoza—his knowledge of the circumstances surrounding the philosopher's death. Georg Hermann Schuller died two years after the event at the age of twenty-nine, and Leibniz held his silence on the matter for the remaining forty years of his life. In the *Theodicy* of 1710, he goes out of his way to mention that he has received a copy of Colerus's recently issued biography, in which Spinoza's doctor is identified as L.M. He even takes the trouble to improve on Colerus's account in one place: he clarifies that the woman the biographer identifies as Spinoza's possible love interest also happened to be the daughter of the notorious Frans van den Enden—who, he reminds us, was executed in Paris in 1674. But Leibniz apparently did not think it worth his while to correct Colerus's misimpressions concerning the identity of the last man to see Spinoza alive.

At this point, the evidence concerning Leibniz's possible participation in a cover-up of the identity of Spinoza's deathbed physician runs out. But it is worth noting that in his very brief life Georg Hermann Schuller established only one claim to fame. As would have been plain to any reader of Spinoza's *Opera Posthuma* of 1678, Schuller was the man who organized the introduction of Leibniz to Spinoza. And it is safe to say that Leibniz, the last survivor of the three, would have been content not to draw attention to the fact that the man who attended the infamous atheist in his last hours also happened to be his own factotum in Holland.

BY 1683, WHEN he contemplated the merits of burning his erstwhile host at the stake, Leibniz's attitude toward Spinoza had undoubtedly undergone a radical transformation since the time seven years earlier when he so eagerly approached the philosopher of The Hague. But the same change of heart is already evident in 1679, when he writes in the past tense of his lapse into Spinozism, and before that in 1678, in his acid commentary on the *Opera Posthuma*. And the central criticism he levels at Spinoza is already evident in his sudden assault on Descartes in early April 1677, just over four months after his voyage to The Hague. Most telling of all, the idea that runs through all of his subsequent refutations of Spinoza—the claim that Spinoza's belief in a necessary aspect in all things is incompatible with the existence of an orthodox deity—is first tied to a stake in the ground in the note dated December 12, 1676.

The conclusion that best fits the evidence available, then, is that Leibniz changed his mind about Spinoza at the very same time that he met Spinoza. Evidently, something happened when the two greatest philosophers of the seventeenth century sat down in the house on the Paviljoensgracht—something possibly unpleasant; something capable, in any case, of dramatically altering the course of Leibniz's life and the subsequent history of philosophy.

14

The Antidote to Spinozism

On a sunny hillside in the Harz Mountains, as the spring of 1684 arrived in lively shades of green, the long awaited prototype windmill blossomed at last. After supervising the final construction of his vaunted invention, Leibniz returned to Hanover to await results of its first trials.

There was no wind.

Amazingly, the inventor of the calculus had failed to observe that the mountainous region where he planned the project simply didn't offer the kind of winds required to power windmills. The hills of Saxony were nothing like the lowlands of Holland. Eventually, a gust blew up in the middle of one night, and, according to a somewhat confused report from a night watchman, the machines creaked into action. There was little chance of striking silver anytime soon.

Leibniz responded to the setback by inventing a new kind of windmill—nothing like the ones that populate the Dutch countryside. According to his new design, a set of flat panels would rotate around a vertical axis, like a merry-go-round. In the summer of 1684, he returned to the mountains and oversaw the construction of his latest invention. The results, however, were not promising; and in any case there still wasn't much wind.

The mining engineers had by now become quite strident in their views that the philosopher-consultant's project amounted to an epic waste of money and time. They proposed that Leibniz conduct an experiment to determine whether his windmills were any more efficient than the preexisting water pumps. The courtier responded with a five-thousand-word essay that shows off his legal training at its finest. His contract, he insists, says nothing about showing that the windmills were *more* efficient than the existing water pumps, only that they would get the water out. He may have been legally correct; but it was not a very effective way to demonstrate that his interests were very well aligned with those of the Duke, his mines, or the rest of the human race, for that matter.

In April 1685, Duke Ernst August finally understood where all this was going and ordered an immediate cessation to work on the windmill project. But with the *schadenfreude* dripping off tongues in Hanover and the general good of humankind still unserved, Leibniz could not bear to pull himself from the mines. Through much of 1685 and 1686, he remained in the mountains, devising still more inventions for the miners. He proposed, for example, installing a circular chain of containers, such that rocks from the surface could be used to pull up loads from the pits. But the miners paid no heed. To a fellow courtier Leibniz complained that the engineers would listen politely to his proposals one day, then suffer memory loss on the next day.

Leibniz's stint in the mines, as with so many of his other adventures, ended with questions about the altruism (or not) of his deepest motivations lingering unanswered. The trouble was not just that his labors in the Harz Mountains produced no benefit to the miners, the Duke, the German economy, or the prospective Academy of the Sciences; it was that the philosopher's behavior throughout the project left radically unclear whether in his own mind the interests of any of these potential beneficiaries could ever have trumped his overwhelming need to ensure his own financial security. But perhaps the doubts can be resolved by considering the adventure from the most global perspective. In the grand plan of the history of philosophy, it sometimes happens that philosophy progresses underground. Like a mine complex flooded with water, its advance may depend on the slow clearing of inundated passageways, one by one, in a seemingly random and invisible way, until at last all the chambers connect and the enterprise breathes with life.

For reasons that lie buried forever in the Harz Mountains, the years Leibniz spent jousting with windmills were the ones in which he at last fulfilled the ambition he had announced in February 1676, to synthesize "a secret philosophy of the whole of things." With the benefit of hindsight, of course, one can scour Leibniz's notes from those years and construct a narrative about how all the connections opened up—and thereby lend the illusion of predictability to the whole process. But in prospect, philosophy is far less susceptible to programming than such narratives tend to suggest.

In the particularly frigid February of 1686, a blizzard swept across central Germany. For two whole weeks, the kinetic courtier was frozen in place. With the drifts piling up outside, he at last found the time to set down his answers to the eternal questions. In the resulting *Discourse on Metaphysics* Leibniz laid out all of the core tenets of his mature metaphysics. He later said it was only from this time that he was satisfied with his metaphysics. His subsequent efforts to refine and reexpress his thoughts offer some interesting changes in tone and emphasis but none in substance.

The *Discourse* came to life with the explicit purpose of furthering the project of church reunion. In the *Catholic Demonstrations* he had mapped out as early as 1671, Leibniz had announced his plan to supply the philosophical foundations for the religion of a unified church. With the *Discourse*, he hoped, he would finally deliver on his promise. As he labored over his precious manuscript in his snowy retreat, the philosopher had one particular reader consciously in mind: Antoine Arnauld, the doyen of Parisian theology. Leibniz was sure that if he could win Arnauld's approval for his new philosophy, then it would be accepted by Catholics and Protestants alike as the basis for a glorious reunification of the Christian church of the west.

But a close reading shows that Leibniz had another, perhaps deeper agenda—and maybe even an additional reader—in mind as he wrote his *Discourse*. In the version of the text that he eventually sent to Arnauld, and which has since become the standard draft, Leibniz describes his new philosophy in the second paragraph of the text as the antidote for the view "that seems to me extremely dangerous and comes very near to that of the latest innovators whose opinion it is that the beauty of the universe and the goodness we ascribe to the works of God are nothing but the chimeras of men who think of him in terms of themselves." But in the earlier draft, in which his internal censors perhaps suffered a momentary relapse, the phrase "the latest innovators" reads simply "the Spinozists." Leibniz's metaphysical system, it seems, was like a new set of windmills—nothing at all like the Dutch kind. With the same spirit and energy with which he set about emptying the Harz mines of water, he now took upon himself the task of clearing the ground of European thought of the seemingly ubiquitous Substance of Spinoza.

God

Modernity reduces God's creation to a silent, colorless, odorless world of weights and measures—a pointless machine—or so it has seemed to many observers. Spinoza embraces this new world—indeed, with his doctrine that God is Nature, he attempts to deify it. But Leibniz does not believe in Spinoza's new deity. And it is this rejection of Spinoza's God that represents the first principle of Leibniz's mature philosophy and the starting point of his own, unique response to modernity.

Any God worthy of the name, says Leibniz, must be able to make choices. That is, God must have an intellect with which to contemplate his options, and a will with which to affirm his decisions. God must have a choice, according to Leibniz's way of thinking, because otherwise he would not have a chance to be good. That is, God must make his choices with the idea that he is doing something that deserves praise. But Spinoza's God makes no choices. It has no will or intellect, at least as we understand those terms. In Spinoza's world, furthermore, "good" is just a term relative to human needs and limitations, no more applicable to God than, say, "delicious," "orange," or, for that matter, "bad." The God of Spinoza, Leibniz concludes, is not a God at all. Spinoza was, as he puts it to the Count von Hessen-Rheinfels, "truly Atheist."

The questions Leibniz raises here concerning Spinoza's doctrine of God are valid ones, and must be contemplated by all those who wish to penetrate to the core of either philosopher's thought. According to Spinoza, God or Nature causes the things of the world in the same way that the nature of a coffee, for example, causes it to be black. But we do not usually say that that the nature of coffee is divine, so why should we say that Nature is God? In the *Ethics*, as a matter of fact, one can substitute the word "Nature" (or "Substance," or even simply an *X*) for God throughout, and the logic of the argument changes little, if at all. So, why use the term "God" at all? What does the name of God add—except, perhaps, some of the crusty and, for Spinoza, impermissible connotations about a divine decision maker who, say, chooses to make coffee black rather than pink? The intuition that motivates Leibniz's position here might be stated this way: what is divine must be in some way beyond or before what is natural, or else it is not divine at all.

In arguing that God must be good, Leibniz puts his finger on a related paradox in Spinoza's thinking. To say that nature is divine is in some way to judge the world—usually, to imply that the world as a whole is good. Nietzsche—whose qualifications as a Spinozist have been insufficiently acknowledged, even by himself—suggests as much when he says that Spinoza "deified the All" in order to "affirm" the world. Spinoza himself says that the world is "perfect." But, according to Spinoza's own logic, the totality of things lies beyond all human judgment. It is neither good nor bad. Now, says Leibniz, if Spinoza cannot say that the world is good, he certainly cannot say that it is perfect, except in the most abstract sense meaning "complete" or "all that there is." He cannot judge or "affirm" the world in the way that one must if one says that it is divine. Therefore, he has no license to give Nature the name of God, as he claims to do.

Even as he rejects Spinoza's concept of God, however, Leibniz retains his deep commitment to the guidance of reason. No less than Spinoza, he finds intolerable the idea of a God without reason, that is, a God who makes up reasons as he goes along, who has the arbitrary power to declare that two plus two is four on one day and then change his mind the next. Like Spinoza, Leibniz now faces one of the defining problems of modernity, namely, how to manage the potentially destructive conflict between God and Nature, or between belief in divinity and the ever expanding power circle of scientific knowledge. Unlike his more orthodox contemporaries, Leibniz is too honest to ignore the claims of reason. Unlike Spinoza, however, he cannot find it in himself to deify the object of the new sciences. His problem, then, is to discover a God of reason—that is, one who answers to philosophical proofs and whose existence is compatible with the findings of science—who nonetheless avoids the Spinozistic pitfall of losing his divinity altogether.

In the *Discourse*, Leibniz first formulates his answer to this problem in a clear and perspicuous way. "God has chosen that world which is most perfect," he writes. That is to say, God is that being which chooses the "the best of all possible worlds."

In his later writings, in which he allows himself the poetic license that accrues to well-ripened visions, Leibniz presents a more vivid representation of this idea of God. In the final pages of his *Theodicy*, a character named Theodorus (Leibniz's alter ego in this instance) falls asleep in a temple and begins to dream. In his reverie, he visits "a palace of unimaginable splendor and prodigious size"—an edifice that, as it happens, belongs to God. The halls in the palace represent possible worlds. As Theodorus wanders through this magnificent construction, he tours a variety of worlds in which things happened very differently than in our own: worlds in which Adam did not eat the apple, for instance, and worlds in which Judas kept his mouth shut.

> The halls rose in a pyramid, becoming even more beautiful as one mounted toward the apex, and representing more beautiful worlds. Finally they reached the highest one which completed the pyramid, and which was the most beautiful of all: . . . for the pyramid had an apex, but no base; it went on increasing to infin-

ity. That is . . . because amongst an endless number of possible worlds there is the best of all, else God would not have determined to create any.

The world at the apex, the best of all possible worlds, it turns out, is the actual world, the one in which we live.

The vision is unmistakably baroque. It is possibly an apt representation of what it feels like to get lost at Versailles, and perhaps it is best read with music of the period in the back of one's mind. (Handel, incidentally, was Leibniz's fellow courtier at Hanover in the year that the *Theodicy* was published.) The passage also oozes the optimism that would later induce Voltaire to satirize Leibniz in the figure of Dr. Pangloss. After all, many would have guessed that our world is one or two levels down from the top of the pyramid, at the very least.

In any case, the crucial and novel feature in Leibniz's account is his characterization of God's choice in terms of possible *worlds*—as opposed to possible *things*. According to Leibniz, God chooses not between, say, allowing Adam to eat the apple or not, but between possible worlds that do or do not include an Adam eating an apple. This marks what Leibniz believed was one of his decisive breakthroughs in the ten years after his journey to The Hague. In his earlier writings, Leibniz's unswerving commitment to the principle of sufficient reason made it difficult for him to conceive of possible *things*. For, inasmuch as everything happens for a reason, there are no isolated accidents or random events in Leibniz's world—everything is part of a single, causal tapestry. "Because of the interconnection of things," he acknowledges at the time of his *Discourse*, "the universe with all its parts would be wholly different from the commencement if the least thing in it happened otherwise than it had." By raising God's choice to the level of possible *worlds*, however, Leibniz can have his principle of sufficient reason and eat it, too, in a sense: that is, he can grant that all things within our world are linked together in a necessary way while still maintaining that the world as a whole does not necessarily have to be the way that it is. "The reasons for the world," he says, "lie in something extramundane."

The concept of possible worlds, according to Leibniz's way of thinking, also neatly solves the problem of God's goodness. Inasmuch as God does not choose particular things, he does not choose things that are evil; rather, he chooses a world that, for some reason, must have evil in it. The reason for this world is the principle of the best, which God applies with perfect precision; and if this world seems to us to have things that deserve the name of evil, we may nonetheless rest assured that God could not have made a better choice.

In order to solidify the conclusion that God must make a choice, Leibniz labors hard to establish a distinction between "moral" necessity and "metaphysical" necessity. God's decision to create the best of all possible worlds, he grants, exhibits a kind of moral necessity. That is, if God wishes to be good, he must apply the principle of the best in his choice of possible worlds. But God's choice does not involve any metaphysical necessity. That is, God is theoretically capable of ordering up a less than ideal world, or no world at all, should he be so inclined.

At this point, the contrast with Spinoza's concept of God could hardly be starker—and that is precisely the point behind the vision. The difference goes back to that simple-sounding question: Does God have a choice? Spinoza says no; Leibniz says yes. Spinoza says that God has only one world to choose from, namely, the one that follows ineluctably from its own Nature. Leibniz counters that God always has the option not to create the world; and, when God decides to go ahead with the project, he faces a choice among an infinite number of possible worlds. Spinoza's God has no need for anthropomorphic encumbrances such as a will or intellect, for it has no choices to contemplate and no resolutions to affirm. Leibniz's God, on the other hand, looks much more like you or me: he must have a capacity for thought and action in order to make his choices. Finally, whereas Spinoza's Substance is well beyond the merely human categories of good and evil, Leibniz's God is the ultimate do-gooder, as he shuffles through all possible worlds hoping to locate "the best."

In sum, Spinoza believes in an "immanent" God; Leibniz argues for a "transcendent" one. Spinoza's God is the immanent cause of things: it creates the world in the same way that an essence creates its properties—that is, in the same way that the nature of a circle makes it round. It is *in* the world (just as the world is in it) and therefore cannot conceivably be associated with any other world or with no world at all. A transcendent God, on the other hand, is the "transitive" cause of things. He creates the world in the same way that a watchmaker makes a watch. He stands outside the world, and he would still be God whether he opted to create this world, another world, or no world at all. He has a certain degree of personhood (which is why we tend to call him "he," in deference to the tradition). Leibniz sometimes uses the phrase "supra-mundane intelligence" to describe his transcendent God. Dropping the polysyllables, we could also say simply that Spinoza's divinity is one that inhabits the "here and now," while Leibniz's resides in the "before and beyond."

The confrontation between Leibnizian and Spinozistic conceptions of divinity, incidentally, continues to characterize discussions to the present, notably in the field of cosmology (never mind the relatively changeless field of theology). Among contemporary physicists, for example, there are those who maintain that the laws of nature are inherently arbitrary. According to their rather Leibnizian view, God (or perhaps a Great Designer) selects from among an infinite range of parameters for the laws of nature, and everything else in the world then unfolds within the chosen regime. Others physicists, however, maintain that the parameters that define the laws of physics may ultimately be determined by the laws themselves, such that nature may account for itself in an utterly self-sufficient way. Such theorists may be said to lean to the side of Spinoza.

In the seventeenth century, of course, the difference between Leibnizian and Spinozan concepts of divinity was hugely—and perhaps essentially—political. Spinoza argues that the deity of popular superstition is a prop for theocratic tyranny. But what Spinoza calls theocratic oppression Leibniz identifies as the best of all possible systems of government. Thus, Leibniz turns the tables and calls Spinoza's concept of God "bad" and "dangerous," on the grounds that it will lead only to "out-and-out anarchy." His own concept of God, Leibniz assures us, will protect civilization—indeed, it will serve as the basis for a Christian republic united under a single church.

Leibniz's insistence on political implications of the metaphysics of divinity is so forceful that it raises the question as to whether his entire philosophy, like Spinoza's perhaps, was essentially a political project. For, inasmuch as it is the universal *belief* in the goodness of God that brings about the desired political ends of unity, stability, and charity, then the facts of the matter—whether God does indeed make choices and is good—don't matter at all. Philosophy, on this assumption, is not the disinterested search for the truth about God, but a highly sophisticated form of political rhetoric.

Mind

Modernity dethrones humankind. It reduces all our thoughts, purposes, and hopes to the object of scientific inquiry. It makes laboratory rats of us all. Spinoza actively embraces this collapse of the human into mere nature. Leibniz abhors it. Even more than he wants to convince us that God is good, Leibniz intends to demonstrate that we are the most special of all beings in nature. In the entire universe, he says, there is nothing more real or more permanent or more worthy of love than the individual human soul. We belong to the innermost reality of things. The human being is the new God, he announces: Each of us is "a small divinity and eminently a universe: God in ectype and the universe in prototype." This is the idea that defines Leibniz's philosophy, and that explains the enormous, if often unacknowledged, influence that his thought has wielded in the past three centuries of human history.

The greatest obstacle Leibniz confronts in his quest to deify the human being is Spinoza's theory of mind. In Spinoza's view, the mind is nothing real; it is merely an abstraction over the material processes of the body. But, counters Leibniz, in the material world, nothing lasts forever; everything is at the mercy of impersonal forces; what passes for "unity" is merely temporary aggregation; and "identity" is a chimera in the never-ending flux of becoming and passing away. If Spinoza is correct, Leibniz concludes, then the human being, too, is merely chaff blowing in the silent winds of nature.

Leibniz's metaphysics is thus best understood as the effort to demonstrate, against Spinoza, that there is another world that is prior to and constitutes the material world; that this more *real* reality consists of indestructible, self-identical unities; and that we ourselves—in virtue of our having minds—*are* the immaterial constituents of this more-than-real world. Of course, as a defender of the immaterial mind, Leibniz now faces the Cartesian mind-body problem in its full glory: He must explain how it happens that the immaterial mind at least appears to interact with the less-than-real material world. So, more precisely, his metaphysics may be understood as an attempt to solve the Cartesian mind-body problem in such a manner as to avoid falling into Spinozistic heresy.

IN ORDER TO rid the world of Spinoza's theory of mind, Leibniz must first annihilate Spinoza's idea of Substance. For, in declaring that God alone is Substance, Spinoza reduces human beings to mere modes of Substance, and thereby renders our minds material and mortal. Leibniz's strategy is therefore to replace the doctrine that God alone is Substance with the claim that there is a plurality of substances in the world. By identifying the mind with these new substances, Leibniz intends to secure for humankind a degree of indestructibility, power, and freedom that his rival philosopher associates only with God. In one of his rare later comments on Spinoza, Leibniz neatly summarizes the difference between the two philosophers on this fundamental point. The author of the *Ethics*, as we know, scoffs at those who regard the human mind as "a kingdom within a kingdom," for, in his view, there is only one kingdom of Nature, one Substance. To which Leibniz responds: "My view is that every substance whatsoever is a kingdom within a kingdom."

The hunch that the world is made up of a plurality of substances appears in some of Leibniz's earliest writings. In the context of his reading of Spinoza's writings upon his return from The Hague, however, he formulates his view in a transparent way. In his notes on Spinoza's letters to Oldenburg as well as on his copy of the *Opera Posthuma*, Leibniz explicitly rejects Spinoza's definition of "substance" as that which is "in itself" *and* "conceived through itself." The second part of the definition, he now asserts, is incorrect: A substance must be "in itself," but it need not be "conceived through itself." Rather, it may be "conceived through God."

An obscure point, it would seem; and yet, if true, it destroys the proof of the Proposition 5 in Part I of the *Ethics* that there cannot be two or more substances in the world. For, that proof turns on the claim that two substances which are "conceived through themselves" can have nothing in common and so cannot be part of the same universe. It is no coincidence, then, that the proposition of the *Ethics* whose proof Leibniz seeks in his first letter to Schuller upon getting to Hanover is Proposition 5 of Part I of the *Ethics*. If he can find the weak point in Spinoza's proof, Leibniz thinks, he will open up the tantalizing possibility that there is not one but a plurality of substances in the world. He further infers—on the basis of quasi-mathematical arguments that would require several more books to elucidate—that the number of such substances must be infinite for roughly the same reason that the number of points on a line is infinite. No matter how small a slice of the universe you take, he says, it will contain an infinite number of substances. In writings dating from the 1690s, he dubs these substances with a name derived from the Greek for "unity," first used by his predecessor Giordano Bruno, and which has since become famous: monads.

The claim that reality consists of an infinite number of monads entails some astonishing consequences, and Leibniz is not shy to draw these out. As substances, for example, monads must be entirely self-contained. That is, they depend on nothing else to be what they are. The most important implication of this is that they cannot interact with one another in any way at all—for, if they did so, one monad could conceivably alter the nature of another monad, and this would imply that its nature depends on the activity of some other substance, which, by the definition of substance, is not permissible. Thus, monads are—in Leibniz's notably poetic language—"windowless." They can't see out, and you can't see in.

It also follows that monads are immortal—they are always what they were and will be, namely, themselves. They have no beginning and no end. In order to make room for God, perhaps, Leibniz somewhat mysteriously allows that at the moment of creation, all monads came into being together, in a single "flash"; and if they should disappear, they must all vanish together in a comparable "flash" of annihilation.

Notwithstanding their evident durability and self-identity, monads do experience change of a sort, for they possess a capability to develop or "realize" themselves according to purely internal principles. In Leibniz's lyrical terms, they are "big [in the sense of "pregnant"] with the future." They may exist in the form of "seeds," he suggests, such as those observed in human semen by scientists such as Jan Swammerdam and Antoni von Leeuwenhoek (both of whom Leibniz met on his journey through Holland).

Here Leibniz appeals to contemporary scientific findings in a manner that cannot but recall the practice of those modern philosophers who likewise attempt to substantiate their metaphysical claims with reference to recent scientific discoveries (in our time, usually quantum mechanics). The rocket science of Leibniz's time was microscopy. The work of the Dutch pioneers in the field, says Leibniz, demonstrates that there are tiny animals everywhere—animals within animals—on no matter how small a scale one looks. Therefore, he concludes, it is quite plausible—nay, practically certain—that if these tiny animals had microscopes, they, too, would find even tinier animals, and so on all the way down without end.

Although all monads exist forever, they nonetheless seem to perdure in the context of very different fellow-monad structures over time. The Leibniz monad, for instance, existed in seed form from the beginning of time. Contrary to popular prejudice, what it acquired on July 1, 1646, was only the agglomeration of fellow monads that make up its outward body. (The fact that Leibniz had two parents vexed the philosopher's followers—who had the monad, mom or dad?—but they did their best to overcome the "problem of sex.") Furthermore, as scientists have shown that even in fires small particles of ash survive in the smoke, it is evident that the Leibniz monad, like its brother monads, will continue to exist indefinitely in microscopic form—perhaps wafting on a piece of dust around its favorite city of Paris, where it will enjoy memories of happier days and receive from God the rewards and punishments appropriate to its deeds.

One of the most striking and controversial inferences that Leibniz draws from the substantial nature of the monad is that a monad's future is written into its essence from the very beginning of things.

He expresses this daring doctrine in terms of logic as well as metaphysics. The "complete" concept of a substance, he says, must contain all the predicates that ever have been and ever will be true of it. For example—and here he invites much aggravation from his critics—the complete concept of "Caesar" ever and always includes the predicate "crossed the Rubicon"; just as the complete concept of "Leibniz," presumably, ever and always includes the predicate "visited Spinoza in The Hague." A monad, one could say, is the ideal subject for a biography: its entire life story unfolds with absolute logical necessity from its singular essence; and so the biographer need only locate this essence in order to settle on an appropriate plot and chapter outline.

The life of a monad does not seem as solitary as it in fact is. Each monad, according to Leibniz, has within itself a "mirror" of the entire universe—a picture of what is happening everywhere at all times and how its own activities "fit in." Thus, monads are essentially mindlike. That is, they have a faculty of *perception* that constructs for them a picture of the "external" world, and a faculty of *apperception* that registers an awareness of this process of perception itself.

By means of these "mirrors" of consciousness, each monad replicates the entire universe of monads within itself; and so each monad is a "universe in prototype." Leibniz refers to this strange vision of worlds within worlds as "the principle of macrocosm and microcosm"—meaning that the microcosm contains or replicates the macrocosm all the way down to the infinitely small. He expresses the same notion in his claim that the ancient doctrine that "All is One" must now be supplemented with the equally important corollary that "One is All."

If Leibniz had been writing in the information age, incidentally, he very likely would have replaced the monad mirrors with laptops running interactive virtual-reality software. Such a metaphor perhaps better conveys the sense in which monads interact with a wider universe only in an internal, "virtual" way, since they cannot really have contact with the rest of the universe at all.

The monad mirrors, in any case, are somewhat scratched and imperfect—no doubt like the silver-backed mirrors that would have caught the philosopher's gaze in Paris. (Or, one could say, the virtual-reality screens have low resolution; or, the software still has lots of bugs.) So, all monads have a confused perception of the world around them. (Save God, of course, whose version of Windows is perfect).

It is the logic of his system—and not arbitrary fancy nor a theory of the subconscious mind, as some have suggested—that compels Leibniz to scratch the mirrors of his monads. The imperfections in individual monads' perceptions play a key role in distinguishing one monad from another, for it is the partial perspective of each monad on the totality that makes it a unique individual with a unique "point of view" as it were. This is what Leibniz means when he says that a monad subsists "in itself" but is not necessarily "conceived through itself." To put it another way: two monads with absolutely perspicuous knowledge of the entire universe would be indistinguishable—in fact, they would both be God, or that through which all substances are conceived.

Equally important, the splotchiness in the mirrors creates the possibility of "free will" in monads, or so Leibniz contends. Although the entire past and future of a monad are embedded in its complete concept, nonetheless, on account of the inferior optics, a monad cannot understand its own essence in a fully perspicuous way. Because it does not know its own future (as God does), the monad is forced to make decisions and behave as though it were free. So, for example, God knew through all eternity that Leibniz was going to visit Spinoza in The Hague; but when Leibniz got off the boat, he faced a choice between walking over to the Paviljoensgracht and stopping in a local coffeehouse for the afternoon.

The obscurity in the monad mirrors, finally, allows us to explain the crucial differences among types of monads. Although in the final analysis monads differ in degree and not kind, they nonetheless fall roughly into three groups, corresponding to what we may think of as rocks, animals, and people. All monads are mindlike to some degree, but only the peoplelike monads have minds, properly speaking. That is, their mirrors—their faculties of perception and apperception—are developed to the point where they have memory and self-awareness. Animal monads have souls, but not minds, strictly speaking, for their apperception or self-awareness tends to be lacking (Leibniz is a little vague on the point; but, in any case, it is worth noting that, compared with the dog-beating Cartesians, he was practically an animal-rights activist, insisting that it is repugnant to view animals as mere machines.) Rocklike monads are extremely passive, and so Leibniz has little to say about them. Note, however, that what we think of as an individual human being consists of one mind-monad dominating an infinite, swirling agglomeration of rocklike body-monads.

With this last observation, the main point of the strange fable of the monads begins to come into focus. Leibniz's purpose is to lay out the context within which the Cartesian mind-body problem may be resolved and the immateriality of the mind preserved against Spinoza's soul-destroying Substance. In the new vocabulary of monads, the mind-body problem may be restated thus: How do mind-monads coordinate their activities with body-monads so that all work together to create a coherent universe in which minds and bodies appear to interact? For example: How is it that, when the Leibniz mind-monad decides to meet Spinoza in The Hague, his body-monads get him aboard the yacht, walk him down along the canals, and knock on his fellow philosopher's door? And how is it that the equally self-contained Spinoza monad happens to organize its body-monads in such a way as to open the door for his visitor?

Phrased in these terms, now, it is evident that, within the Leibnizian system, the mind-body problem no longer refers to something that is logically impossible, but only to something that seems ludicrously improbable. That is, Leibniz does not have to explain how two radically different classes of entity—minds and bodies—may interact with each other; he simply takes it as given that all substances are of the same mindlike nature and that they do not interact with one another at all. The remaining problem is only that it seems very unlikely, to say the least, that all these monads would coordinate their internally driven activities in such a way as to produce a coherent world—that the Leibniz mind-monad should not decide to visit Spinoza, for example, while the rest of him goes for a cup of coffee.

This understanding of the problem sets the stage for what Leibniz claims is his single most magnificent bequest to humanity: the doctrine of "the pre-established harmony." Although each monad acts according to its own, purely internal laws of development, Leibniz maintains, each is so designed that the world within which it perceives itself to be acting coheres exactly with the world within which all the other monads perceive themselves to be acting. Thus, for example, when the Leibniz mind-monad decides to call on Spinoza, the Leibniz body-monads just happen to be planning a walk up the Paviljoensgracht, too.

Leibniz's choice of a musical metaphor to describe the coordination of monad activities seems very much in the spirit of his age. In the late seventeenth century, the delights of contrapuntal music became widely celebrated, great architecture was praised as "frozen music," and even the orbits of the planets around the sun were said to have agreeably musical properties. Sometimes, though, Leibniz uses a different metaphor, one drawn from another of the wonders of his age: the watch. Mind and body, he says, are like a pair of perfectly constructed and perfectly synchronized watches. They tell the same time throughout eternity, not because they are causally linked to each other, nor because anyone intervenes to adjust one to the other, but because each on its own progresses through the same series of seconds on its own devices. (It is interesting to note that in Leibniz's day watches were notoriously imprecise, and could be counted on to diverge appreciably from one another by the end of each working day; but the race was on to build one of sufficient reliability to be used in measuring the longitude of ships at sea.) In the information age, we would probably favor a different metaphor: although each monad runs its own virtual-reality software on a stand-alone basis, we could say, the virtual reality of each monad is perfectly consistent with the virtual realities of all the other monads.

Needless to say, the extraordinary degree of mutual compatibility among monads is far greater than could ever be attributed to any merely human watchmaker or even any immortal software corporation. In fact, says Leibniz, the pre-established harmony is manifestly the handiwork of God. When the Almighty creates the infinite infinity of monads in the big flash, he designs each in such a way that its internal principle of activity harmonizes perfectly with those of all the others. The doctrine of the pre-established harmony may also be understood as a generalized and perhaps more elegant version of Malebranche's occasionalism. According to the latter, God intervenes on every occasion where there is an interaction of mind and body, in an endless series of real-time miracles. In Leibniz's world, God intervenes only once, at the moment of creation, in an original miracle whereby he programs the infinite infinity of monads with such astonishing skill that they sing in harmony for all eternity.

The pre-established harmony also lines up neatly as the apparent replacement for Spinoza's doctrine of parallelism. Spinoza, we should recall, claims that mind and body operate in parallel because they are really the same thing seen from two angles, like two sides of the same coin. Leibniz implicitly agrees that mind and body appear to operate in parallel, like two clocks ticking away side by side; but, on his account, they do so only by the grace of God's impeccable craftsmanship, for they are in themselves radically independent of each other.

God's intervention on the mind-body problem is so wondrous, Leibniz adds, that it amounts to another proof of his existence and of his goodness. The proof belongs to an ancient theological tradition, one that flared in the seventeenth century but that has always smoldered somewhere in the hearth of the human imagination. Leibniz's question—How is it that all the monads manage to get along so well?—is a generalization over some much simpler questions that have been asked many times before: How is it that apples are just the right size for our mouths? How is it that the water we need to live falls so abundantly from the sky? With minor changes in vocabulary, the same type of question may be heard in places even today: How is it that the apparently arbitrary parameters of the physical laws of the universe, some would ask, are set at precisely those values that make life in the universe possible? How can such complex phenomena as intelligent life be the result of an evolutionary process that has no purpose or designer? The argument that only God could account for such improbable developments as bite-sized apples, congenial cosmological constants, intelligent life, and the pre-established harmony is generally called "the argument from design." Spinoza, Hume, Kant, and many other philosophers have long since pointed out that the logic of the argument is hardly compelling: it establishes a probability, not a certainty; and the probability of an event that is absolutely unique is in any case indefinable. But, as Leibniz understood, mere quibbles about logic do little to diminish the enduring appeal of the argument.

The story about monads and the pre-established harmony clearly reinforces—and is intended to reinforce—Leibniz's political vision. To the *respublica Christiana* and the Empire of Reason, Leibniz now adds a third name for his political ideal: the City of God. The citizens of this heavenly metropolis, he says, are the thinking monads of the world—i.e., all people—and the harmony they exhibit among themselves is a reflection of God's glory. A pillar of the theocratic order represented in the City of God is the doctrine of personal immortality encoded in the monadology. Indeed, Leibniz maintains that without universal belief in rewards and punishments in the afterlife, people will behave very badly and anarchy will consume society. Thus, at stake in his refutation of Spinoza's theory of mind is the preservation of Christian civilization.

Yet, notwithstanding their creator's medieval-sounding politics, Leibniz's monads have a curiously modern edge, too. The City of God is a monarchy, to be sure, with God as its king. But, among its earthly denizens, a certain kind of egalitarianism reigns. All monads are created equal; each embodies the All, and each reflects the full glory of God; and so each has certain basic rights of citizenship. Indeed, Leibniz specifically opposes slavery, for example, on the basis of the equality of monads. The universal equality of monads also finds expression in Leibniz's thoroughgoing cosmopolitanism: "Justice is that which is useful to the community, and the public good is the supreme law—a community, however, let it be recalled, not of a few, not of a particular nation, but of all those who are part of the City of God and, so to speak, of the state of the universe." Although Leibniz's legacy was later commandeered by Germans in the name of nation building, the philosopher himself never wavered from the universality of his ideal. In the context of a tiff among the various European academies, for example, he writes: "Provided something of consequence is achieved, I am indifferent whether this is done in Germany or France, for I seek the good of mankind. I am neither a phil-Hellene nor a phil-Roman, but a phil-anthropos."

Leibniz was indeed a phil-anthropos, and this was perhaps both the central message embedded in his monadology and the chief point of contrast with the reviled Spinoza. For, according to the latter, the human being is nothing exceptional, and it is merely ignorance and vanity that lead humankind to imagine that we "are the largest part of nature." But, according to Leibniz, the human being is every-thing—the point and the substance of the world. The modern secu-lar state, when viewed from a global perspective, looks much more like Spinoza's free republic than Leibniz's City of God; and yet, para-doxically, many of the beliefs that guide individuals within the mod-ern world—the faith in the sanctity of the individual, the ideal of charity, and the unique purpose of humankind—would seem to fol-low directly from Leibniz's essentially antimodern theocratic project.

One the most intriguing features of Leibniz's monadological vision is the most obvious one: that it seems to describe an *ideal*. The City of God serves Leibniz as a vision whose realization is the goal of all of his efforts (and those of like-minded individuals). In some passages, Leibniz even makes this rather modern notion of progress explicit: "We must also recognize that the entire universe is involved in a perpetual and most free progress, so that it is always advancing toward greater culture." And yet, logically speaking, the City of God is a representation of the actual world, not of an ideal one. We *are* monads, after all; we are already immortal and we necessarily live according to the laws of the pre-established harmony. This conflation of—or perhaps confusion between—representations of the real and depictions of the ideal is a fundamental feature of Leibnizian meta-physics, and perhaps even raises the question as to whether the entire system of monads and harmonies was less a representation of life as we know it than some sort of visionary utopia.

"ALL THIS, I acknowledge, I understand not at all," wrote the English philosopher Samuel Clarke in response to Leibniz's attempt to explain his ideas about substances and the pre-established har-mony, and there is no shame in admitting as much even today when presented with the monadological philosophy in bare outline. Bertrand Russell frankly confesses that, on first reading, Leibniz's metaphysics struck him as "a fascinating fairy tale, coherent, perhaps, but wholly arbitrary." Possibly Hegel provides the most useful guidance on the matter: "Leibniz's philosophy appears like a string of arbitrary assertions, which follow one another like a metaphysical romance," he acknowledges. "It is only when we see what he wished thereby to avoid that we learn to appreciate its value."

There is in fact a single thread that may lead one safely through the labyrinth of the monadology. The astonishing and bizarre features of the monads—the windowlessness, the pregnancies, the splotchy mirrors, the infinite replications of the infinite universe, and the pre-established harmony—all follow with admirable logical rigor from the premise that substantiality (i.e., absolute unity, self-identity, freedom, and permanence) is a quality of individual minds, and not of nature as a whole. What Leibniz is *for* is often difficult to grasp; but what he is *against* fits neatly into one word: Spinoza.

Salvation

Leibniz, like Spinoza, finds happiness in the love of God. But, as the two philosophers have very different ideas about the nature of both God and love, they inevitably arrive at very different destinations on their respective journeys to salvation.

According to Spinoza virtue is its own reward. Therefore, the question of personal immortality can have no bearing on our salvation, for the wise man has no need of additional rewards in a purported afterlife to justify virtue in this life. Leibniz, on the other hand, takes the more usual view that in this life, at least, virtue often goes unrewarded, and evil often goes unpunished. Belief in the immortality of the soul, he argues, is therefore essential if we are to have faith that the calculus of rewards and punishments in the universe will ever add up to justice. The doctrine of personal immortality is thus vital to our happiness. Indeed, says Leibniz, Spinoza's attack on the doctrine of personal immortality, if successful, can serve only to bring great misery to the human race. (It is curious to note once again that, according to the logic of Leibniz's arguments, it is the *belief* in and not the *fact* of immortality that matters for our happiness. Even if the soul were mortal, we could still find a Leibnizian kind of bliss, provided we were able to convince ourselves otherwise.)

The difference between Leibniz and Spinoza on happiness, as on all subjects, comes down to their different attitudes toward God. For Spinoza, the intellectual love of God is the highest form of reason. But, as we know, this brainy love is not of the kind that can be returned. Spinoza's Substance is utterly indifferent to humanity's concerns. For Leibniz, on the other hand, the only love worthy of the name is the kind that promises punctual and copious repayment. Spinoza's unrequited love of God, Leibniz maintains, is in fact *unreasonable*:

> Spinoza thinks that the mind can be greatly strengthened if it understands that what happens, happens necessarily. But the animus of the sufferer is not rendered content through his compulsion, nor does it feel evils any the less on that account. The soul is happy if it understands that good follows from evil, and that what happens is for the best if we have wisdom.

In the *Theodicy* he adds that Spinozistic dogmas concerning the "brutish" necessity of things "destroy the confidence in God that gives us tranquility, the love of God that makes our happiness." His own doctrines, by contrast, guarantee that God does everything with our good in mind, and thus they give us the happiness and tranquility we need. The crucial difference between the two philosophers comes down to this: Spinoza finds happiness in loving God; Leibniz finds it in God loving us back. (Or, again, more precisely, Leibniz finds happiness in the *belief* that God loves us back.)

LEIBNIZ'S METAPHYSICS, no less than Spinoza's, is a personal confession and involuntary memoir—a kind of ontological hologram of the character of its creator. With its agile synthesis of an extraordinary range of philosophical issues and ideas, it reflects the highest aspirations of Guilielmus Pacidius, the Great Peacemaker of All Thought. In its fantastical and poetic moments, it captures something of the richness of the imaginary life of the man who conceived of the Egypt Plan and sparred with windmills. With the impossibly intricate arrangement of its many moving parts, it embodies the incomparable cleverness of the inventor of the most advanced arithmetical calculating machine of his day. In its excess of ingenuity—for it can hardly be overlooked that the system is sometimes *too* clever—it mirrors something of the philosopher's irrepressible vanity. Its very quirkiness reads like a signature—Leibniz's way of reminding the world that this was *his* system.

There is in the monadology, too, something of that legalistic sensibility—the strange gap between the author and his own arguments so characteristic of Leibniz from his earliest works. As ever, the philosopher evinces surprise and delight in his own ratiocinations; words like "advantageous," "useful," and "pleasing" trip lightly off his tongue. In all of his philosophical investigations, he never discovers the kind of thing that others might call a "grim truth." He is always the lawyer—a highly polished, politically appointed public defender, with tremendous courtroom presence and a knack for parsing culpability with infinitely refined distinctions. He leaves us in no doubt as to what it is that he would like us to believe. Yet he can never entirely avoid raising a nagging question as to whether *he* believes what he says.

Was Leibniz in his heart of hearts truly convinced that reality consists of an infinity of pregnant, windowless, splotchy substances? Or was he just rustling up the theory of the case that would rescue God from the seemingly inevitable verdict of malpractice?

Whether he believed it or not may be impossible to determine; but the fact that he *would have liked* to believe in his monadological world seems quite certain. The philosophy of Leibniz expresses, above all, the neediness of its creator. His is essentially a metaphysics of reassurance, intended to strengthen within us the comforting convictions that God cares for us, that we never die, and that all is for the best in the best of all possible worlds. At some level, it surely represents the mature philosopher's answer to the craving for security and the longing for paternal guidance that he first bared to the world as a schoolboy. And it is this all too human cry from the heart that made his work so universal in the later history of philosophy.

Leibniz, perhaps alone with Spinoza, grasped the general direction of modern history. But, unlike his eerily self-sufficient rival, he had a far greater concern with the price that humanity would have to pay for its own progress. He understood that even as science tells us more and more about *what* everything is, it seems to tell us less and less *why*; that even as technology reveals utility in all things, it seems to find purpose in nothing; that as humanity extends its powers without limit, it loses its faith in the value of the same beings who exercise that power; and that, in making self-interest the foundation of society, modern humankind finds itself pining for the transcendent goals that give life any interest at all. Leibniz saw modernity in the first instance as a threat rather than an opportunity. In all of his philosophical labors, his aim was to protect our sense of purpose and self-esteem from this threat, to rescue an old set of values from the depredations of the new. And there was no more dangerous and powerful exponent of the new than Spinoza.

Leibniz's mature metaphysics, in brief, was a confrontation with the philosophy of the man he met in The Hague. Yet Leibniz did not consolidate his mature views until ten years after the encounter. The spectacular artifice of the monadology was the fruit of a debate that took place in his own mind with an interlocutor long since dead. It reflects what he might have wished had happened in the house on the Paviljoensgracht, perhaps, but not what actually occurred. In fact, it reads like the interior monologue of one who keeps reliving a certain moment, replaying the event from different angles, rehearsing his own responses, adding voice-over commentary, tweaking his memories and editing key passages until at last, on final playback, he scores the victory that he longs to believe was rightfully his.

15

The Haunting

"I can't tell you how distracted a life I am leading," Leibniz confided to one of his friends in late middle age. "I have so much that is new in mathematics, so many thoughts in philosophy, so numerous literary observations of other kinds, which I do not wish to lose, that I am often at a loss what to do first. . . ."

The first item on his list of distractions was a genealogy. Following the implosion of his mining venture, Leibniz needed a new peg on which to hang his hopes for career security. He proposed to Duke Ernst August that a thorough history of the Brunswick clan would enhance the prestige of the Duchy of Hanover, and the Duke happily appointed him as the family historian. In return for performing the labor, Leibniz suggested, the Duke should double his salary. In the event, he settled for having his existing salary converted to a pension for life.

It proved to be less of a bargain than Leibniz might have hoped. After forty years of rolling the genealogical stone up the hill only to have it fall back down on top of him, the philosopher managed to bring the history of the Brunswicks only up to the eleventh century. But the project did offer one overwhelming benefit: It gave Leibniz the excuse to leave Hanover. At the age of forty-one, he set off on what he promised his employers would be a two-and-a-half-month journey for the purpose of gathering genealogical data from royal houses in Germany and Italy. He stopped in dozens of cities and towns all the way down to Naples; took in renowned collections of coins, fossils, and caterpillars; attended private showings of operas; visited all the major libraries; met with leading experts on China, Kabbalism, mining technology, chemistry, mathematics, and anatomy; and returned home two and a half years later with a carefully tallied bill of 2,300 thalers in expenses and a fistful of somewhat defensive-sounding letters in which he insisted that he had performed no inconsiderable labor on behalf of the Duke of Hanover during his travels.

Leibniz's political activities, too, consumed much of his energy in his years of plenty. At the age of fifty, in recognition of his able assistance in, among other things, securing the elevation of the Duke of Hanover to Elector of the Holy Roman Empire, he was promoted to privy counselor of justice, the second-highest civil rank in the land. His incessant petitions for increases in pay began to meet with occasional success. Including the income from moonlighting with neighboring principalities, his receipts rose to a vertiginous 2,000 thalers per year—11 Spinoza Units. When he eventually got the Society of the Sciences going in Berlin and became its first president, he began to draw another 600 thalers annually from that source. By the standards of the time, he was becoming a very wealthy man.

In his later years, the great philosopher also devoted much time to cultivating his friendships with the ladies of the court, notably Duchess (later Electress) Sophia and her daughter, Sophia Charlotte, the first queen of Prussia. Sophia had two things her husband, Duke Ernst August, conspicuously lacked: a sense of humor and an interest in philosophy. Upon reading Spinoza's *Tractatus* in 1679, for example, she declared it "admirable" and "completely in accord with reason." She enthused that her second son, Friedrich August, "knows Descartes and Spinoza almost by heart" and regarded her eldest, Georg Ludwig—the future King George I of England—as the thick one on account of his lack of interest in metaphysics. When she learned of

Spinoza's death, she quipped that a churchman must have poisoned him, because "most of the human race lives by deceit."

Leibniz later said that his *Theodicy* was the record of conversations he had with Sophia's daughter, Sophia Charlotte, in the gardens of the family's summer palace. Sophia Charlotte, it seems, was even more of a handful than her mother. "Here is a letter of Leibniz," she pouts to a friend. "I love this man; but I am angry that he treats everything so superficially with me." On her deathbed, according to the legend passed on by her grandson, Frederick the Great, the still vivacious queen is reported to have said to the hovering prelates: "Do not torment me, for I go now to satisfy my curiosity on the principle of things that Leibniz has never been able to explain to me; on space, infinity, being, and nothingness. And I prepare for my husband the King the spectacle of a funeral, where he will have a new opportunity to display his grandeur."

Leibniz became so comfortable in the company of aristocrats that at some point it seems he decided to make himself one. His began to sign his letters with a small and illegible squiggle between his first and last names—a squiggle that grew in confidence until it unmistakably represented a *v*, as in Gottfried Wilhelm *von* Leibniz. But the courtier was never ennobled, and there is no evidence that he ever brought himself to part with the money that would have been required to purchase such a distinction. Eventually, the squiggled ennoblement vanished from his letters as mysteriously as it had arisen.

Notwithstanding the travel, the hack work, the chatty princesses, and all the other demands on his time, Leibniz in his later years never relented in the heroic level of his intellectual activity. He churned out hundreds of letters to learned correspondents every year; prepared treatises on chemistry, optics, economics, and "the true laws of matter"; drafted up new problems and solutions in the "science of infinities" (i.e., the calculus); conducted thought experiments on the universal characteristic; performed intricate analyses of the theological issues at stake in church reunion; revised the entire system of laws in Germany; composed thousands of lines of Latin in poetry in perfect meter and rhyme; and tinkered with his arithmetical calculating machine, which he was sure would one day soon be ready for practical use.

The reckless curiosity, the tireless dedication to learned pursuits, the delight in subtle argumentation, the multiple and constantly shifting layers of motives, the insatiable hankering for security, the yearning for Paris or something like it, the careerism and the politicking, the ceaseless dance along the line that separates order from chaos, and all the rest of the dazzling, omnimaniacal Leibniz show continued without interruption for the remaining thirty years of the philosopher's life. As he grew older, Leibniz became more Leibniz.

One day in his later life, a young nobleman visited the world's last great polymath and left us with an intimate portrait of the philosopher at home in his maturity:

> Although he is more than sixty years of age, and makes a strange appearance clad in fur stockings, a dressing gown lined with the same material, large socks made of felt, instead of slippers, and a long, singular looking wig, nevertheless he is a very polite and social person, and entertained us with remarks on politics and various literary topics. I succeeded at length in breaking off the conversation for the purpose of asking him to show me his library. . . . But, as I had been led to expect would be the case, he declined. . . . Other persons assured me, however, that the books in his library were very numerous and valuable; but that it was a peculiarity of Leibniz's, that he liked to worm in it alone. Not even the Elector himself, therefore, could get a chance of seeing it, the Herr Privy Counselor always alleging that it had not been put in order.

Leibniz's own writings from later life paint much the same portrait of a chatty, eccentric, and sometimes rambling elder statesman in the republic of letters. They read like the syllabus for an entire university written with the zest of a society tabloid. They reveal a mind crowded with memories of people, places, and ideas; fired with undiminished desire to know; and brimming with higher learning, political trivia, hot buttons, and white lies.

The peculiar costume of fur and felt, incidentally, was Leibniz's one concession to age. From around his fiftieth year, he suffered increasingly from a painful form of arthritis. Quite sensibly, however, he avoided the doctors of the time—who, with their leeches and lancets and noxious potions did far more damage than the illnesses they purported to treat—and preferred instead to pursue a sartorial therapy of his own design.

With Leibniz, inevitably, as with almost all aging philosophers, a certain amount of intellectual sclerosis set in, too. In his later years, the elements of the metaphysical system he first outlined in the *Discourse* became so self-evident to him that he often saw no need to argue for them. They became a fixed part of his reality, and his deepest philosophical pleasure came less from formulating his propositions than from seeing their truth reflected back to him in the statements and activities of others.

Those who viewed the spectacle of the philosopher's performance from afar might well have supposed that the encounter in The Hague now belonged to the dead part of personal history; it was just another long forgotten scene in the endless variety show of his life. By the time of the *Theodicy* in 1710, in fact, Leibniz virtually edited out of existence what little remained of the encounter in his letter to Count Ernst of 1683. The rendezvous with Spinoza now counted as the equivalent of a chance encounter at sea: "I saw M. de la Court as well as Spinoza on my return from France through England and Holland, and I learned from them some good anecdotes concerning affairs of those times." On the matter of his prior correspondence with Spinoza, Leibniz seemed content to put the subject to rest with a casual lie: "I wrote to him one time a letter concerning optics, which was inserted in his [posthumous] works." The claim that he wrote to the humble lens grinder "one time," of course, is directly contradicted by evidence contained in the very same volume of Spinoza's posthumous works.

In his later philosophical writings, as a rule, Leibniz mentions the name of Spinoza only in the spirit of caricature. The "famous Jew" is almost always twinned with Hobbes, that other malefactor of modern materialistic atheism, and is reliably presented as the spokesperson for a patently absurd metaphysics of "brute necessity." "One need not refute an opinion so bad," he says in a typical comment on Spinoza's doctrine that God alone is Substance. He describes Spinoza's philosophy in general as "pitiful and unintelligible" and shows no interest in engaging his rival's arguments in any direct or detailed way. Year by year, his official posture on Spinoza calcified like the joints in his stiffening body.

But, behind Leibniz's ever shifting public façades, the ghost of Spinoza was far from leaving the courtier-philosopher in peace. At the core of Leibniz's restless endeavors lay a permanent anxiety. It was an anxiety that expressed itself in an astonishing variety of ways: in the frantic search for financial security and social status, in the dread of Hanoverian provincialism, in the desperate schemes for repairing a fractured church, in fears of political revolution, and in frenetic attacks on a range of fellow philosophers, from Descartes to Locke to Newton. But it was, at bottom, always the same anxiety. And, in the fullness of time, it came to acquire a name, a name that stood for everything that Leibniz could neither abide nor evade. In the forty years after he departed from The Hague, Leibniz was always running; but he was running in circles, never quite able to extricate himself from the orbit of the man he met in November 1676.

Church Reunion

When Leibniz submitted a condensed version of his *Discourse on Metaphysics* to Antoine Arnauld in 1686, his hopes were high that Protestants and Catholics would soon be taking communion together in a universal church. But Arnauld handed Leibniz a humiliating set-back. To Count Ernst von Hessen-Rheinfels, who served as mediator in the discussion, the theologian offered this assessment of Leibniz's metaphysics: "I find in these thoughts so many things which terrify me, and which all men, if I am not mistaken, will find so shocking, that I do not see of what use such a writing can be, which all the world will reject." Arnauld's primary initial concern had to do with Leibniz's concept of freedom of the will, or lack thereof. If "ate the apple" is a necessary predicate of "Adam" for all eternity, Arnauld reasoned, then Adam was not really free; and if he was not free, he did not sin; and if he did not sin, there is no church.

Leibniz wrote back immediately to defend himself from such dire accusations. The correspondence continued through another four letters from each side through 1686 and 1687 until Arnauld called a stop to it. Two years after Arnauld cut him off, the resilient philosopher wrote one more letter, clearly hoping to resume the discussion. But Arnauld died four years later without replying.

The Leibniz-Arnauld correspondence offers a rich source of insights on the central questions of the monadological philosophy. Leibniz at one point even considered publishing the correspondence, and later scholars have generally regarded it as one of the philosopher's major works. The scholars also like to point out that their man eventually got the theologian's grudging acknowledgment that perhaps he did not deny freedom of the will after all, so maybe he won the argument in the end.

In truth, the only point that Arnauld established to his own satisfaction was that Leibniz was not a heretic and that at least he meant well. In a separate letter to Count Ernst, after deciding to bring the conversation to an end, Arnauld makes his judgment of Leibniz and his metaphysics brutally plain:

> He has some opinions on physics which are truly strange, and that do not appear in the least sustainable. But I was careful to give him my thoughts in a way that would not injure him. It would be much better if he would stop at least for some time these sorts of speculations in order to apply himself to the greatest affair that there can be, which is the choice of the true religion.

Evidently, in Arnauld's judgment, Leibniz's grand intellectual synthesis could make no contribution whatsoever to the project of reunion. It is also apparent that the theologian put up with the otherwise fruitless exchange because he was keen to convert Leibniz to Catholicism. In his follow-up letter to Leibniz, Count Ernst, too, begs the philosopher to come over to the one true church. The two ardent Catholics, as it turns out, viewed the prospective conversion of Leibniz as a way of getting to his employer, the Duke of Hanover, and his wife, Sophia, who remained defiantly Protestant. The grand conversation about metaphysics of church reunion, it seems, was just a roundabout form of religious politics as usual.

Leibniz was by no means dissuaded from pursuing the reunion project. Rebuffed by Arnauld, he raised his sights to one of the most powerful figures in the Catholic world of the time, Jacques-Bénigne Bossuet, the Bishop of Meaux. Bossuet was Louis XIV's premier spiritual adviser. He was dour, severe, and neither unfamiliar with nor averse to the pleasures of exercising immense political power. He was just then articulating the ideological foundations for the expulsion of the Huguenots, in which hundreds of thousands of the French Protestants were tortured, raped, murdered, and otherwise induced to leave their homes, all at great expense to French economy and society, but to the profound satisfaction of the King and his counselor, who at last saw their nation united under a single church. Bossuet's intellectual contributions to his country included a book in which he used extensive citations from the New Testament to demonstrate that the rule of Louis XIV was ordained by God. In between acts of ethnic cleansing and scholarly tasks, the Bishop took time to campaign against the new opera in Paris—a form of entertainment that, he was convinced, involved putting Satan's words to music.

As Bossuet was a rather busy man, Leibniz corresponded mainly with a circle close to the Bishop: the French theologian Pelisson, who published an argument in favor of the infallibility of the pope; the Abbess of Maubuisson, who happened to be Princess Sophia's sister; and Marie de Brinon, a former schoolmistress and the secretary to the Abbess. According to Sophia, Brinon was extraordinarily eloquent—for she never stopped talking.

The topic of the day was heresy. Specifically, Leibniz needed to know whether the Catholics planned to stick to the decree made in the Council of Trent in the sixteenth century to the effect that Protestants were heretics. Seven years of correspondence and a number of lengthy manifestos concerning the nature of heresy spilled from Leibniz's plume before he understood that his interlocutors had no interest in negotiating the Catholic Church's right to make infallible judgments concerning just who would or would not count as a heretic. Bossuet was imperturbable in his convictions on the matter. "And so we get a clear idea of the real fundamental meaning of the words Catholic and heretic," he said, firmly laying down the law. "A heretic is one who has his own opinions. What does having an opinion mean? It means following one's own ideas, one's own particular notions." It should perhaps be counted in Leibniz's favor that Bossuet was eventually provoked to call him "opinionated" and "a heretic."

Toward the end of the exchange, Leibniz finally let his temper fly. He dashed out a scathing letter to Marie de Brinon:

> I admire the solidity of your judgment . . . when you do not speak to me of sending to Hell everything that is not Roman. . . . Keep, if you like, purgatory, transubstantiation, and all your seven sacraments; keep even the Pope with all his clergy, we will not oppose you in that. Keep yourself from two things only, namely, harming the honor of God by a cult of creatures which gives a bad impression to many people; and from injuring the charity which one owes to men by a sectarian and condemning spirit.

The sarcasm in the comments about "all your seven sacraments" here distinctly favors the view that the philosopher never put much stock in the religious doctrines he first set out to prove as a twenty-two-year-old. Transubstantiation and the rest of the paraphernalia of orthodoxy, it seems, were mangy horses to be traded for the sake of the grander goal of creating a unified church. The only doctrine that really mattered to Leibniz was the principle of charity that sustains any rational religion. Sadly, we will never know how the loquacious schoolmistress might have responded to Leibniz's sudden fit of honesty, for it seems that the philosopher never posted this letter. Instead, he stuffed his indignation back in his desk drawer and sent out a more diplomatic reply.

In retrospect, it is curious that Bossuet and his supporters should have corresponded with Leibniz at all. After all, Bossuet was at that moment providing the world with a very clear example of his preferred method for church reunion in his horrific policy of extirpating the Huguenots from France. Eventually, all was revealed in a letter Sophia received from her sister's secretary. Brinon, it seems, had been praying all along for Sophia's conversion. At the same time, Pellison, whose work on papal infallibility began the whole exchange, was doing his part by praying for Leibniz's conversion. Just as was the case with Arnauld and Count Ernst, it seems, while Leibniz produced learned arguments in support of universal peace, his counterparts were interested mainly in securing his personal and unconditional surrender.

His apparent inability to accept that his Catholic interlocutors were far more interested in his and his employers' confessional status than in his metaphysics made Leibniz seem oddly disconnected from reality. Even more surreal was his apparent conviction that with his fine-spun ratiocinations concerning the infinite infinity of monads he would induce sympathy for the renegade churchgoers of the north among the likes of Arnauld—never mind the opera-hating, Protestant-killing Bossuet and his coterie of fanatics. In fact, Leibniz *was* out of touch—but only because he was too far ahead of his time. His theological counterparts did not understand the threat posed by Spinoza, for they did not yet understand the nature of the modern world emerging around them. In their eyes, Leibniz could only have seemed slightly unbalanced, a man sending fantastical phalanxes of monads to battle with invisible, personal demons. In Leibniz's eyes, on the other hand, his fellow reunion enthusiasts were blind to the looming crisis of the new century. They saw reunion as little more than the renegotiation of the decrees of medieval councils. They did not understand, as Leibniz did, that it was just one front in a cosmic struggle between two forms of modernity: his own, and that of his titanic and seemingly omnipresent rival.

Stopping Locke

In 1689, around the time that Leibniz was cruising the Grand Canal in Venice, John Locke returned from exile in Holland to England in the wake of the Glorious Revolution aboard the same vessel that ferried a new monarch, William of Orange, to the sceptre'd isle. In his suitcase, Locke carried the manuscript of his *Essay Concerning Human Understanding*. When it was at last published under England's newly tolerant regime, Locke's work caused a sensation in the European republic of letters. With Voltaire's lavish endorsement, it became a pillar of the classical French Enlightenment, and had a direct influence on the framers of the United States Constitution. Today, the *Essay Concerning Human Understanding* is usually regarded as the founding work of modern, empiricist philosophy.

Leibniz was shocked. After a French translation appeared in 1700 (his English was never very good), he set to work on a massive, point-for-point response. The *New Essays on Human Understanding* is Leibniz's longest and in some ways his best philosophical work. It takes the form of a dialogue between one Philalethes, a Frenchman who obligingly cites passages by Locke from memory, and Theophile, Leibniz's favorite alter ego. Needless to say, Theophile gets the better of the argument, but not before Philalethes manages to moot some interesting issues.

Like his life in general, Leibniz's book appears at first glance to be radically disorganized. He attempts to stick to the structure of Locke's *Essay*, which is itself a rather cumbersome and patchy effort, but his enthusiasms consistently get the better of him, sending him off on many colorful digressions—about medical practices of the time, how to deal with extraterrestrials, interesting personalities he has encountered, and so on. As one has come to expect, however, there is a greater unity to the work than meets the eye.

Leibniz returns obsessively to a theme raised in one particular paragraph in Locke's *Essay*. The offending passage reads: "We have the Ideas of Matter and Thinking, but possibly shall never be able to know, whether any mere material Being thinks, or no; it being impossible for us, by the contemplation of our own Ideas, without revelation, to discover, whether Omnipotency has not given to some Systems of Matter fitly disposed, a power to perceive and think. . . ." "The author's philosophy," Leibniz thunders in reply, "destroys what appears to me most important—that the soul is imperishable." The fine print of Locke's text, of course, makes clear that his suggestion is conjectural or hypothetical: *maybe* matter can think, he says; we just don't know. But Leibniz entirely overlooks the hypothetical character of Locke's assertion. In his view, the dreaded chain of inferences is obvious: Locke says that the mind *might* be a material thing; therefore, there is no reason to think that the mind is *not* a material thing; therefore, the *soul* may be regarded a material thing, too; therefore, for all we know, the soul is *perishable*. In fact, the guiding purpose of Leibniz's five-hundred-page effort in the *New Essays* is to refute Locke on this point. My essay is "almost finished," he tells a friend. "I am above all concerned to vindicate the immateriality of the soul which Mr. Locke leaves doubtful."

In Leibniz's view, Locke's rejection of the immateriality of the mind is closely linked to another, even more devious heresy. If matter has the power to think, he infers, then matter and thought may well be viewed as two attributes of the same substance. Indeed, Lady Masham, the daughter of the philosopher Ralph Cudworth and Locke's friend, writes to Leibniz arguing from a Lockean point of view: "My question in the case would be this: whether God could not . . . create an unextended substance, and then unite it to an extended one . . . there appearing to me no contradiction in the coexistence of thought and soliditie in the same substance." In Leibniz's mind, of course, the lady's somewhat confused attempt to render thought and extension as attributes of the same substance is perfectly scandalous, and can only lead to the conclusion that the world consists of but one substance. So sure is Leibniz that Locke himself is guilty of some such commitment to substance monism that in the preface to the *New Essays* he goes out of his way to take an otherwise mystifying swipe at the doctrine of the world-soul, "a notion whose impossibility is clearly shown by my system alone, perhaps."

Locke's vague conjecture that matter might be able to think, of course, is Spinoza's avowed doctrine. The inference that the materiality of the mind implies the mortality of the soul—an inference Locke himself rejects—is one that Spinoza endorses explicitly. And, the idea that "thought and soliditie" might just be attributes of the same substance is very simply a logical precursor to Spinoza's doctrine that God alone is Substance. Leibniz's magisterial refutation of the founder of British empiricism, in brief, is a covert assault on the man he met in 1676. Furthermore, Locke—like Descartes before him—is really just a feeble imitation of Spinoza: he "leaves in doubt" that which his dark master pitilessly destroys.

In 1704, just as Leibniz was reviewing his final drafts of the *New Essays*, he received the news that John Locke was dead. He decided to withdraw his work from publication, for he was loath to publish a criticism of a man who could no longer rise to his own defense, or so he said. The *New Essays* did not see print until 1765.

Leibniz's unstated intuition that Locke was something of a Spinozist, incidentally, is probably more insightful than is generally allowed in modern interpretations of the great empiricist's work. Locke wrote much of his *Essay* while living in exile in Holland from 1683 to 1688, during which time he purchased all of Spinoza's works and mingled in circles that included some suspiciously freethinking characters. Furthermore, the parallels between his work and that of Spinoza extend well beyond those suggested by Leibniz. To be sure, as a conciliation-minded member of the Christian establishment, Locke toned down or obfuscated some of the more radical implications of his Spinozism—a task for which his inimitably wobbly prose was particularly well suited.

Grand Politics

From the Polish Succession of 1669 to the English Succession of 1714, Leibniz threw himself into all of the major (and many of the minor) political affairs of his time. On the surface, much of his work seems to have been intended to serve particular, local purposes—usually those of his employer of the time, which in most cases was the Duke (later Elector) of Hanover. But a broader look at Leibniz's political activities in fact reveals that they were governed (where possible) by a grand vision for the future of western civilization—and an overwhelming anxiety about the actual direction of history.

The specific and most pressing imperative of Leibniz's geopolitical strategy was to contain Louis XIV. The philosopher's first major political project, the Egypt Plan, was conceived with this strategy already in mind. In 1683, Leibniz openly derided the Sun King in a scathing piece of political satire, *Mars Christianissimus*. Louis could have been one of "the delights of the human race," he writes in that work; but instead he has become "the scourge of Europe."

Leibniz's strategy of containment achieved its finest expression in the context of the pair of related succession crises that convulsed

European politics at the turn of the eighteenth century. With the approach of the death of the sickly King Charles II of Spain, Louis XIV maneuvered to place his grandson on the Spanish throne. The rest of Europe, not least the Hapsburgs, of course, had very different hopes for the future of Spain. Upon Charles II's death in 1700, Louis XIV and his Bourbon clan nonetheless claimed the Spanish crown, and there ensued a complex series of conflicts involving all the major powers of Europe and leading to the loss of hundreds of thousands of lives across the continent.

At the same time, over in England, Queen Anne (sister-in-law of and successor to William) was having no luck in breeding an heir to the throne. Louis XIV, true to form, plotted to put one of the Catholic Stuarts in charge of England. Many feared that such an outcome would reduce England to a vassal state of France. In what must count as a spectacular piece of genealogical luck, the alternative contender for the throne was none other than Leibniz's friend and patroness, Sophia, the Electress of Hanover, who happened to be the granddaughter of James I, the first Stuart king of England, and the closest Protestant in the line of succession.

For Leibniz, the prospect that France might now rule the two next most powerful countries in Europe represented a tremendous danger to civilization. He leapt into the succession crises on the side of all those who were opposed to Louis XIV. With his *Manifesto for the Defense of the Rights of Charles III* and other writings in favor of the Hapsburg candidate, he hoped to persuade the Spaniards to spurn the Sun King's efforts to claim their throne. With the *Considerations on the Question of the English Succession* as well as in many of his letters, he struggled to advance the Hanoverian cause in England.

Leibniz's animus toward Louis XIV marks an interesting paradox in his political thought. In his theoretical writings, Leibniz champions the idea of a continent-wide Christian republic under a single monarch. Given that Louis XIV was a monarch whose ambition it was to unite Europe under a single church, one might well wonder why the philosopher found him to be such a scourge. It wasn't just a matter of defending Germany from its most powerful neighbor, as it turns out; nor was Leibniz driven solely by the desire to install his employer on the throne of England. (Though he did advertise his willingness to move to London—rather too eagerly, in the view of his fellow courtiers—should the Hanoverians require his services there.) In fact, Leibniz viscerally opposed Louis XIV because he believed that the Sun King's brand of absolute monarchy represented a form of secular decadence: a corruption in which both reason and religion were reduced to mere show of words in the service of a thoroughly irreligious, deceitful, and self-interested ruling elite.

In his polemic against the Bourbon succession in Spain, for example, he paints a chilling picture of life in France: "The people are trampled upon without mercy and reduced to bread and water by tithes, taxes, imposts . . . and all of this to serve the insatiability of a Court which cares not at all about the subjects which it already has, and which seeks only to augment the number of miserable people by extending its estates."

As he works his way up to the catalogue of horrors of the *ancien régime*, Leibniz seems to reach a climax with the declaration that to admit the French to Spain would be "to open the door to dissoluteness and to libertinage." At last he reveals the thing that he fears most about Louis XIV: "The worst thing of all is that atheism walks today with its head up in France, that pretended great wits are in fashion there, and that piety is turned to ridicule." The atheistic spirit of France, he thunders, is a "venom" that none can resist. Wherever the Sun King sets foot, the poison spreads. The toxin to which Leibniz refers here, of course, consists of modern, materialistic, and atheistic ideas—ideas to which he himself was exposed during his years in Paris.

There can be little doubt just who, in Leibniz's mind, first manufactured these venomous ideas. In the *New Essays*, he at last puts a name to the deed. Spinoza, he acknowledges, led an exemplary life. But his followers are capable of "setting fire to the four corners of the earth." Worst of all are those ideas, the horrific ideas emanating from The Hague: "I find that similar ideas are stealing gradually into the minds of men of high station who rule the rest and on whom affairs depend, and slithering into fashionable books, and are inching everything towards the universal revolution with which Europe is threatened." In Leibniz's nightmare scenario, then, the corrupt rule of Louis

XIV prepares the ground on which the slithering Spinozists flourish, and these serpents of materialism then spread their soul-destroying ideas and bring about a global revolution in which western civilization collapses into anarchy. The program at the core of all of Leibniz's political activities throughout his career can be summarized in a single slogan: Stop Spinoza.

Newton's Repulsive Law of Attraction

Isaac Newton conceived the essentials of his version of the calculus during his *anni mirabiles* of 1664–1666, when he was in his early twenties. For the next twenty years, he kept the discovery almost entirely to himself. It wasn't all that hard for him to do: he lived by himself in Cambridge, in a house where all the furnishings were colored red, he took his meals alone (when he could remember to eat), and he dutifully gave lectures to mostly empty classrooms.

When Leibniz conceived the essentials of his version of the calculus in the autumn of 1675, he was not yet aware that Newton had achieved substantially the same results ten years previously. The next summer, through Henry Oldenburg's mediation, Newton informed Leibniz that he had come upon a method answering to the requirements of the calculus (though he did not provide details). Leibniz responded by divulging to Newton the basics of his own method. Both then kept their silence for another eight years. In 1684, incensed to learn that his old friend Tschirnhaus had tried to spill the beans about the calculus (and take credit for them, too), Leibniz published a sketch of his method in his famous article in the *Acta Eruditorum*, "A New Method of Maxima and Minima and Also Tangents, and a Singular Kind of Calculus for Them."

A number of able mathematicians around Europe grasped the significance of Leibniz's discovery, and soon enough the courtier of Hanover, who was everything the Cambridge don was not in terms of human relations, commanded a frenzied web of calculus aficionados in Germany, France, Switzerland, and the Netherlands.

In 1687, Newton published his *Principia Mathematica*, which is generally regarded as one of the two or three most important works in the history of science. In that work, he stakes his claim to independent discovery of the calculus (though he does not detail his method). He lets on that he had ten years earlier informed "that most skilled geometer G. W. Leibniz" of his discovery and "that famous person replied that he too had come across a method of this kind, had imparted his method to me, which hardly differed from mine except in words and notation." Leibniz made no objection to the claim, and indeed wrote to Newton urging "you, who are a perfect geometer, to continue as you have begun" and to publish the details of his method.

And there the affair should have ended. It was, at bottom, a case of bright minds thinking alike and of trees falling in forests with nobody to hear them, followed in good time by the appropriate mutual recognition of independent achievement. It all began to turn sour with the intervention of Nicolas Fatio de Duillier, a young, brilliant, and excitable Swiss mathematician who achieved a degree of personal intimacy with Newton unmatched by any other mortal and that has since raised more than a few prurient eyebrows. More than ten years after the publication of the *Principia*, Fatio asserted that Newton was the "first" inventor of the calculus. "As to whether Leibniz, its second inventor, borrowed anything from him," he added, "I prefer to let those judge who have seen Newton's letters and other manuscript papers . . . which I myself have examined."

For another decade the conflict simmered at a low boil, the antagonists and their seconds content to restrict themselves to unsavory insinuations. All-out war began in 1710, when an English writer published an article bluntly accusing Leibniz of plagiarism. Understandably outraged, Leibniz demanded an independent inquiry from the Royal Society. In 1712, the Society duly organized a commission, which delivered its verdict: the accusation of plagiarism stands. The *de facto* chairman of the inquiry and author of its report on Leibniz was Isaac Newton.

An anonymous article appeared in the German press defending Leibniz and reversing the charge: Newton, the unnamed author declaims, plagiarized Leibniz. Leibniz was forced to disown the article, claiming that it had been put out by a "zealous friend." But it soon became clear to all parties that the "zealous friend" in question was Leibniz himself. In England, meanwhile, appeared an anonymous review of the dispute, according to which Newton was the innocent victim of Leibniz's chicanery. The "anonymous" author, it turns out, was Newton himself.

The priority dispute over the calculus outlived even its two obstreperous protagonists and was not definitively put to rest until scholars finally set the record straight in the twentieth century. At first glance, the whole sorry affair seems to represent a case of supersized egos with undersized scruples clashing in the context of overheated national rivalries and suboptimal publication practices. It was all those things, too, but it was also something else.

From the moment *Principia* appeared, Leibniz demonstrated far greater anxiety about Newton's physics than his mathematics. In February 1689, shortly after reading Newton's work, Leibniz published another article in the *Acta Eruditorum* arguing that the movements of the planets may be explained in terms of a complex, invisible, and fluid vortex centered on the sun. The manifest purpose of the exercise was to provide an alternative to Newton's physics, according to which planetary movements are the consequence of the law of gravitational attraction. In order to make his claims appear independent of and even prior to Newton, incidentally, Leibniz asserted that his knowledge of the *Principia* was only secondhand. As Newton later suspected, however, Leibniz was fibbing: notes made in his personal copy of the *Principia* date from before the time he wrote the article.

Over the next two decades, Leibniz regularly took swipes at Newton's repugnant law of gravity. In 1710, ominously, he noted that the theologically suspect John Locke took great comfort in Newton's idea of action at a distance. By 1715, Locke and Newton were quite mixed up in Leibniz's mind. In his correspondence battle with Samuel Clarke—who was understood by all to represent his friend and neighbor Newton—Leibniz opened the attack on his antagonist in the priority dispute with the strange observation that "Natural religion seems to be very much in decline in England. . . . Several make souls corporeal, others make God himself corporeal: Mr. Locke and his followers are doubtful at least whether souls are not material and naturally perishable."

Why did Leibniz find Newton's law of attraction so repulsive? And why did he link it with Locke's conjectures about the materiality of the mind? In a letter to one of his French allies, Leibniz frankly acknowledges the anxiety that lay at the bottom of all his dealings with Newton:

> After [admitting the law of attraction], it will be permitted to imagine all the shams that one would want; one could give to matter the power of thought, and destroy the immateriality of the soul, which is one of the principal foundations of Natural Theology. Thus one sees that M. Locke, who is not very persuaded of this immateriality, seizes avidly on M. Newton's idea.

According to Leibniz's way of thinking, the chain of inferences is so obvious that it hardly needs stating: Newton's law of gravity implies that matter can move by itself, without the need for any mindlike principle of activity. But from this it follows that matter might acquire the force of thought. And, as the case of Locke shows, merely to suggest that matter might think is *ipso facto* to destroy the immortality of the soul. Newtonian physics, in sum, is a Trojan horse: it conceals a horde of atheistic ideas that, if permitted entry, will overrun the citadel of European civilization.

Leibniz's attribution of such hideous designs to Newton is highly problematic, to say the least. The great physicist devoted much of his spare time to proving precisely those theological doctrines Leibniz accused him of subverting. In truth, the heresies that Leibniz attempted to pin on his rival in the priority dispute—that matter can move by itself; that matter can think; that the soul is material; that the soul is mortal—clearly belong to another philosopher. When Leibniz looked at Newton—no less than when he looked at Descartes and Locke—he saw Spinoza. And this fact, as much as the usual story about supersized egos facing off across the Channel, explains much of the strange intensity, if not the origin, of the most inglorious dispute in the history of mathematics.

The Yellow Peril

In a Europe whose Eurocentrism was at its narrowest peak, it is eloquent testimony to the breadth of Leibniz's intellectual interests and to the sincerity of his desire to reconcile all of humanity in a single City of God that he took great interest in the history, religion, and philosophy of the Chinese. It has been said that the word "China" appears more frequently in his writings than "monad" or any of the other terms of his metaphysics.

Leibniz's fascination with the Middle Kingdom dates at least from the time of his epic voyage to Italy, where he met the Jesuit Claudio Grimaldi (1638–1712), who had spent seventeen years as a missionary in Beijing. The principal topic of discussion among European sinologists at the time was how to manage the proselytizing of the Christian religion in China. Should the local rites associated with Confucianism be regarded as secular and therefore compatible with Christianity? Or are they in fact heathen rituals, deserving of harsh repression? Does Chinese religion include concepts compatible with the Christian God and the immortality of the soul? Or is it paganism—or, worse, atheism?

True to his peacemaking disposition, Leibniz took a very conciliatory stance. In his China writings, he maintains that missionaries should not attempt to suppress local traditions, but rather should incorporate any rites that did not directly contradict the Christian message. Furthermore, he offers a highly favorable judgment on the philosophy that underlies most of Chinese theology. His argument, in brief, is that Chinese philosophy, especially in its ancient form, looks very much like his own philosophy; and since he is a good Christian, so are the Chinese.

Specifically, he asserts that most of the Chinese religious thinkers acknowledge a "supra-mundane intelligence"; that the more astute ones have discovered the "soul"; and that perhaps all that is lacking is to introduce them to the latest developments in Europe—"by acquainting them with the true systems of the Macrocosm and the Microcosm"—in order to include them within a universal Christian church. He even hints that the most sophisticated Chinese may be there already. The principle of the *li*—a core concept in much of Chinese thought—may be read not just as the proposition that All is One, says Leibniz, but also as the proposition that One is All. This, of course, would render it a version of his own monadology, than which no finer specimen of Christian metaphysics may be conceived.

Alas, the melancholy monadologist notes with dismay, there is a "bad" version of philosophy afoot in China. This bad philosophy is almost entirely the work of modern Chinese thinkers—"heterodox and atheistic scholars . . . who are permitted in China to utter their impieties with impunity, at least orally."

These malevolent unbelievers, says Leibniz, manage to twist the true meaning of the principle of the *li*. They deviously attempt to render the *li* as "the soul of things as if it were their essence"—that is, as if it were some sort of universal Substance. They put forward the evil dogmas that everything occurs by "brutish necessity" and that there are no "spiritual substances." The bad Chinese philosophers, in other words, are retailing the execrable ideas Leibniz elsewhere attributes to a certain, infamous, European atheist. And, indeed, in summarizing his case against the Middle Kingdom's homegrown deviants, Leibniz at last identifies the real object of his concern: "One could perhaps claim that . . . one can conceive of [the *li*] as the prime form, that is, as the Soul of the World, of which the individual souls would only be modifications. This would follow the opinions of several ancients, the Averroists, and in a certain sense even the opinions of Spinoza." Elsewhere Leibniz describes Averroës (the Arab philosopher Ibn Rushd) as essentially a Spinozist *avant la lettre*; thus we may infer that the bad Chinese are Spinozists to a man.

"If by misfortune Atheism should prevail in Europe and become the doctrine of the most learned," just as it has in China, Leibniz goes on to say, then missionaries from China would have the right to look at ancient texts in Europe and "to ridicule the ridicule" of the Atheists. For all of his interest in China, it seems, Leibniz never quite managed to get Europe off his mind. China, in the final analysis, was a kind of laboratory experiment in modernization, a cautionary example of what might happen here at home, should Spinoza succeed.

Heal Thyself

Leibniz's paranoia about Spinozism was a general feature of the age in which he lived. The universal impulse to expose Spinozistic conspiracies had something of the air of a highbrow witch-hunt (and it is interesting to note that the lowbrow variety was very much in fashion at the time, too). In more recent times, one could find an analogue in the anti-Communist crusades of the mid-twentieth century. A typical feature of such affairs, in any case, is that the accusations eventually fall on precisely those who make the accusations themselves. The case of Leibniz was no exception to the rule.

In 1712, a Dutch professor named Ruardus Andala published a tract accusing Leibniz of plagiarizing Spinoza. One of Andala's pupils followed suit with another book making essentially the same charge. In 1723, some years after Leibniz's death, the German theologian Joachim Lange asserted that the entire system of the pre-established harmony was nothing but the Spinozan philosophy under a new name. (To be fair, however, it must be pointed out that Lange was of the sort who believed that the remote cause of all philosophy was Satan himself.)

The suggestion that Leibniz had some deep and unacknowledged attachment to Spinozism soon spread beyond the bastions of orthodoxy. Gotthold Lessing, the eighteenth-century critic whose reading of Spinoza played a crucial role in reviving the philosopher's fame, said of Leibniz: "I fear that he was himself a Spinozist at heart." Johann Gottfried Herder, who sensibly declined any access to his subject's inscrutable interior, declared: "What Leibniz was in his heart I may not know; but his *Theodicy* just as many of his letters show that, precisely in order not to be a Spinozist, he thought through his system." More recently, Bertrand Russell has said, in a typical analysis of the philosopher's notes: "Here, as elsewhere, Leibniz fell into Spinozism whenever he allowed himself to be logical; in his published works, accordingly, he took care to be illogical."

The suggestion that Leibniz's mature philosophy retains some unstated attachment to Spinozism, however, invariably arouses controversy among those who care about such matters—as it should. In his mature metaphysics, after all, Leibniz contradicts every central doctrine of Spinoza's philosophy, and in his public and private comments on any number of other subjects he engages in ceaseless, if covert, warfare on Spinozism in all its forms. Given the obvious, then, one should ask: What grounds could there possibly be for suspecting a hidden link between Leibniz and his nemesis?

It is our good fortune that Leibniz had a chance to respond to the charges. In 1714, one of Leibniz's correspondents gently inquired whether perhaps there might be some Spinozism in the doctrines of the monadology. Leibniz's reply:

> On the contrary, it is precisely by means of the monads that Spinozism is destroyed. For there are as many true substances— as many living mirrors of the Universe, always subsisting, as it were, or concentrated Universes—as there are Monads; whereas, according to Spinoza, there is but one sole substance. He would be right, if there were no Monads.

On first reading, the meaning of Leibniz's words is plain enough: he unequivocally rejects the Spinozistic philosophy. On second reading, however, we seem to enter the labyrinth all over again. Here Leibniz draws an inference that is perhaps obvious from a consideration of his metaphysical system but that must nonetheless sound very troubling to the many who are not yet convinced of the truth of the monadology. For, as he now makes explicit, if the infinite, sizeless, windowless, mutually harmonized substances of which he writes do not exist, then Spinoza is correct. Not: that both he and Spinoza might be wrong; but: that if he is wrong, Spinoza is *right*. At the very least, this represents a spectacular promotion for the philosopher of The Hague. After forty years of avoiding as much as possible the mention of his name and publicly dismissing his philosophy as so bad it need not be refuted, Leibniz suddenly declares that Spinoza—and not Plato, Aristotle, Epicurus, or any other great philosopher from the past—offers the only real alternative to his own philosophy.

Even in his response to the charge of Spinozism, it seems, Leibniz could not shake the obsession that led to the charge in the first place.

He had already sensed the presence of his rival in the most unexpected places—in Locke's *Essay*, Newton's physics, Descartes's metaphysics, Louis XIV's politics, the history of Chinese philosophy—and
now he saw it lurking in the shadow of his very own philosophical
system, determined to break free should his own arguments fail to
destroy it. The strange ubiquity of Spinoza in Leibniz's world, in fact,
requires that we leave open the possibility that his restless vigilance
on the matter perhaps followed from some awareness of just how
close he was himself to succumbing to the danger; that he feared
Spinozism so much because he thought that it just might be *true*; and
that, in a manner of speaking, he perceived the influence of his rival
everywhere because he mistook the tint in his own spectacles for a
certain dark aspect of the outside world.

16

The Return of the Repressed

Imagine a pair of friends returning separately from travels abroad, each describing a favorite city whose unpronounceable name they have forgotten. Your friends are wildly different in character, background, and aesthetic sensibilities; not surprisingly, they seem to have taken an interest in wildly different cities. As your friends are quite competitive, furthermore, they soon take to criticizing each other's choices. Each celebrates the virtues of his city by contrasting them with the alleged failings of the other's. As the discussion progresses, however, you begin to suspect that they are talking about the same city. In fact, you hear nothing in what they say that could confirm that they are *not* talking about the same city. Yet there is still no doubt that the city in question *means* something very different to each of your friends; that the two *saw* very different things in their travels. Now imagine that your friends are named Leibniz and Spinoza, and that instead of a particular city they are discussing the nature of the universe. The question then is: Do they share the same philosophy? Or, in other words, is philosophy about *what* you see, or the *way* you see it?

God

It is a startling fact that Spinoza considered and rejected something very like Leibniz's transcendent concept of God before the two philosophers met. In a letter dating from 1674, Spinoza writes: "He who affirms that God could have refrained from creating the world is declaring in an indirect way that it was made by chance, since it proceeded from an act of will which might not have been. Since this belief and this view is quite absurd, it is commonly and unanimously admitted that God's will is eternal and has never been indifferent." The idea that God has the option not to create the world, of course, is a defining feature of Leibniz's concept of divinity. Spinoza's critique of that concept begins with a premise with which Leibniz must agree: that God must have reasons for what it does. When God creates the world, Spinoza therefore infers, it cannot do so by whim or accident, but because some reason compels it to do so. Since that reason is always there—it is "eternal"—then it is "quite absurd," as Spinoza puts it, to speak of God as having the option not to create the world.

Spinoza's comments on a proto-Leibnizian concept of God anticipate a set of criticisms later offered by others in direct response to Leibniz. The debate boils down to a simple question: Does Leibniz's God really have a choice? Many have argued that he does not. Leibniz seems to add fuel to the fire under his feet with comments such as "everything [is] settled in advance" and "God's decree [to actualize the best of all possible worlds] is immutable."

A version of the critique runs like this: How do we know that this is the best of all possible worlds? It cannot be because we observe it to be so—for, to sift through all possible worlds and rank them according to their merits requires the kind of omniscience that only God has. It must therefore be because the choice of the best of all possible worlds follows from God's nature. In other words, God chooses the best of all possible worlds because it is in his nature to be good. God could not do otherwise because if he did so he would not be good, and therefore he would not be God. But this implies that God does not have a choice at all. He must create this world, exactly as it is, if he is to deserve the name of God.

At this point in the argument, of course, the mature Leibniz would concede that a transcendent God must have a sufficient reason for his actions. But, the author of the *Theodicy* would add, the reason for this world is a "moral" one and not a "metaphysical" one; specifically, it is the "principle of the best," to which God appeals in justifying his decision to create the world. Unfortunately for Leibniz, Spinoza has already anticipated this response. People like Leibniz, he sneers in the *Ethics*,

> seem to posit something external to God that does not depend upon him, to which in acting God looks as if it were a model, or to which he aims, as if it were a fixed target. This is surely to subject God to fate; and no more absurd suggestion can be made about God, whom we have shown to be the first and only free cause of both the essence and the existence of things. So I need not spend any more time in refuting this absurdity.

Leibniz's God, according to Spinoza, is not a free agent, but rather is beholden to some preconceived idea about the good—"a fixed target." More generally, Spinoza's point is that Leibniz's transcendent God is not a God *of reason*, for it must act in some arbitrary way, according to externally presented criteria over which it has no control. The only way out for those who believe in a God of reason, Spinoza implies, is to regard the "good" for which God allegedly aims as something internal to God's own nature. But this, of course, would be to accept a version of Spinoza's own concept of an immanent deity and reject the very idea that God chooses among possible worlds.

Spinoza's implicit critique of the distinction between "moral necessity" and "metaphysical necessity" was made quite explicit by Leibniz's later critics. In his exchange with Leibniz, for example, Samuel Clarke argues that "*necessity*, in philosophical questions, always signifies absolute necessity; *hypothetical necessity* and *moral necessity* are only figurative ways of speaking." The twentieth-century philosopher Arthur Lovejoy is even blunter: "The distinction Leibniz here attempts to set up [between moral necessity and brute metaphysical necessity] is manifestly without logical substance; the fact is so apparent that it is impossible to believe that a thinker of his powers can have been altogether unaware of it himself." But a good indication that the matter here runs much deeper than a simple logical error is that the literature is also not short of scholars willing to defend Leibniz's distinction.

The trouble with Leibniz's transcendent God, expressed in the most general terms, concerns the very nature of the choice Leibniz asks God to make. Leibniz often seems to imply that God's choice is something like the selection of an entrée from a menu of dishes. But, in fact, the nature of the choice God makes is very different from that faced by the typical restaurant patron. It is not a choice between *this* and *that*, but between *something* and *nothing*—or, more precisely, between anything at all and absolutely nothing. God's choice must take place outside, before, or beyond this (or any other possible) world. And yet it must be a rational choice; that is, it must involve comparing possible options and maximizing preferences. The question that troubles Leibniz's more acute critics is: Is such a transcendental choice conceivable? Is it possible to imagine a choice that takes place without also imagining a world within which to make it? Can you do it?

Leibniz, it seems, could not. Indeed, in the *Theodicy*, he goes to the trouble of providing a detailed description of the "higher" world within which God's transcendental choice is allegedly made— namely, the fabulous, pyramid-shaped palace of all possible worlds. We may prefer to imagine a different setting—say, we could picture God shuffling cards in a weighty game of cosmic solitaire, or stopping in for a treat at a cosmic diner. Spinoza, for his part, had Leibniz's God either sculpting from a model or firing arrows at a bull's-eye. In any case, it seems impossible not to imagine some sort of scenario within which God's transcendental choice occurs. The question then arises: Who created this higher world? Who constructed that beautiful, baroque pyramid, the green felt card table, the bow and arrow—i.e., all the constraints, norms, and preferences according to which all possible worlds are defined and judged?

If we say that this higher world is God's creation, too, then we seem to acknowledge that there is only one possible world from which God may choose—namely, this higher world—and all the so-called possible worlds aren't really "worlds" at all, but merely features of the one true world created by God, like the blocks of a pyramid. At the end of that road lies Spinozism. If we say that this higher world has always been there and has always been the way it is, on the other hand, then we make God one of its creatures and we subject God to its rules, and he acts unfreely—i.e., according to its nature and not his own. In a sense, God is no longer God, but just a logical operator within the scheme of some preexisting nature. At the end of that road lies atheism—or, one could say, a form of Spinozism without Spinoza's belief in the divinity of nature.

Indeed, some such charge is what Spinoza implicitly levels at Leibniz. The label of "fatalism" that Spinoza hurls against (people like) Leibniz, ironically, is the same that Leibniz tosses at Spinoza in his later works. Had Spinoza lived long enough, he might have accused Leibniz of being a godless Spinozist—after clarifying that he himself was not one. Perhaps the most curious feature of Spinoza's implicit critique of Leibniz, though, is its tone. Spinoza's dismissal of a proto-Leibnizian concept of God as utterly absurd hardly suggests much room for negotiation on the subject from Spinoza's end. Indeed, his contemptuous treatment of the idea offers an intriguing clue as to how he might have responded if and when Leibniz let slip his commitment to it when they met in 1676.

Mind

One might have hoped that Leibniz's theory of mind, as represented in his monadology, would lead us safely out of this labyrinth of Spinozistic Leibnizes and Leibnizian Spinozas. The monads, after all, are where Leibniz draws his line in the sand: Spinoza would be correct, if there were no monads. But this line in the sand turns out to be something of a mirage, too.

Leibniz's readers have frequently complained that the monads belong to a thoroughly deterministic cosmos, in which history unwinds like the ticking of a second hand through eternity. Arnauld —oddly echoing Spinoza—accuses Leibniz of propounding a view "more than fatalistic." "Once [God] has chosen," Leibniz acknowledges, once again adding fuel to the fire, "one must grant that everything is included in his choice, and that nothing can be changed." Life in Leibniz's world, practically speaking, would seem to be indistinguishable from life in Spinoza's world.

Leibniz, of course, responds that the monads' ignorance of their own true nature requires that they act as if they were free. That is, God knows Caesar will cross the Rubicon, but when Caesar stands on the banks of the river, he faces a momentous decision. Thus, Caesar, like the rest of us, has free will. The best reason to think that Leibniz's argument in favor of free will is as bad as it sounds is that it is indistinguishable from Spinoza's argument *against* free will. This surprising coincidence is evident in a moment when Leibniz lets down his guard and speaks frankly. The will, he says, "has its causes, but since we are ignorant of them and they are oft-hidden, we believe we ourselves independent. . . . It is this chimera of imaginary independence which revolts us against the consideration of determinism, and which brings us to believe that there are difficulties where there are none." These words could have been simply lifted out of the *Ethics*, where Spinoza writes that "men believe they are free . . . because they are conscious of their volitions and desires, yet ignorant of the causes that have determined them to desire and will." Leibniz was—and, at least in the privacy of his personal notebooks, understood himself to be— a determinist.

Of course, it is possible to be a determinist and still not be a Spinozist, and, at first glance, that is precisely the niche that Leibniz seems to want to occupy. Spinoza's determinism is closely linked to his doctrine of parallelism, according to which mind and body pursue parallel paths through life because they are the same thing viewed from different perspectives. Spinoza's determinism, in other words, translates into the claim that all of our mental acts may ultimately be mapped into physical processes, which themselves operate necessarily according to laws of cause and effect. Leibniz's determinism, on the other hand, arises from within the mind itself, and not from interaction between mind and body, for he allows no such interaction. That is, it is because all predicates are contained within the concept of a monad that it follows a predetermined path through life. According to the doctrine of pre-established harmony, mind and body move in parallel only because God has seen fit to harmonize the predetermined activities of independent mind- and body-substances, and not because they are two attributes of the same substance.

While the theoretical difference between Spinoza's parallelism and Leibniz's pre-established harmony is easy to understand, however, the practical implications of this difference are much harder to see. How, one should ask, might a neutral observer detect whether he happened to be in a Leibnizian universe rather than a Spinozan one? In both cases, after all, every mental act without exception occurs alongside a corresponding physical event. As a matter of principle, there would be no way to establish through any observation whether this apparent unity of mind and body is the consequence of an underlying identity, as Spinoza suggests, or an amazing coincidence, as Leibniz argues. As early as 1712, and then again in the 1720s, Leibniz's critics said flatly that there was no way to tell the difference. In fact, they said, Leibniz's pre-established harmony is a plagiarism of Spinoza's doctrine of parallelism.

Leibniz, of course, insists all over again that his form of parallelism is different because, whether we observe so or not, it occurs by the will of God, not through the common identity of mind and body in substance. But, unfortunately, this approach does not forestall the collapse into Spinozism for long. The pre-established harmony is the prime example of a choice that, according to Leibniz, is "morally" necessary but not "metaphysically" necessary. God has the metaphysical option, Leibniz implies, to create a disharmonious universe, even if it is morally incumbent upon him to favor a harmonious one. If, however, Leibniz's distinction between "moral" and "metaphysical" necessity is specious, then we would have to conclude that the pre-established harmony follows necessarily (*tout court*) from the nature of God, and that the parallelism in Leibniz's world is every bit as logically necessary as that which obtains in Spinoza's world.

Supposing we allow Leibniz the distinction between moral and metaphysical necessity, the question still remains: Is a "disharmonious" universe metaphysically possible, as he implies? According to

Leibniz's principle that One is All, each individual monad entails the entire existing universe of monads, in the sense that its internal "mirror" replicates the activities of all the other monads, no matter how many or how far. Choose one monad, in other words, and you choose the entire universe. In a disharmonious universe, however, the "universe" within each monad would have nothing to do with the "universe" outside. A mind-monad might be in Paris, for instance, while its body is in Hanover (or, better, nowhere at all—for there is no obvious sense in which the body a monad thinks it has should refer to any outside monad at all). Choose two or more monads, in other words, and you choose two or more universes that have nothing to do with one another. But, if monads belong to universes that have nothing to do with one another, then they cannot be conceived of as belonging to the same universe. Even God, through whom all substances must be conceived, would not be able to imagine such disparate substances as belonging in any sense to the same universe. But if disharmonious monads do not belong to the same universe, then a disharmonious universe is not possible. And if a disharmonious universe is not possible, then Leibniz's God has only harmonious possible universes to choose from, which is to say that in all possible universes mind and body are harmonious, which is to say that the parallelism of mind and body exhibits just as much logical necessity in Leibniz's world as it does in Spinoza's.

The dangerous and unexpected convergence of Leibniz's views on the mind-body relation with Spinoza's also raises a worrisome challenge to his doctrine of personal immortality. To be sure, Leibniz ever and always avows his faith in personal immortality, and repeatedly chastises Spinoza and his proxies for their belief in "an immortality without memory." However, as a consequence of his commitment to a form of parallelism, Leibniz is forced to acknowledge that even in its before- and after-lives, the mind-monad remains tied to some parallel manifestation of body-monads. Before life, roughly speaking, we are something like seeds; after life, we reside in microscopic form somewhere in the ashes, for example. As a further consequence of his own parallelism, Leibniz is compelled to acknowledge that our faculties of perception are greatly influenced by the kinds of body-

monads with which we are surrounded. He hastens to add that even
a mind-monad buried in a speck of ash will control some set of sub-
ordinate body-monads, thus forming an organic structure. But,
Leibniz's assurances about the fire-resistant properties of monads
notwithstanding, many have found it difficult to believe that immortality as a cinder is all that it is cracked up to be. Perhaps understandably, the skeptics question whether the perceptive faculties of the
average speck of ash may attain a degree of acuity sufficient to permit it to bask in the rewards or suffer the punishments that Leibniz
insists must come its way in the course of its eternal afterlife.

The implosion of the doctrine of immortality reflects an even
deeper crisis in Leibniz's thought concerning the very idea of individuality. In his effort to secure the absolute permanence and unity
of the individual soul against all outside influence, Leibniz is forced
to represent the body and all of its activities as the workings of an
infinity of monads external to the individual mind-monad. The question then naturally arises: Why not ascribe to this outside infinity of
monads *all* of the attributes that we use to define our identities—
beginning with height and weight but not ending with our memories, preferences, and passions? Instead of preserving the sanctity of
the individual, Leibniz may be inadvertently engaged in a deconstruction of individuality itself—which, of course, is exactly what
Spinoza accomplishes in his system.

All of the suggestions that Leibniz is some sort of Spinozist can be
mapped into the claim that monads are not true substances, as Leibniz maintains, but rather something more like modes of a single Substance. Leibniz himself acknowledges the centrality of the matter
when he says that Spinoza would be right, if there were no monads.
All of the challenges to the substantiality of monads in turn come
down to a question about the relation between monads and God.

In his metaphysical system, Leibniz strives to maintain a delicate
balance between God and the monads. For example, he avers that
monads are eternal and indestructible—as indeed substances must
be—but then turns around and allows that God can create them or
annihilate them all in a flash. He grants monads freedom in their own
eyes—which is as it should be for all substances—but then seems to

take away their freedom in God's eyes. These and other tensions in the City of God come to a head in a simple question: Is God a monad?

It would seem a straightforward question, the sort to which the great monadologist would have a ready answer. Yet Leibniz is surprisingly cagey on the subject. His best hint comes in the phrase that God is the "monad of monads." One would have thought that, after three centuries of effort, the Leibniz scholars would have reached a consensus on just what Leibniz means by "the monad of monads." But such is not the case. Some argue that God must be a monad, others that he cannot be. In fact, there is no answer that works within the constraints of the Leibnizian system.

Consider the possibility that God is not a monad. This makes sense: since God chooses to "flash" the monads into existence, he must exist before the "flash." In that case, however, it follows that the monads exist and have their properties only in virtue of the properties and/or deeds of this flashing, nonmonadic entity. But if monads depend on some other entity in this way, then they are not substances, for a substance by definition depends on nothing else to be what it is. Rather, the so-called monads must in fact be considered merely "modes" of substance. And since God is the only entity that does not depend on some other entity to be what it is, then God alone is substance. Hegel sums it up nicely: "There is a contradiction present. If the monad of monads, God, is the absolute substance, and individual monads are created through his will, their substantiality comes to an end." If God is not a monad, in short, then Leibniz is a Spinozist.

Needless to say, Leibniz would now rush to open the other door. So, consider the option that "the monad of monads" is indeed a monad. But, if God is a monad, then by definition he cannot interact with other monads, for otherwise he would determine their essence and they his. If he cannot interact with them, he cannot create them. As a monad, in fact, God may have concourse with his so-called creations only in a "virtual" way, by means of the pre-established harmony. If God acts only through the pre-established harmony, then he can't be said to create that either. And whatever it is that God does— if there is anything at all left for him to do—all of it follows with absolute, logical necessity from his monadic essence. That is, the fact that he will "create" this particular universe (if he can) is already contained within his concept, in the same way that "cross the Rubicon" is a necessary predicate of "Caesar." Indeed, given the lemma that to choose one monad is to choose its entire universe, it follows that once God exists, then the universe such as it is exists with rigorous necessity. So God can hardly be said to have a choice about anything—except insofar as, like Caesar, he is ignorant of his true nature. In short, if God is a monad, he isn't God at all; he's just another one of us. Russell alludes to this eventuality when he remarks that Leibniz's monadism should have impelled him to an even greater heresy than Spinozism. To put it crudely: if God is a monad, Leibniz is an atheist.

Salvation

Those still hoping for a hard and fast distinction between the Leibnizian and Spinozan philosophies might look forward to building the fence somewhere along the path to salvation. After all, it seems embarrassingly obvious from their different lifestyles, if nothing else, that the two philosophers represent very different ideas about the nature of human happiness. Unfortunately, the differences between the two on salvation turn out to be no less elusive than the putative differences between monads and modes.

Leibniz's determinism inevitably draws him very close to Spinoza's ethical positions—and even opens him up to attack from the same, orthodox antagonists. For example, to the extent that God's decision to create the best of all possible worlds is "immutable," as Leibniz has it, then it would seem pointless to pray to him, just as it is pointless to pray to Spinoza's God in hopes of some alternative outcome of events. Inasmuch as everything a monad ever does is already contained within its concept, furthermore, then it would take a legalistic mind of tremendous power to demonstrate that monads commit sins of their own free will. Russell goes so far as to accuse Leibniz of "discreditable subterfuges" in his efforts to conceal the fact that all sin for him is "original sin, the inherent finitude of every created monad."

Leibniz attempts to finesse the issue by suggesting, for example, that monads can choose to do good by guiding their efforts according to the "presumptive will" of God. Exactly how one goes about presuming God's will Leibniz leaves somewhat unclear; but a Spinozist would undoubtedly infer that the "presumptive will" of God is a metaphorical way of alluding to the realization of our own essential and inherently finite natures, for that is what forms our contribution to the realization of God's plan for the universe. But this maximization of the individual *conatus*, of course, is precisely the path Spinoza proposes to take in his *Ethics*.

Leibniz's tendency toward a Spinozism in ethics extends beyond his commitment to some form of determinism and penetrates into his very idea of self-realization, or happiness. Because it has a *conatus* of sorts, each monad wants to "become what it is," as it were; and anything that contributes to this project of perfecting the self counts as pleasure, whereas whatever detracts from it is pain. "Pleasure is nothing but the feeling of an increase in perfection," explains Leibniz. But these words could easily have been lifted from Spinoza's *Ethics*. The more "active" a monad is—which is to say, the more it realizes its own nature, as opposed to submitting passively to the domination of other monads—the happier it is. "We will be happier the clearer our comprehension of things and the more we act in accordance with our proper nature, namely, reason," Leibniz clarifies. "Only to the extent that our reasonings are correct are we free and exempt from the passions which are impressed upon us by surrounding bodies." It is passages like this one—which, again, could simply have been cribbed from the *Ethics*—that lead Russell to suggest that, in his ethical philosophy, "Leibniz no longer shows great originality, but tends, with slight alterations of phraseology, to adopt (without acknowledgment) the views of the decried Spinoza." In fact, Leibniz's unswerving commitment to the guidance of reason leads him inexorably toward the identification of freedom and happiness that is the defining feature of Spinoza's ethics.

IN THEIR REPORTS on their travels into the very heart of things, Leibniz and Spinoza seem at first glance to describe radically different universes. One discovers a numberless horde of animated substances, the other a singular mass of undifferentiated substance;

one finds souls that never die, the other no souls at all; one sees a world in which everything happens for a reason, the other a world in which everything just happens.

Yet, when we look for observable effects and practical consequences that might serve to distinguish the two worlds in question, the discrepancies seem to evaporate upon inspection. The world according to Leibniz is a reasonable one; it is a law-abiding, all-determining cosmos that is the proper subject of scientific investigation, a world unencumbered with inscrutable deities, where the individual remains for all practical purposes at the mercy of external forces, and in which we have the responsibility to seek happiness by realizing ourselves. The world Leibniz describes, in brief, is the one first properly observed by Spinoza.

Ultimately, the differences between the two philosophers have to do not with the nature of the world as each sees it, but with the meaning or value each ascribes to it. Spinoza identifies the law-abiding, all-determining nature that serves as the object of scientific investigation with God. Leibniz does not. Indeed, Leibniz's philosophy is at its clearest and most sincere in the negative. Its founding principle remains: Nature is *not* God; that is to say, a Being that makes no choices and cannot be called good does not deserve the name of God. The monads exist for no other purpose than to make this negation, which remains standing even as the rest of Leibniz's philosophy collapses into something observationally indistinguishable from Spinozism.

In this there is revealed something essential about the nature of Leibniz's philosophy and its peculiar relationship with that of Spinoza. The monadology is best understood as an attempt to show that one may grant the existence of a universe in every way indistinguishable from the one Spinoza describes and still cling to old hopes about God and immortality on the basis that these matters lie beyond the limits of anything that can be observed or proved by Spinoza and his ilk. Leibniz's avowed proof of the immateriality of the mind is really just an argument that Spinoza's materialism does not rule out the possibility of an undetectable spiritual force behind all apparently mechanical actions; his proof of the pre-established harmony is just an argument that the parallelism Spinoza observes can never be definitively shown to be the result of an identity, rather than mere coincidence; his proof that the world has a designer is just an argument that Spinoza fails to prove absolutely that there is none; and his proof of the existence of a transcendent God is really just an argument that an immanent God is not a God. Leibniz's philosophy as a whole follows the pattern he established as a young man in his early defense of transubstantiation. In the final analysis, he does not leave us with a set of positive doctrines, but with a series of negations. His work amounts to a deconstruction of modern philosophy in general and of Spinozism in particular. It is defined by—and cannot exist without—that to which it is opposed. It is, in essence, a reactive philosophy.

Perhaps the best way to summarize Leibniz's problematically self-subverting position is to say that he was a Spinozist who did not believe in Spinoza's God. One logical outcome of such a position, of course, is precisely that toward which Leibniz tended whenever he attempted to distinguish himself from Spinoza: namely, that there is no God at all. The author of the system of the pre-established harmony spent a lifetime branding the author of the *Ethics* as an atheist; but it was Leibniz who sailed much closer to the winds of unbelief.

All of which puts us in a better position to understand in general terms what transpired on those windy days in November 1676—even if the details of the event must remain forever beyond our knowledge. In a philosophical as well as a literal sense, Spinoza opened a door for Leibniz. He revealed to his visitor a reality that, for all practical purposes, the young man recognized as the world within which he situated his own philosophy. In frank and sometimes brutal language, he showed Leibniz what it means to be a modern philosopher. Yet Leibniz did not behold this reality in the same way that Spinoza did. When he looked into the black opal eyes of his host, he did not find a new divinity. He saw instead the death of God. His philosophy was in many respects an attempt to shut the door that he wished he had never opened. But it was too late: he was already standing on the other side.

17

Leibniz's End

The clouds began to gather over Leibniz's political career around the turn of the eighteenth century, sometime after the death of his second Hanoverian patron, the Elector Ernst August. The Elector's son and successor, Georg Ludwig, showed little appreciation for the court *érudit*. He derided the aging philosopher as "a living dictionary" and "an archaeological find." Leibniz, it turns out, still appeared in public wearing the enormous wig and the baroque costume of his gilded youth in Paris. He had not noticed that in the intervening decades his style had long since gone out of fashion. In the eyes of the young nobles at court, the natty dresser had become a nutty professor.

Mainly, Georg Ludwig complained about Leibniz's "invisible books." Decades had passed since the philosopher undertook the project of tracing the genealogy of the House of Brunswick, but he had yet to produce a single volume on the subject. It probably didn't help that, when Georg Ludwig brought up the matter of the missing books, Leibniz turned around and said that he would be hard-pressed to find the time for the project unless, perchance, he should receive an annual pension of 2,000 thalers for life. He also put forward his conviction that he should be promoted to vice chancellor—the highest civil rank in the land.

Georg Ludwig was not amused. Irked by the philosopher's habit of vanishing on long and unexplained journeys, he decreed that his living dictionary henceforth should seek his personal permission to leave Hanover. The Elector then took great pleasure in denying Leibniz's repeated requests for leave to travel. After a while, the fun wore off, and in order to save himself the trouble of having to turn down his minion's incessant petitions, the Elector effectively put Leibniz under house arrest until such time as he should have completed the promised history of the Brunswick clan.

But the wily philosopher snuck out anyway. At the age of sixty-two, he undertook a secret trip to Vienna. There he met with, among others, the ambassador from the court of Peter the Great, with whom he discussed a plan for promoting the sciences in Russia. In letters posted back to the Elector and his mother, Sophia, from Vienna, however, he maintained that he was in the spa town of Karlsbad, tending to his ailing health. From Vienna, the errant philosopher next journeyed to Berlin in the company of the Russian ambassador. In his letters back to Hanover, he retailed a novel story: having been rejuvenated by the mineral waters of Karlsbad, he said, he was now visiting some remote and inaccessible universities in Saxony in order to perform research for the history book. In Berlin, Leibniz dined with many more of the great and good, though he carefully avoided contact with the resident ambassador from Hanover. Unfortunately, a member of the Russian embassy mischievously let slip to a member of the Hanoverian embassy that the great philosopher had been spotted enjoying himself immensely in Vienna.

Georg was furious. Sophia wrote to Leibniz somewhat tartly that her son was now offering a reward for anyone who could bring him in. The chastised courtier returned hastily to his place of employment, where the Elector personally rebuked him. Leibniz apparently did not take the message to heart, for in a long, written response to the Elector, he fabricated yet another story about his trip (this time he claimed that he bumped into the Empress in Karlsbad, and she dragged him kicking to Vienna). He further complained vigorously that the Elector's attitude toward him was most unkind, and he alerted his employer to a fact that he found disgraceful: the historian of the House of Brandenburg received a 3,000 thaler pension for his efforts—more than double what the Brunswickians were promising their genealogist.

As cups ran over with yellow bile on both sides of the employment dispute in Hanover, Leibniz suffered another blow to his career. In 1710, the members of the Berlin Society of the Sciences met in the absence of their nominal president and, inexplicably, elected a new director. The "cabal," as Leibniz called them, neglected to tell him whether or not this meant he was no longer president. When the Society held its grand, official inauguration in Berlin on January 19, 1711, in any case, the man who had dedicated much of his life to making its existence possible was not in attendance.

Unhappy in Hanover and unwelcome in Berlin, Leibniz made robust efforts to seek employment elsewhere. Paris was still on the top of his list; and London was rising fast with the prospect of a Hanoverian succession; but the most promising immediate opportunities were to be found in Vienna. In late 1712, Leibniz once again set off for the capital of the Holy Roman Empire in search of imperial favor, scattering in his wake the usual variety of false alibis.

Sophia implored the AWOL philosopher to return. But Leibniz sent back one excuse after another. At first it was the plague in Vienna. If he left the city, he complained, he would run the risk of a hostile reception from peasants in unaffected rural areas. (Sophia quipped that he seemed to prefer the pestilential air of Vienna to the stale air of Hanover.) Then it was his health. (Eckhart, who ended up doing much of the legwork on the *History of the House of Brunswick*, didn't buy it: "The gout is just an excuse." Leibniz would never finish the project, he predicted, because he "is too distracted, tries to do everything, and wants to get himself mixed up in everything.") Much to Leibniz's sorrow, Sophia died suddenly in the summer of 1713; but her funeral was not enough to draw him out of the imperial capital. Late that year, with his mother no longer there to cool his temper, Georg Ludwig lost his patience. He cut off the wandering monadologist's salary.

The harsh move failed to have the anticipated effect. It seems that by this time Leibniz had secured a position in Vienna as imperial privy counselor and was drawing a hefty salary from the Holy Roman Emperor. Nonetheless, he wrote back in early 1714 promising that nothing could keep him from returning to Hanover by summer. But the summer found Leibniz still in Vienna, working to establish an Imperial Society of the Sciences.

Then in August arrived the long awaited news: Queen Anne of England was dead. The crown of England passed to King George I— also known as Georg Ludwig, Elector of Hanover. No plague or empress could now stop Leibniz's rush back to Hanover. He let his correspondents know that they should forward his mail to the Court of St. James in London. He arrived breathless in Hanover on September 14, eager to continue the journey on to the English capital.

But the palace of Hanover was empty of life. Leibniz's disappointment was keen as he learned that King George had departed to claim his new realm three days previously. Worse, the new monarch had left instructions that, should the family historian ever be located, he be asked to remain in Hanover for the time being. Still not inclined to take George at his word, Leibniz immediately approached Caroline, the new king's daughter-in-law, and asked if he might go to London with her. But she and her entourage left without him on October 12.

Meanwhile, the King's minister, having received correspondence in London on the philosopher's behalf, wrote a stern letter ordering him to remain in Germany until the history of the House of Brunswick was complete. Leibniz wrote back asking if he could come to London and serve as the historiographer of England instead. According to Caroline, the King snapped back: "He must show me that he can write history first; I hear that he is diligent." By this time, George I had presumably discovered that Newton's antagonist in the priority dispute was about as popular among his new subjects as smallpox. The Court of St. James delivered its final word: Leibniz was grounded. He was not to be allowed out of Hanover until he turned in his history.

Bad news from Berlin soon added to the slings and arrows from London. For the five years since he had been unceremoniously kicked off his perch as leader of the Society of the Sciences, Leibniz had continued to draw his presidential salary of 600 thalers. In 1715, the bookkeepers finally got their act together, and the Society cut off his salary. Leibniz howled with indignation, but, as the new leaders of the Society pointed out, the money had been intended to cover his expenses, and since he had not shown up to any meetings for the previous four years nor otherwise performed any work for them, he could hardly claim to have run up any bills on their account.

Leibniz spent his seventieth and final year no less prodigiously than all those that had gone before. In correspondence with the leading mathematicians of Europe, he explored new approaches to the calculus and fended off accusations of plagiarism from Newton's supporters. He debated natural theology with Samuel Clarke. He wrote a discourse on Chinese theology. He cultivated a new friendship with a French Jesuit in hopes that he might finally receive the call to take a position in Paris.

Though it hardly showed in the pace of his work, Leibniz's health was deteriorating rapidly. His arthritis now caused excruciating pain with the slightest movement. As part of his program of home remedy, the ailing courtier would sometimes lie on a flat board for days at a stretch. He complained of pain in his kidneys, and developed a tumor in his right leg. But he took it all as a philosopher should: "I suffer from time to time in my feet," he told a friend. "Occasionally the disease passes to my hands; but head and stomach, thank God, still do their duty."

In May 1716, King George returned to Hanover to enjoy a hunting holiday. Perhaps because the beautiful spring weather lifted his mood, he relented somewhat in his ire toward his wayward historian. He granted a resumption of Leibniz's salary, which had been held in abeyance over the previous two and a half years. Sadly, the gain was offset in September when the Holy Roman Emperor decided that the Viennese taxpayers were not getting their money's worth from the privy counselor who was under house arrest in Hanover.

As the summer gave way to autumn, Leibniz remained confined in the town he had been trying to leave for the previous forty years of his life. Reviled in London, scorned in Berlin, ignored in Vienna and

Paris, he rounded the final lap in the race of life in the rather depleted condition that at one time or another inevitably befalls those who live by the favor of others.

YET, EVEN AS the rain fell pitilessly on Leibniz's personal career, the sun never stopped shining in his metaphysical writings. In the land of the monads—the best of all possible worlds—it was always high noon. At the age of sixty-eight Leibniz penned a pair of essays on the central doctrines of his metaphysics: the *Monadology*, and the *Principles of Grace*. He presented the latter to the warrior-prince Eugène of Savoy, who, on the theory that the philosopher's writings were as precious as diamonds, locked the sparkling manuscript safely in a jewelry chest, where it remained until some years after the author's death. Leibniz's last essays, more than any other of his works, are responsible for the impression that the philosopher was something of an ontological poet or perhaps even a confabulator.

Leibniz in his sunset writings no longer pretends to argue for his views. The ever stranger propositions simply follow one another like the lyrics of a metaphysical ballad or the transcription of a séance. The last musings of the monadologist have often evoked a sense of wonder in readers. They are "a kind of telescope, which showed me another universe, which presented to me an enchanted perspective . . . almost magical," said the Swiss philosopher Charles Bonnet in 1748. Herder, too, thought that Leibniz had introduced us to "another world" with his "reflective poetry." Where some saw a wonderland, however, others complained of that old superficiality or corelessness—the void that sometimes seemed to occupy the place of Leibniz's heart. Frederick the Great snidely called Leibniz's masterwork a "Monadenpoeme." "In this philosophy everything is spirit, phantom and illusion," said the great eighteenth-century mathematician Leonhard Euler.

Strangest of all was that sometimes Leibniz himself seemed to nod in the most subtle of ways at the surreal and possibly illusory character of his own thought. In a passage not published until 1948, for instance, he almost seems to be chanting as he writes that each monad contains:

the entire past, and even the whole infinitely infinite future, since each moment contains an infinity of things each one of which encloses an infinity, and since there is an infinity of moments in each hour or other part of time, and an infinity of hours, years, of centuries, of eons in the whole of future eternity. What an infinity of infinities infinitely replicated, what a world, what a universe, apperceptible in whatever corpuscle one cares to choose.

Of course, according to the proper, literal reading of such a text—in which one ascribes propositions to philosophers in the same way that one affixes attributes to substances—Leibniz here affirms that, according to the latest science, the universe in which we live has some astonishing logical properties. "What a wonderful world!" he sings, like a Louis Armstrong of seventeenth-century metaphysics. This is Leibniz in his incarnation as the great optimist, always looking at the sunny side of God's creations, strutting blindly into Voltaire's satirical grasp.

But, according to a second, more compelling reading, the "world" Leibniz asks us to celebrate seems to be not the real one, but an imaginary one—the fairy-tale land of pregnant, windowless monads. Look at my monads, Leibniz seems to say. Aren't they beautiful? Wouldn't it be nice if the real world were so intricate, so well constituted, so harmonious with our innermost needs and desires? The City of God, as it appears in Leibniz's final writings, shines ever more like an ideal, like a place just over the next hill, rather than a description of the world in which we live. And perhaps it is not too much to suppose that at some point in later life the philosopher came to accept that this ideal was an impossible one—the kind that marks the end point of fantasy rather than of action.

Indeed, the brilliance of Leibniz's metaphysical visions grew in direct proportion to his deepening gloom on the future of European civilization. By the time of his last, glowing thoughts on the monads, he despaired that Europe had fallen victim to a "spiritual epidemic." He foresaw anarchy and revolution. And he understood that his vision of a united Christian republic belonged to the past, not the future. The gap between the world he described in his monadological writings and the world such as he experienced it only grew with time, until at last perhaps even Leibniz could no longer entirely overlook it.

There was some sadness in this knowledge, an aftertaste more wistful than bitter. When in his final years he heard of the idealistic Abbé de St. Pierre's utopian plan for establishing perpetual peace by means of continental federalism, for example, Leibniz told a friend that a better alternative would be to return the church to its medieval role as the central power of Europe:

> But it would be necessary at the same time for the ecclesiastics to resume their old authority and that an interdiction and an excommunication make kings tremble, as in the time of Nicholas I or Gregory VII. Here is a plan which will succeed as easily as that of M. l'Abbé de St. Pierre; but since it is permitted to write romances, why should we condemn the fiction which would recall the age of gold to us?

The best of all possible worlds, it seems, has no gold in it; ours is an age of lead. The grand project of unifying the churches—the task that had consumed the greatest part of his labors in the fifty years of his working life—Leibniz here reduces to little more than a pleasing diversion, an exercise in creative writing. The impression that the great monadologist was a Panglossian optimist turns out to be as thin as a coat of silver on the back of a mirror. He was in fact one of history's great pessimists.

Leibniz's philosophy, in the final analysis, was not of this world; it was a mirage that marked the end point of his ceaseless activity, an illusion of stasis conjured out of perpetual motion. Leibniz was that part of us that is always striving, the element of desire for something new, something better than what we have—something that usually ends up looking like a hologram of the past, the imaginary idyll of a youth that never was. He was the Great Gatsby of his time, always believing in the green light in the distance, the ever receding destination of all our efforts. Perhaps only in the last years of his life did he understand that the end was a fiction, and that the price paid for living too long in one's dreams was a kind of hollowness in the present.

Leibniz never quite lived in the world of monads; he always only aspired to. In the universe of the monads, there is nothing more permanent, sure of its identity, and secure from material depredations than the individual self. In the grubby world in which the monadologist struggled for physical and political survival, however, there was nothing more fragile and less sure of its identity than that same self. The great courtier of Hanover spent the better part of a decade underground in the Harz Mountains; he took on Sisyphean assignments such as researching the genealogy of an inbred family of aristocrats; and he pressed frantically for new jobs and higher salaries with a passion that others could describe only as greed—all because he did not believe that the self could withstand the merciless assaults of material forces. He craved praise, brooked no contradiction, and tended to burst spontaneously into the kind of effusive self-congratulation that others could view only as the mark of extraordinary vanity—because at some level he did not believe that the self could otherwise preserve its precarious identity in an indifferent world. He spared no effort to guard himself against "dangerous" philosophical views—such as, principally, those of Spinoza—because he did not believe that the self would always remain true to itself.

In the Empire of Reason Leibniz advocates in his political theory, the absolute truth sits on the throne; even God must answer to the immutable laws of justice, beauty, and reason. But in the political world Leibniz inhabited during office hours, nothing demonstrated less power than the unaided truth. From attempting to dupe the Poles into accepting a German king in 1669 to bedazzling Louis XIV with the prospect of Egyptian glory in 1672, from finessing the elevation of the House of Hanover by means of purportedly neutral intervention with the Holy Roman Emperor in 1692 to manipulating the English Succession by means of anonymous pamphlets later disowned in 1704, there was hardly a stratagem Leibniz pursued in his long and colorful political career that did not make use of deception. And this same lack of faith in the efficacy of the unvarnished truth seems to have penetrated to the core of his philosophical and theological work, too. In his eagerness to reunite a divided religious world, Leibniz did not scruple to lay at the foundation of the future church a number of doctrines in whose truth it is quite implausible to maintain he believed.

In the City of God that Leibniz glorifies in his philosophy, the principle of charity reigns supreme. But in Paris, Hanover, and the other cities in which he resided, Leibniz seems to have assumed that self-interest is the only reliable motivator of the human being. Whether the philosopher placed his personal good above the public good is perhaps a matter from which he may seek protection from epistemological barriers; that he acted on the assumption that *other* people, as a rule, were inclined to do so, however, seems beyond dispute. Leibniz trusted no one. Indeed, he seems to have been so convinced that others would not support humanitarian quests such as his own that he was forced to take huge amounts of time off from those quests in order to secure for himself the money and power required to pursue them. Human beings are so self-interested, he insinuated, that without the promise of personal rewards and punishments in the afterlife, they can hardly be counted on to support the public good in this life.

The stage on which Leibniz acted out his life belonged to another philosopher. The idea of the "self" he presupposed in his actions was not the permanent unity of his monadology, but the fragile collection of passions that emerges from Spinoza's theory of mind. The political field within which he sought employment was not the Empire of Reason, but the secular order represented in Spinoza's works, according to which power is the first language of politics, and truth is spoken only rarely, and mostly in jest. And the premise of his daily practice was not the principle of charity, but Spinoza's doctrine that all people and all things act first and foremost out of self-interest. Like his God, Leibniz wanted to live only in the before and beyond; but like the rest of us, he never really left the present. The truth at the bottom of the great courtier's multifarious way of being is just this: Leibniz acted like a *Spinozist*—and yet he was nothing like *Spinoza*.

And therein lies the final clue to understanding the event that took place in November 1676. When Leibniz sat down with Spinoza in the house on the Paviljoensgracht, he acquired the kind of thing that philosophers have sought and for which they can only—in the fullness of time—be grateful: a form of self-knowledge. Spinoza showed him who and what he was. For Leibniz, it was a very hard kind of knowledge. In took forty years of life for it to percolate slowly through his being, until at last it expressed itself in a certain kind of acceptance. Leibniz was one of the great performers, a master of managing perceptions, of holding up the looking glass that allows us to flatter ourselves in flattering him. If, just before that final bow, the wig slipped off its perch, exposing something of the artist underneath, then we should imagine that he saved for us a sly wink and wan smile of farewell, comfortable at last in the role that was his to play.

IN EARLY NOVEMBER 1716, the philosopher's hands and shoulders seized up. He spent eight days lying in bed, attended by his secretary and his coachman, aggressively fending off suggestions that he should be seen by a doctor. On the ninth day he learned that a certain famous physician whom he had met previously at a spa and who was known for his able care of local aristocrats happened to be in Hanover. Starting to get delirious, he agreed to accept a house call.

The philosopher greeted the doctor with a lengthy lecture on the nature and genesis of his ailments. His discourse turned heated and incoherent. He began to use strange terms borrowed from alchemy and digressed at length on recent successes by a certain Florentine in converting half an iron nail into gold. "The patient's story . . . was a feverish fantasy about making gold," the doctor recorded gravely in his notes.

The doctor exchanged glances with the secretary, prescribed a few potions, and departed. The secretary, who later wrote down his version of events, suggested to the dying man that a pastor come to give him the last sacraments.

"Fool, what should I confess?" the philosopher scoffed. "I have stolen or taken from no one."

The secretary reminded his master that he would soon pass into eternity.

"Also are other men mortal."

The secretary left his master for the evening.

On the following evening, the secretary heard a noise in the philosopher's chamber. He rushed in to find the patient attempting to burn some papers in the candle flame. The exhausted philosopher closed his eyes and sank into his secretary's arms.

The secretary pleaded with him once again to accept the sacraments.

The philosopher opened his eyes wide but said nothing.

"Does my lord not recognize me?" the frightened assistant asked.

The philosopher opened his eyes wider. "I know you very well," he said calmly. He asked for his nightgown, and the secretary yelled for the coachman to bring it.

As the secretary struggled to pull the robe on his master's stiff body, the philosopher released a noxious cloud of gas. The smell was so evil that the secretary felt a sharp pain in his head. At last the philosopher relaxed, closed his eyes, and fell into a gentle sleep.

Leibniz died one hour later, at 10:00 P.M. on Saturday, November 14, 1716.

LEIBNIZ'S SOLE HEIR, his nephew Friedrich Simon Loeffler, arrived twelve days later, just in time for the official inquest. The examiners found among the deceased's possessions a large number of valuable books, a trove of manuscripts and letters, the arithmetical calculating machine, and a little black box. Inside the box they found cash and securities valued at over 12,000 thalers. When Loeffler's wife heard the news, she was so astounded at their sudden good fortune that she fell to the floor in a frenzy and died of joy.

Eckhart took upon himself the funeral arrangements. He commissioned an elaborate coffin and issued invitations to the entire court of Hanover for the burial on December 14. King George and his friends, as it happens, were vacationing in a nearby hunting lodge, within easy reach of the cemetery.

None attended. No doubt Leibniz's disfavor with the King kept many of the courtiers away. According to Eckhart, though, they declined to attend because they had come to view the philosopher as an unbeliever. The absence of any signs of orthodox belief in his last hours, it seems, marked no change in behavior from the preceding decades. Leibniz never went to church, says Eckhart, despite being harangued on the subject regularly by the local ministers.

As neither the court nor Leibniz's rich and recently widowed heir thought it worth the trouble to memorialize the dead atheist, his remains were interred with little ceremony in an unmarked grave. (Eventually the omission was made good with a simple copper plate, in which is inscribed Ossa Leibnitii [The Bones of Leibniz].) There were no six state carriages or throng of followers such as ushered Spinoza into Hades. According to a young Scottish acquaintance who happened to be in Hanover at the time, the funeral rites were so meager that "you would have thought it was a felon they were burying, instead of a man who had been an ornament to his country."

The Berlin Society of the Sciences allowed its founder's death to pass unremarked, as did the Royal Society of London. Eventually, the Royal Academy of Paris, at the insistence of the Duchess of Orléans, made space for Fontenelle's belated eulogy of the great philosopher.

Leibniz affected hundreds of lives during his seventy years; and even the harshest judgment of his career must allow that his work in furthering the sciences and arts has been of indirect benefit to countless millions more. Yet, to judge by his funeral, it would seem that he died, like a windowless monad, having touched no one very deeply at all.

18

Aftermath

Justice is no more assured in the history of thought than it is in the rest of human experience. In the crucial half century after his death—the crucible of modernity—Spinoza was arguably the most important philosopher in the world. Yet, his influence was mostly negative and almost always unacknowledged. The incalculable impact he had on Leibniz is only one example, albeit the finest, of the immense but nearly invisible power Spinoza wielded over his contemporaries.

Eventually, of course, the tide of history turned in Spinoza's favor, and the ideas first expressed in the *Tractatus Theologico-Politicus* and the *Opera Posthuma* suddenly became as ubiquitous as water. Other writers inevitably waded in, however, and claimed credit for having discovered the ocean. Soon, the old controversies were forgotten, and the new historians mistook the earlier, malign suppression of Spinoza for a form of benign neglect. The philosopher of The Hague, they concluded, vanished from history shortly after his death, his works read by few and understood by almost none. Even the omnipresent Leibniz, they noted, had little to say about the fellow philosopher with whom he had the pleasure of conversing for a few days in November 1676.

Leibniz was no more fortunate in his posthumous fate than his rival. In the years immediately following the great monadologist's demise, a young professor of mathematics named Christian Wolf found public favor in Germany with a shelf-bending series of works that were said to be inspired by Leibniz. Sadly, the Leibnizian-Wolfian philosophy, as it came to be called, mainly served to provide ample evidence in support of the truism that none can wreak more damage on a philosopher's reputation than his own followers. Wolf's philosophical works, as the Germans realized somewhat after the rest of Europe, were exceeded in their volume only by their banality. Wolf managed to replicate most of the absurdities of the system of the pre-established harmony while removing all of the original author's elegance and panache.

In early years of the Enlightenment, Leibniz achieved popularity as the spokesperson of a soft-core version of the new faith in reason. In the eyes of many, his *Theodicy* in particular seemed to promise a happy third way between the hard truths of science and the seemingly outmoded doctrines of orthodox belief. Unfortunately, popularity brought scrutiny, and scrutiny soon led to scorn. With Spinoza largely forgotten and the profound nature of the challenge he represented still poorly understood, Leibniz's metaphysical system baffled most of its readers. Like a dialogue with every other line removed, the monadology lay exposed to incomprehension and ridicule, which it promptly received in undue measure. In England, where resentments over the priority dispute with Newton still festered, Leibniz became the butt of satire from wits such as Jonathan Swift. The unkindest cuts, however, came from France. "Can you really maintain that a drop of urine is an infinity of monads, and that each one of these has ideas, however obscure, of the entire universe?" scoffed Voltaire.

As the Enlightenment stumbled through revolution and reaction, both Leibniz and Spinoza emerged from obscurity in strange new incarnations. Spinoza's most popular and enduring persona dates from an evening in 1765 when Gotthold Ephraim Lessing picked up a dusty copy of the *Opera Posthuma* and discovered between its covers a mystical pantheist. The most infamous atheist of the seventeenth century became the "God-intoxicated man" of Novalis. Even today, the dreamy, reclusive spiritualist dominates the public image of Spinoza. The political revolutionary who sought to overthrow theological tyranny and deconstruct the very idea of spirituality has long been forgotten.

The battered ghost of Leibniz found new life, too—in a pair of separate and curiously incompatible incarnations. On the one hand, the author of the *Monadology* was celebrated as a "literary" philosopher, the inventor of "the unconscious," and the purveyor of a magical and romantic vision that could take us well beyond the limits of scientific rationality. On the other hand, somewhat later, Leibniz was hailed as a pioneering logician. Russell and others who sought to place the study of logic at the foundation of philosophy claimed to see in Leibniz's metaphysics an astonishingly prescient and coherent application of fundamental principles of logic.

In the histories of philosophy that dominate the trade, it was Immanuel Kant who sealed the fate of the two greatest philosophers of the seventeenth century. In his effort to tame philosophy into a discipline suitable for the modern academy, Kant trained his attention on the methods whereby philosophers purported to justify their claims to knowledge. He divided his immediate predecessors into two groups: the empiricists, who allegedly relied on sense experience to base their claims to knowledge, and the rationalists, who were said to derive their truths from pure reason. According to Kant's peculiar scheme, Leibniz and Spinoza wound up playing on the same side of history. Together with Descartes—the man Leibniz loathed and Spinoza regarded as seriously confused—they became the three rationalists. Leading the empiricist opposition was John Locke—the same whom Leibniz regarded as a wobbly crypto-Spinozist. He was joined by the Irish philosopher George Berkeley, whose view that physical objects are only ideas in the head strikes most readers as distinctly unempirical, and David Hume, whose ideas about the mind and causality look remarkably like those of Spinoza.

Hegel, who very much liked to see history move along in groups of three, strongly championed Kant's version of events; and the British, who were pleased to see a trio of their greatest philosophers of the period lined up against three continental musketeers, were more than happy to go along with the story, too. As a result, in philosophy classes to the present, where irony tends to be a scarce commodity in any case, Spinoza and the man who dedicated his life to expunging Spinoza's name from the world's memory are presented as happy partners on the same side of a debate about the epistemological foundations of academic philosophy. Only very recently have scholars begun to rescue Leibniz and Spinoza from the revisionist schemes of their philosophical successors.

In the conventional histories of philosophy, Leibniz and Spinoza ultimately fall victim not to progress but to the idea of progress—an idea that first gained currency toward the end of the eighteenth century and that has since been taken up with gusto by all those who have a stake in presenting philosophy as a respectable, quasi-scientific discipline. Once we set aside suspect narratives of the history, however, it becomes clear that, far from being left behind by their modern successors, Leibniz and Spinoza remain unsurpassed today as representatives of humankind's radically divided response to the set of experiences we call modernity. Much of modern thought simply wanders in the space between the two extremes represented by the men who met in The Hague in 1676.

The active response to modernity inaugurated by Spinoza has supplied the basic theory for the modern, liberal political order, as well as the underpinnings of modern science. Its aim is to show us how to be moral in a secular society, and how to seek wisdom where nothing is certain. In its religious or mystical moments, it is the experience of a new kind of divinity—or perhaps the revival of one that was lost to the western world during the period of theocratic rule. Its effects are easily discerned even in thinkers who publicly derided Spinoza—Locke, Hume, Voltaire, and Nietzsche, to name some examples.

And yet, although the world we live in is perhaps better and more originally described by Spinoza, the reactive form of modernity that began with Leibniz has in fact become the dominant form of modern philosophy. Anxious over the apparent purposelessness of the world revealed by modern science; bitter about the threatened demotion of humankind from its special place in nature; alienated from a society that seems to recognize no transcendent goals; and unwilling to assume personal responsibility for happiness—a needy humankind has reinvented the Leibnizian philosophy with abandon over the past three centuries.

Kant's attempt to prove the existence of a "noumenal" world of pure selves and things in themselves on the basis of a critique of pure reason; the nineteenth-century-spanning efforts to reconcile teleology with mechanism that began with Hegel; Bergson's claim to have discovered a world of life forces immune to the analytical embrace of modern science; Heidegger's call for the overthrow of western metaphysics in order to recover the truth about Being; and the whole "postmodern" project of deconstructing the phallogocentric tradition of western thought—all of these diverse trends in modern thought have one thing in common: they are at bottom forms of the reaction to modernity first instantiated by Leibniz.

All begin with the conviction that there is some vital aspect of experience which escapes modern thought. All maintain that the purpose of life begins where modernity ends. All claim to discover the special and elusive meaning of existence through an analysis of the putative failures of modern thought. And all remain indissolubly attached to precisely that which they oppose.

Leibniz's latter-day followers call the extramodern mystery at the core of existence any number of names: Being, Becoming, Life, the Absolute, the Will, nonlinear rationality, and more. But it is no different in principle from what Leibniz calls the principle of activity, the immortal soul, and, finally, the monad. The modern Leibnizians produce an equally diverse set of labels for that to which they are opposed: mechanism, instrumental reason, the Enlightenment, western metaphysics, phallogocentrism, and so on. But their nemeses are in the end the same thing that Leibniz calls materialism, the philosophy of the moderns, "the opinions of certain recent innovators," or, in moments of clarity, Spinozism.

LIKE ALL GOOD philosophers, Leibniz and Spinoza must eventually come to a rest somewhere outside of history. The two men who met in 1676 in fact represent a pair of radically different philosophical personality types that have always been part of the human experience. Spinoza speaks for those who believe that happiness and virtue are possible with nothing more than what we have in our hands. Leibniz stands for those convinced that happiness and virtue depend on something that lies beyond. Spinoza counsels calm attention to our own deepest good. Leibniz expresses that irrepressible longing to see our good works reflected back to us in the praise of others. Spinoza affirms the totality of things such as it is. Leibniz is that part of us that ceaselessly strives to make us something more than what we are. Without doubt, there is a little piece of each in everybody; equally certain is the fact that, at times, a choice must be made.

Leibniz was a man whose failings were writ as large as his outsized virtues. Yet it was his greed, his vanity, and above all, his insatiable, all too human neediness that made his work so emblematic for the species. With the promise that the cruel surface of experience conceals a most pleasing and beautiful truth, a world in which everything happens for a reason and all is for the best, the glamorous courtier of Hanover made himself into the philosopher of the common man. If Spinoza was the first great thinker of the modern era, then perhaps Leibniz should count as its first human being.

Spinoza, on the other hand, was marked from the start as a *rara avis*. Given his eerie self-sufficiency, his inhuman virtue, and his contempt for the multitudes, it could not have been otherwise. Yet the message of his philosophy is not that we know all that there is to know; but rather that there is nothing that cannot be known. Spinoza's teaching is that there is no unfathomable mystery in the world; no other-world accessible only through revelation or epiphany; no hidden power capable of judging or affirming us; no secret truth about everything. There is instead only the slow and steady accumulation of many small truths; and the most important of these is that we need expect nothing more in order to find happiness in this world. His is a philosophy for philosophers, who are as uncommon now as they have always been.

Notes

Full biographical information for most sources cited in these notes can be found in the following section. For lists of abbreviations used for primary texts, see pages 332–33. Thus, for example, in the first note below the source is *Gottfried Wilhelm Leibniz: Sämtliche Schriften und Briefe* ("A"), series II, volume 1, page 535.

1. The Hague, November 1676

11   "the most impious . . .": Antoine Arnauld, cited by Leibniz in A II.i.535.

11   "that insane and evil man . . .": Bishop Pierre-Daniel Huet, cited in Friedmann, p. 204.

11   "horrible" and "terrifying": A II.i.172.

11   "intolerably impudent": To Thomasius, A II.i.66.

11   "I deplore that a man . . .": A I.i.148.

12   "When one . . . compares one's own small talents . . .": Diderot, *Encyclopédie*.

12   "It is so rare for an intellectual . . .": Orléans, p. 282.

12   His limbs, it was said: For these and other colorful descriptions of Leibniz in person, see Guhrauer, especially the final chapter.

12   "He is a man who, despite . . .": Klopp ii.125; Müller, pp. 27ff.

13   "I love this man . . .": Sophia Charlotte, cited in Guhrauer ii.248.

13   "To be a follower of Spinoza . . .": Hegel, iii.257.

13   he famously replied: "I believe in Spinoza's God": Clark, pp. 413ff.

13   "well-formed body": Freudenthal, p. 3.

13   "beautiful face": Freudenthal, p. 59.

13   "pleasing physiognomy": Freudenthal, p. 237; see also Nadler (1999), p. 155.

13   "so that one might easily know . . .": Freudenthal, p. 59.

14   "a few hours": To Ernst von Hessen-Rheinfels, A II.i.535.

14   "anecdotes concerning the affairs of those times": *Theodicy*, sec. 376.

14   "waste time in refuting": *Theodicy*, sec. 173.

14   "many times and at great length": To Gallois, A II.i.379.

15   "You know that I once went a little too far . . .": A VI.vi.73.

2. Bento

18   "the kind of monster . . .": Limborch, cited in Meinsma (1909) p. 532.

19   For the history of Jews in Spain and Portugal, see Nadler (2003) and Raphael.

19   "in a free and unimpeded way": See Nadler (1999) and (2003) on the Portuguese Inquisition.

20   Isaac's in-laws: For Spinoza family history, see especially Gullan-Whur.

21   "the most beautiful city in Europe": Freudenthal, p. 3.

21   "love nothing so much as their freedom": Israel (1995), pp. 1ff.

21   "It is hardly to be imagined . . .": Temple, p. 106.

21   "This *simulacrum* of liberty . . .": A IV.i.357ff.

23   "From Spain came the Portuguese Jews . . . ": A IV.i.358, 357.

23   "Ritch merchants, not evill esteem'd off . . .": Gullan-Whur, p. 8.

24   "I saw giants in scholarship . . .": Nadler (1999), p. 61.

24   "Nature endowed him . . .": Freudenthal, p. 36

24   "He was not yet fifteen . . .": Freudenthal, p. 24.

25   When he was around ten: Freudenthal, p. 20.

25   "a celebrity among the Jews . . .": Freudenthal, p. 4.

26   the offending rabbi off to Brazil: See Nadler (1999) and (2003) for interesting detail on Morteira and the Jewish community in Amsterdam.

26   "He admired the conduct . . .": Freudenthal, p. 4.

26   "not at all vain . . .": Freudenthal, p. 4.

28   four hundred establishments: Durant and Durant.

28   "She was rather frail . . .": Freudenthal, p. 37.

29   "it was a pity . . .": Freudenthal, p. 9.

29   "That nothing ought to be admitted . . .": Freudenthal, p. 39.

30   "under the age of twenty": Freudenthal, p. 4.

30   "one cannot decently avoid . . .": Freudenthal, p. 5.

30   "How does it appear . . .": Freudenthal, p. 5.

31   "had nothing but hatred . . .": Freudenthal, p. 6.

31   an attempt was made: Freudenthal, p. 29ff., 41.

33   "Whether he was mindful . . .": Freudenthal, p. 8.

33   "I am aware . . .": Paraphrase of Freudenthal, p. 8.

33   "The lords of the Mahamad . . .": Freudenthal, pp. 115ff.

35   "I enter gladly . . .": Freudenthal, p. 8.

35   "Since we have the rare good fortune . . .": TTP Pref.

36   "that odd philosopher . . .": Oldenburg, ii.549.

36   The blue-blooded physicist Christiaan Huygens: Freudenthal, p. 191.

37   ". . . all the notions whereby . . .": E I Ap; cf. also TTP 6.

37   "I know it in the same way . . .": L 76.

37   "courteous and obliging": Freudenthal, p. 60.

37   "his knowledge, his modesty, and his unselfishness": Freudenthal, p. 237.

3. Gottfried

40   as the historian Lewis White Beck: Beck, pp. 196ff.

41   Gottfried first distinguished himself when he was three days old: For this and following citations from Leibniz's personal recollections, see Guhrauer, xii.appendix.

42   "I preferred books to games": Müller, pp. 6ff.

43   "The 'foretaste' of the history of philosophy . . .": A II.i.14.

44   "already equal to the investigation . . .": A VI.i.5.

47   "I expressed my thoughts . . .": Recollections in Guhrauer, ii.appendix.

49   "Being familiar with the whole history of philosophy . . .": Müller, p. 13; A I.i.8.

49   "A true friend desires his friend's good . . .": A IV.i.34.

52   "the very hills skipped like lambs for delight . . .": A VI.iii.152ff.

53   "I believed it unworthy . . .": See Fischer, p. 46.

53   "The human mind cannot rest . . .": A IV.i.179.

4. A Life of the Mind

55   "Jew who is an impudent atheist": Nadler (1999), p. 158.

58   "The masses can scarcely imagine . . .": E IV Ap 28.

59   "Those who know the true value of money . . .": E IV Ap 29.

59   "gruel made with raisins . . .": Freudenthal, p. 58.

59   "plain and common" and that "he paid . . .": Freudenthal, p. 61.

59   "which usually dintinguishes . . .": Freudenthal, p. 17.

59   "the affectation of negligence . . .": Freudenthal, p. 17.

59   "My relatives shall inherit nothing from me . . .": Freudenthal, p. 59.

60   "the Israelite achieves an admirable polish": Freudenthal, p. 191.

61   "it is not out of necessity . . .": L 44.

62   "in harmony with reason": E IV Ap 20.

62   "our philosopher was not . . .": Freudenthal, p. 23.

63   "it is part of the wise man to recreate . . .": E IV P45 C2 Sch.

63   "Things are good only insofar . . .": E IV Ap 5.

63   "late-night studies": L 9.

64   "love of solitude": Freudenthal, p. 16.

64   "never quitted his solitude . . .": Freudenthal, p. 16.

64   "his most intimate friends . . .": Freudenthal, p. 12.

65   "a great many friends . . .": Freudenthal, p. 57.

65   "filles de qualité . . .": Freudenthal, p. 195.

65   "His conversations had such . . .": Freudenthal, pp. 22ff.

66   "The free man who lives among the ignorant . . .": E IV P70.

66   "there is nothing in nature more useful . . .": E IV P35 C2 Sch.

66   "Man is a God to Man": E IV P35 C1.

66   he defines "honorable": E IV P37 Sch1.

67   "a man good to associate with . . .": Freudenthal, p. 31.

67   "Your religion is all right . . .": Freudenthal, p. 61.

67   "As for our group . . .": L 8.

68   "Either Adam's forbidden act . . .": L 18.

68   "I gather . . . that you are deeply devoted": L 19.

69   "I hardly believe that our correspondence . . .": L 21.

70   "I hope that when you have thought the matter over . . .": L 27.

70   "a book full of studious abominations . . .": Freudenthal, p. 75.

72   "With such reluctance did I recently tear myself away . . .": L 1.

72   "I would by all means urge you . . .": L 7; L 11.

72   "entertains me with a discourse . . .": Oldenburg ii.549.

72   "a certain odd philosopher": Freudenthal, p. 190.

73   "Atheists are usually inordinately fond . . .": L 43.

5. God's Attorney

76   "They are those who honor God . . .": A IV.i.535ff. On the inter-
      pretation of Leibniz's political philosophy, I am greatly indebted to
      Riley and have paraphrased some of his arguments, albeit in
      reduced form.

78   "conciliatory eclectic": Mercer, pp. 23ff.

78   "I have been astounded by a new system . . .": *New Essays*, G V.64.

79   "mother of all my inventions": A II.i.160.

79   "It seems to me, as I have told Your Excellency . . .": A II.i.489.

80   same thing as "the Empire of Reason": See PW, p. 107.

81   "I do not see anything that is more important . . .": A I.iii.273.

86   "There is nothing, I think, . . .": A II.i.172.

87   "I know of no one who has philosophized . . .": A II.i.58.

87   "Pardon that an unknown one . . .": A II.i.59.

88   "Bubbles are the seeds . . .": G IV.184ff.

88   the product of "proud ignorance": See Hofmann, pp. 24ff., and
      Loemker.

89   a letter he addressed to his future employer: A II.i.159ff.

89   so obese that he rarely moved: See Hirsch, pp. 104, 119.

91   "I can suggest much to others . . .": Letter to Placcius, September
      5, 1695; cited in Guhrauer.

92   "is the most knowledgeable and powerful city in the universe": A
      I.vii.638.

94   "We must always adapt ourselves . . .": Klopp vi.188.

6. The Hero of the People

96   "It wo'd stumble any one's belief . . .": James Howell, preface to
      Giraffi.

97   a portfolio of charcoal: Freudenthal, p. 56.

97   "a certain . . . Spinosa, born of Jewish parents . . .": Freudenthal, pp.
      118ff.

98   "The prejudices of the theologians . . .": L 30.

98   the Koerbagh brothers: Cf. Meinsma and especially Israel (2001)
      for excellent detail on the Koerbagh story; also Freudenthal, pp.
      119ff.

100   "the supreme mystery of despotism . . .": TTP Pr.

101   "the dispelling of ignorance would entail . . .": E I Ap.

101   "The more every man endeavors and is able . . .": E IV P20.

101   "To act in absolute conformity with virtue . . .": E IV P24.

103   "If he knew that [the doctrines of faith] were false . . .": TTP 14.

104   "the same be seized and suppressed . . .": For analysis of this and following quotes, see especially Israel (2001), pp. 276, 228, 284.

104   "the most vile and sacrilegious . . .": Freudenthal, p. 122.

105   "would deserve to be covered . . .": For this and following, see Friedmann, p. 204.

105   "mightily in vogue among many": See Israel (2001), p. 284.

105   "All the strong spirits . . .": Freudenthal, p. 30.

105   "In the humble and pensive solitary . . .": Cited in Hazard, p. 127.

105   "for it is not for nothing . . .": Reynier van Mansvelt, *Adversus anonymum theologico-politicum* (1674), cited in Friedman, p. 205.

106   "could not live in security . . .": Freudenthal, pp. 22ff.

106   "The virtue of a free man . . .": E IV P69.

107   "no virtue can be conceived prior . . .": E IV P22.

7. The Many Faces of Leibniz

110   "You have treated this intolerably impudent work . . .": A II.i.66.

110   "last year was published a most pestilent book . . .": A I.i.142.

110   "I have read Spinoza's book . . .": A I.i.148.

111   "the terrifying work . . .": A II.i.172ff.

111   "Mr. Spinoza, celebrated doctor and profound philosopher, at Amsterdam": L 45.

112   "Mr. Dimerbruck [*sic*] does not live here . . .": L 46.

112   "paid great attention to your . . .": L 70.

112   "I believe I know Leibniz through correspondence . . .": L 72.

112   On the back of a recently discovered copy: Paper delivered by Ursula Goldenbaum at The Young Leibniz Conference, Rice University, Houston, April 2003.

113   "The author of the book . . .": A II.i.205.

113   "The Jew Spinoza, who bears . . .": A II.i.193.

113   "That Spinoza is the author . . .": A II.i.208.

114   "You have seen without doubt the book . . .": A I.i.193.

115   "there is a Supreme Being who loves . . .": TTP 14.

115   letter to a friend named Magnus Wedderkopf: A II.i.117.

115   "whatever occurs does so through God's . . .": TTP 6.

116   "For it is necessary . . .": A II.i.117.

117   "The more I got to know Leibniz . . .": Hirsch, p. 11.

117   "It is always risky to speculate on motives . . .": Rescher, p. 160.

118   a much more complex phenomenon that deserves the name "multiplicity": Friedmann suggests as much.

118   "all things to all men": Beck, p. 240.

119   The real author of the letter, of course, was Leibniz: A I.i.251ff.

8. Friends of Friends

121   "this is a most neat place in all respects": Samuel Pepys, *Diaries* (Berkeley: University of California Press, 1970) vol. 1, 14 May 1660.

122   "two-penny pieces": See Gullan-Whur, p. 248.

122   "He told me that on the day . . .": Freudenthal, p. 201.

123   the visiting heretic was also seen chatting: Freudenthal, p. 30.

123   "a very bad Jew and hardly a better Christian": Freudenthal, p. 195.

123   "since there is nothing so deceitful . . .": Freudenthal, p. 22.

124   "Fear nothing . . .": Freudenthal, p. 65.

126   Little is known about Schuller. For details on Schuller, see Steenbakkers, pp. 51ff.

127   "Even if I were the follower . . .": See Nadler (1999), p. 329, and *Studia Leibnitiana* (1981), pp. 61–75.

127   "queer impression": L 63.

127   "to return to a most trustworthy . . .": L 63.

128   "At the time some things seemed . . .": L 61.

128   "anything that may seem in any way . . .": L 62.

129   "While I was engaged in this business . . .": L 68.

129   "work to discover exactly as possible . . .": Freudenthal, pp.148, 152.

130   "showed his irreligious character . . .": Meinsma, p. 532.

130   "I see at last what it was . . .": L 75.

131   "the death and burial of Christ . . .": L 78.

131   "To seek to turn all this . . .": L 79.

9. Leibniz in Love

132   Paris came of age in the seventeenth century. See Bernard, Sauval, Lister, and Lough.

134   "black, stinking, of an intolerable odor to strangers": For this and following descriptions of Paris, see Bernard, p. 197.

136   "I believe I will always be an amphibian": A I.i.445.

136   It was one of those ages: See Durant and Durant.

136   "I speak in Parisian, as you can see": A I.i.397.

136   "He is a man who . . .": Klopp ii.125; Müller, pp. 27ff.

137   "being impelled by the instinct of *delectatio*": G I.57.

138   "It is necessary to snare the world . . .": A IV.i.567.

138   "There is in France a great freedom . . .": PW, p. 157.

141   greeted him with "great applause": A II.i.230.

142   "Please allow me to advise you . . .": A III.i.533ff.

143   "As it is from grand princes . . .": A I.i.504.

143   "excellent people": A II.i.230.

143   "Never has a foreigner . . .": Friedmann, p. 193.

143   "Paris is a place where it is difficult . . .": A I.i.491.

144   "the liberality of princes . . .": A I.i.400ff.

146   "Having by my labor and the grace of God . . .": A I.i.428.

148   "A man like me . . .": A I.i.492.

149   "there is here [in Paris] an infinity . . .": A I.i.417.

151   a letter of introduction from Henry Oldenburg: A III.i.275.

151   "Sending Tschirnhaus to us . . .": A III.i.327ff.

151   "There arrived a young man . . .": LoC, p. 131.

151   "habit of stealing things": GM ii.51, 130, 233.

152   dismissed it all as mere playing with symbols: GM i.375.

152   "established a close friendship . . .": L 70.

154   "I believe I know Leibniz . . .": L 72.

154   he sent off a letter to Jean-Baptiste Colbert: A I.i.505.

155   "Tschirnhaus has told me . . .": A VI.iii.384; LoC, p. 40.

10. A Secret Philosophy . . .

156   "Spinosa's book will be about God . . .": A VI.iii.384; LoC, p. 40.

156   a single sheet of paper: Friedmann would disagree. He maintains
        that Leibniz's summary of Spinoza from Tschirnhaus here shows he
        understood little of Spinoza's thought. I think Friedmann is simply
        wrong on this point.

157   "the theory that it is all arranged . . .": Quoted by Steven Wein-
        berg, *New York Review of Books*, Oct. 21, 1999.

158   "I do not differentiate between . . .": L 6.

159   "is the immanent cause of things . . .": L 73; E I P18.

159   "All things, I say, . . .": L 73; cf. E I P15.

160   "deified the All . . .": Nietzsche iii.512.

160   "Things could not have been produced . . .": E I P33.

162   "God gives no laws to mankind . . .": ST ii.24.

162   "to ascribe to God those attributes . . .": L 23.

162   "If a triangle could speak . . .": L 56.

163   "I know it in the same way . . .": L 76.

166   "Such is the view of this illustrious man . . .": E V Pref.

167   "They appear to go so far . . .": E III Pref.; cf. also TP ii.6.

167   "Man is a part of Nature . . .": ST ii.18.

168   "Thinking substance and extended substance . . .": E II P7 Sch.

168   "Mental decision on the one hand . . .": E III P2 Sch.

169   "Nobody as yet has learned . . .": E III P2 Sch.

169   "In proportion as a body . . .": E II P13 C Sch.

171   If a stone tossed in the air: E I Ap; L 58.

171   we have particular volitions: E II P49.

171   "only an idea of our willing . . .": ST ii.16.

171   The mind does not know itself: E II P23.

171   the idea of each modification of the body: E II P27.

172   "the human mind . . . has not an adequate . . .": E II P29.

173   "You will not be able to deny . . .": L 76.

174   "I shall consider human actions . . .": E III Pref.

174   "Pleasure" is the state: E III P11.

175   "Nothing but grim and gloomy superstition . . .": E IV P45 Sch.

176   the more we seek our own interest: E IV P20.

176   "Hence we clearly understand . . .": E II P49 Sch.

176   "Insofar as we understand . . .": E IV Ap32.

177   "the human mind cannot be . . .": E V P33.

179   "It cannot be said that God . . .": ST ii.24.

179   "He who loves God cannot endeavor . . .": E V P19.

180   "Gradually it has become clear to me . . .": Nietzsche, iii.571
       (*Beyond Good and Evil*, i.6).

11. Approaching Spinoza

183   *The Elements of a Secret Philosophy*: A VI.iii.473; DSR, p. 22.

184   "There seems to be . . .": A VI.iii.474; DSR, p. 24.

185   "God is not something metaphysical . . .": A VI.iii.474; DSR, p. 26.

185   In a letter of February 28, the Duke's secretary: A I.i.510.

186   "fourteen days . . .": A I.i.512.

186   "Is the mind the idea . . .": A VI.iii.518; DSR, p. 74; also A
       VI.iii.510; DSR, p. 60.

186   "It seems to me that the origin of things . . .": A VI.iii.518; DSR,
       p. 76.

187   "figure and motion" from "extension, taken in an absolute sense":
       L 82.

188   The secretary to the Duke was now flatly mystified: A I.i.515ff.

188   On September 26, the Hanoverian ambassador: A I.i.516ff.; A I.ii.3.

189   "certain metaphysical mysteries . . .": A VI.iii.570; LoC, p. 219.

190   "my old design of a rational writing . . .": Cited in Friedmann, p. 78.

191   "I seem to have discovered . . .": A VI.iii.572ff.; DSR, pp. 90ff.

191   "[Spinoza] defines God . . .": A VI.iii.384.

191   "It can be easily . . .": A VI.iii.573.

192   "If only those things . . .": A VI.iii.573.

192   "One could say: all things are one . . .": G i.129.

193   "A metaphysics should . . .": A VI.iii.573ff.

194   "You know I went a little . . .": A VI.vi.73.

12. Point of Contact

196   "many times and at great length": To Gallois, A II.i.379.

197   "Spinoza did not see . . .": Freudenthal, p. 201.

198   "The famous Jew Spinoza . . .": Freudenthal, p. 220.

198   "that discerning Jew": A VI.vi.455.

198   "says what he believes . . .": A II.i.535.

198   "I know that there are people . . .": A VI.vi.462.

198   "It can be acknowledged . . .": A VI.vi.462.

199   "That a Most Perfect Being Exists": A II.i.271ff.; A VI.iii.578ff.;
       DSR, p. 100.

13. Surviving Spinoza

204   "I will have made the trip at my own expense": A I.ii.10.

204   "I may not now dream only of living . . .": A I.ii.13.

204   the philosopher told his friends, it was well worth it: A II.i.378.

204   To Tschirnhaus he confided: Cited in Müller, p. 51.

205   Leibniz also had no shortage of ideas: A I.ii.74ff.

207   he designed a unique system: Cf. A I.iii.35–45, 47–48.

207   "If all possibles were to exist . . .": A VI.iii.581ff.; DSR, pp. 102ff.

207   added some additional notes in the margins: To my knowledge, the
       two sets of notes (in different ink) are not dated; so my placing the
       second set after November 1676 is speculative.

208   "If all things emanate of necessity . . .": G i.124.

208   reply of February 6, 1677: A II.i.303ff.

208   "Why you have not delivered . . .": Freudenthal, p. 202.

209   "I fear that [Spinoza] will not . . .": A II.i.303.

212   "After [Spinoza] gave orders . . .": See Steenbakkers, p. 58.

212   "before and after [Spinoza's] death . . .": A II.i.382.

213   "God willing, I shall give you . . .": See Steenbakkers, p. 60.

213   "It seems that death . . .": A II.i.304.

214   "I am greatly relieved . . .": A II.i.304.

215   "I was vexed to discover . . .": Cited in Friedmann, p. 139.

215   "a rather mean spirit": A II.i.500.

215   "It seems that Mr. Leibnits wishes . . .": G iv.333.

215   "nor do I approve of his dangerous idea . . .": A II.i.306.

216   The editors carried out their feverish labors: See Israel (2001) for more detail.

216   he plotted a secret journey to Amsterdam: A I.ii.272; A III.ii.118; Müller, p. 49.

217   "Spinoza died this winter . . .": A II.i.379.

217   "What Spinoza says about the certainty . . .": A II.i.301.

218   takes pains to calm: A II.i.382.

219   "the letter is no danger to you . . .": A II.i.405.

219   "The Posthumous Works of the late M. Spinosa . . .": A II.i.393.

219   "How much better and more true are the Christian ones": A II.i.394.

220   "empty, pretentious device": For Leibniz's marginalia on the *Ethics*, see G i.122ff.

220   "When I considered . . .": PPL pp. 404ff.

221   "these new lights . . .": A VI.vi.73.

222   "had a certain self-effacement . . .": For this and following, see PPL, p. 338.

224   "If matter assumes all forms possible successively . . .": A II.i.505ff.

224   "is nothing but a chimera . . .": A II.i.501.

225   "Descartes thinks in a whisper . . .": Friedmann, p. 118. See also G iv.346: Descartes's philosophy "leads straight to the sentiments of Spinoza."

225   "immortality without memory": A II.i.502.

225   "One hopes that [Leibniz] will return . . .": G iv.333.

225   "I would never have mentioned . . .": G iv.341.

225   pension of 1,200 thalers: A I.ii.200–203.

225   "I have the affair of the windmill . . .": A I.ii.188.

226   The philosopher promised Ernst August: A I.iii.44.

226   From 1680 to 1686, he made: A I.iii.xix.

226   "that in this business all mathematical speculations . . .": A I.iii.xxxix.

226   "own interest, and not that of the mines": A I.iii.109.

227   "a dangerous man and evil to deal with": A I.iii.66–80; Hirsch, p. 151.

227   letter to Count Ernst von Hessen-Rheinfels of August 14, 1683. A II.ii.535.

14. The Antidote to Spinozism

233   His contract, he insists, says nothing: A I.iv.xlff., 176ff.

233   Leibniz complained that the engineers would listen: A I.iv.259ff.

237   "God has chosen that world which is most perfect": *Discourse on Metaphysics* 6; PPL, p. 470.

237   "The halls rose . . .": *Theodicy*, sec. 416.

238   "Because of the interconnection . . .": G ii.42.

238   "The reasons for the world lie in something extramundane": PPL, p. 790.

241   "a small divinity and eminently a universe . . ." TI ii.554; cited in Riley.

242   "My view is that every substance . . .": PE, p. 280; Friedmann, p. 175.

245   "the principle of macrocosm and microcosm": WoC, p. 117.

250   "Justice is that which is useful . . .": Cited in Riley, p. 260.

250   "Provided something of consequence . . .": G vii.456.

251   "are the largest part of nature": TTP 6.

251   "We must also recognize that . . .": PPL, p. 797.

251   "All this, I acknowledge . . .": LCC, p. 109.

251   "a fascinating fairy tale . . .": Russell, p. xvii.

252   "Leibniz's philosophy appears like a string . . .": Hegel, iii.330.

253   "Spinoza thinks that the mind . . .": PE, p. 280.

253   "destroy the confidence in God . . .": *Theodicy*, sec. 177.

15. The Haunting

256   "I can't tell you how distracted . . .": Letter to Placcius, September 5, 1695, cited in Guhrauer.

257   "admirable" and "completely in accord with reason": See Israel (2001), p. 84.

258   "most of the human . . .": Israel (2001), p. 84.

258   "Do not torment me . . .": Aiton, p. 266, citing Schnath, p. 572.

258   Leibniz became so comfortable in the company: See Hirsch, p. 415.

259   "Although he is more . . .": Cited in Guhrauer.

260   "I saw M. de la Court . . .": *Theodicy*, sec. 376.

260   "I wrote to him one time . . .": Freudenthal, p. 220.

261   "I find in these thoughts . . .": G ii.15.

262   "He has some opinions on physics . . .": A I.iv.443; G ii.110.

263   "And so we get a clear idea . . .": Cited in Hazard, p. 199.

264   "I admire the solidity of your judgment . . .": A I.xiv.741; also cited in Riley, p. 239.

266   "We have the Ideas of Matter . . .": Locke, *Essay Concerning Human Understanding*, IV.iii.6.

266   ". . . destroys what appears to me . . .": A VI.vi.48n.

267   "I am above all concerned . . .": G iii.473; also cited in Jolley (1984), p. 102. Jolley makes a strong case that Leibniz's central goal in the *New Essays* was to defend the doctrine of the immaterial, naturally immortal soul. My only additional claim is that the attack from which he wished to defend this doctrine was an essentially Spinozistic one.

267   "My question in the case . . .": G iii.360.

267   "a notion whose impossibility . . .": A VI.vi.59.

268   "the delights of the human race": PW, pp. 121ff.

269   the Hanoverian cause in England: See Klopp, viii.250ff.

270   "The people are trampled upon without mercy . . .": PW, p. 159.

270   "The worst thing of all. . .": PW, p. 158.

270   "I find that similar ideas . . .": A VI.vi.455.

272   "you, who are a perfect geometer . . .": Hall (1980), p. 109.

272   "As to whether Leibniz . . .": See Hall (1980) and Hofmann for more detail on the quarrel between Newton and Leibniz.

273   As Newton later suspected: Hall (1992), p. 259.

274   "After [admitting the law of attraction] . . .": Leibniz to Hugony, 1714, cited in Jolley (1984), p. 65.

275   the word "China": See WoC, Introduction.

275   "by acquainting them with the true systems . . .": WoC, p. 116.

276   "heterodox and atheistic scholars . . .": WoC, p. 127.

276   "brutish necessity": WoC, p. 128.

276   "spiritual substances": WoC, p. 114.

276   "One could perhaps claim that . . .": WoC, p. 96.

276   Elsewhere Leibniz describes Averroës: *Theodicy*, sec. 9–10.

276   "to ridicule the ridicule": WoC, p. 84.

277   Ruardus Andala: For the early history of the Leibniz-Spinoza affair, see Stein, pp. 3ff.

277   "Here, as elsewhere, Leibniz fell . . .": Russell, p. xi.

278   "On the contrary, it is precisely . . .": G iii.575; PPL, p. 1077.

16. The Return of the Repressed

281   "He who affirms that God . . .": L 54.

281   "everything [is] settled in advance": G vi.107ff., 131.

281   "God's decree . . . is immutable": G vi.445, vi.131, vi.390; GM iii.2, iii.534.

282   "seem to posit something external . . .": E I P33 Sch 2.

282   "*necessity*, in philosophical questions . . .": LCC, p. 99.

282   "The distinction Leibniz here attempts . . .": Lovejoy in Frankfurt, p. 320.

285   "has its causes, but since . . .": TI ii.482; also cited in Riley, p. 77.

285   "men believe they are free . . .": E I Ap.

289   "There is a contradiction present . . .": Hegel, iii.342.

290   Russell alludes to this: Russell, pp. 38, 172.

291   "Pleasure is nothing but . . .": PPL, p. 335.

291   "We will be happier . . .": PPL, p. 431.

291   "Leibniz no longer shows great originality . . .": Russell, p. 5.

17. Leibniz's End

294   "a living dictionary" and "an archaelogical find": Müller, p. 186.

296   Sophia quipped: Klopp ix.415.

296   "The gout is just . . . mixed up in everything": Müller, p. 343.

298   "I suffer from time to time . . .": Du v.428.

299   "a kind of telescope . . .": Jolley (1995), p. 467.

299   "In this philosophy . . .": Euler, *Opera Omnia*, xi.305.

300   "the entire past, and even . . .": TI ii.553.

301   "But it would be necessary . . .": PW, p. 184.

304   "The patient's story . . .": Cited in Guhrauer and in Ritter (1916).

304   The secretary, who later wrote down his version: See Hirsch for full citation.

18. Aftermath

308   "Can you really . . .": Voltaire, *Oeuvres*, xxii.434.

310   Only very recently have scholars: See especially Israel (2001).

A Note on Sources

On the interpretation of Spinoza's philosophy I claim no originality, but the reader should be aware that I have favored a certain shift in emphasis from the consensus view. In contemporary histories, Spinoza tends to be portrayed first and foremost as a metaphysician or "system builder." I have presented him primarily as a political and moral philosopher—one who turned to metaphysical system building as a means of expression rather than an end in itself. In histories of philosophy since the days of Immanuel Kant (including my own, incidentally), Spinoza is typically classified as a "rationalist" (i.e., a philosopher who believes that knowledge derives principally from pure reason, as opposed to sensory experience). Along with a number of other recent commentators (see Mason, for example), I now find this label to be worse than useless; Spinoza was, if anything, closer to the positions of radical empiricism. In his more popular incarnations, Spinoza typically appears as an otherworldly figure, a mystic, or "God-intoxicated man," as the German critic Novalis put it. While I accept that such a view captures an essential aspect of his character, I think it fails entirely to grasp the central lesson of his philosophy.

According to the most widely accepted versions of the history of culture, Spinoza was immediately forgotten upon death, not to be reread until late in the eighteenth century. I take the view that Spinoza was indeed vividly remembered by his contemporaries (not least Leibniz) and hugely influential, if in a clandestine way. On this point I must acknowledge a great debt to Jonathan Israel's recent study, *Radical Enlightenment*, which I cannot recommend highly enough to readers interested in learning more about the period.

Leibniz, too, is traditionally classed as a "rationalist" and therefore lumped together with Spinoza. The label is hardly more illuminating in his case than it is in Spinoza's, and the idea that the two philosophers should share the same label seems especially perverse. In most versions of the history of philosophy, Leibniz never manages to escape Voltaire's satirical representation of him in *Candide* as Dr. Pangloss, the sunny optimist who insists in the face of earthquakes and other calamities that all is for the best in the best of all possible worlds. I have argued, of course, that this caricature of Leibniz as a metaphysical Pollyanna is entirely superficial.

The defining question concerning any interpretation of Leibniz's philosophy, taken independently of Spinoza, is whether it should be classed as an early "modern" one or a gravely tardy "medieval" one. I staunchly defend the view that Leibniz's thought should be regarded as modern, through and through. That having been said, I note that his work represents a species of modern thought best described as "reactive," inasmuch as it involves a characteristically modern repudiation of modernity in the name of values that are imagined to have been realized better in, among other places, the medieval world.

On the interpretation of Leibniz's philosophy, the crucial point on which I differ from most (though not all) commentators, of course, is in the degree of importance I assign to his relationship with Spinoza. Among those who care about such matters, Leibniz's relationship to his predecessor is a particularly fraught subject, and probably no significant statement about it can be made that will not elicit violent disagreement from some quarter. A number of very credible interpreters maintain that Leibniz was Leibniz before he studied or met Spinoza and remained so ever after, and that therefore the link between the two is philosophically inconsequential. Perhaps the majority of observers accept that Leibniz went through a phase in which he sympathized with Spinoza with respect to one particular set of issues, after which he set off on his own, independent course. I am in the minority when I claim that Spinoza was the dominant influence in Leibniz's mature work—although I hasten to add that in my view that influence was overwhelmingly (yet problematically) negative, and that the later Leibniz was certainly never a "Spinozist" in any ordinary sense of that term. I think I am alone in maintaining that the physical meeting between the two philosophers marks the decisive turning point in Leibniz's philosophical development, although I am not alone in locating a significant turning point within the three-year period that begins with the meeting.

• • •

The modern debate about the relationship between Leibniz and Spinoza properly begins with Stein (1890). In the years preceding his visit to The Hague, says Stein, Leibniz was in agreement with Spinoza on all the essential points in philosophy. In the two- to three-year period after The Hague, Stein continues, Leibniz began to move slowly away from his mentor, even while remaining "Spinoza-friendly." Not until 1684, he claims, did Leibniz formulate his mature philosophy and come to the recognition that he could not abide Spinoza.

Stein's analysis was influential, and is cited favorably by Russell, among others. Unfortunately, Stein did not have at his disposal a comprehensive collection of Leibniz's works, and a number of his conclusions wither in the light of evidence now available. Although Leibniz clearly did find something very intriguing in Spinoza's thought in the period before they met, it is simply not true that the two philosophers were in agreement on the essential matters in philosophy. It is even less true to say that Leibniz waited until he was thirty-eight to come up with some of the core ideas of his mature philosophy. Stein's description of the period 1677–1679 as "Spinoza-friendly" seems particularly inapt: this was the time in which Leibniz described Spinoza in notes to himself as "devious" and "obscure," among other things, never mind what he said to correspondents.

Friedmann (1946; 1962) corrected many of the errors in Stein's account and settled the matter to the satisfaction of most scholars. Friedmann maintains that Leibniz developed the core convictions of his philosophy before having met Spinoza and that he saw Spinoza mainly through the somewhat distorting prism of his own interests and preconceptions. The link between the two, Friedmann therefore concludes, is inconsequential: Leibniz "was never a Spinozist." Recently, Christia Mercer has made the same case indirectly. From an exhaustive study of Leibniz's early philosophical works, she concludes that his metaphysical system existed in prototype before he had any contact with Spinoza or his writings; therefore, she argues, Spinoza cannot have had much influence on his thought.

One significant problem for Friedmann's (and by extension, Mercer's) line of interpretation is that Leibniz himself seems not to have agreed with it. In the famous comment in the *New Essays*, after all, Leibniz has his spokesperson Theophile confess that "in another time I went too far and began to lean to the side of the Spinozists." Friedmann deals with this inconvenient piece of evidence by arguing that Leibniz was attributing to the fictional Theophile a philosophical past that was not his own. But this simply will not do: in the preface to the *New Essays*, Leibniz says explicitly that he has chosen to express his own views through Theophile; and he was long in the habit of using fictional spokespersons to articulate views that he himself held without reserve or irony. In his anxiety to refute Stein, it seems, Friedmann oversteps the mark, and thus finds it impossible to explain how it came to pass that Leibniz himself believed that he had come perilously close to lapsing into Spinozism.

Friedmann does indeed correct the important factual problems in Stein's account, in my view; but his account falls short because he fails to address some philosophical preconceptions that, ironically, he shares with Stein. Both critics assume, to put it somewhat cryptically, that the Leibnizian philosophy is one thing, and the Spinozistic one another. That is, they imagine that Leibniz's philosophical system is an uncomplicated, self-identical substance, like a chemical compound, and that it happens to be very different from Spinoza's substance. Either it came into being before making contact with Spinoza, in which case it has nothing to do with Spinozism, as Friedmann maintains, or it arrived afterward, in which case there is the possibility of influence, as Stein argues.

But in truth, Leibniz's philosophy was never any one thing. It was a basket of positions, tropes, and stereotyped reactions that evolved over time. It represents no slight on the great philosopher—nor does one have to subscribe to dialectical idealism—to acknowledge that his philosophical "system" was neither simple nor entirely self-identical. This was especially true in his early work. Many of the central doctrines of Leibniz's mature philosophy—when phrased in very abstract terms, such as the principle of individuality, the principle of harmony, and so forth—may be found in embryonic form in his earliest works. But there are plenty of other embryos to be found in Leibniz's early work, too. Indeed, had Leibniz been fired from his post as a courtier and become an embittered Spinozist in later years, undoubtedly scholars would have been able to prove that he had been one before he met Spinoza, too. There is no coherent, universal synthesis of Leibniz's philosophical positions among his early writings for the simple reason that such a synthesis did not exist in his mind. Even his mature work, furthermore, fails to be entirely self-sufficient, and without constant vigilance tends to slide in quasi-Spinozistic positions.

This inherent disunity in Leibniz's thought is, I think, the key to taking the understanding of his relationship with Spinoza beyond the level of analysis provided by Stein and Friedmann. It is too simple by an order of magnitude to say either that Leibniz was a Spinozist, with Stein, or that he was never a Spinozist, with Friedmann. The truth is that, before he knew anything about Spinoza, Leibniz was against Spinoza; and yet, at the same time, he also had a Spinozistic side. The encounter with Spinoza was crucial to his philosophical development because it forced him to confront this division within his own thought. Spinoza presented him with a problem he devoted his philosophical labors to solving, namely, how to suppress the dangerous Spinozist within himself. Absent the dalliance with Spinoza, Leibniz would have remained a conservative thinker; but he would not have been an essentially modern one, and his philosophy would not have originated the reactive form of modernity. To make a long story even more complicated: It is quite plausible to say that, before, after, and during their encounter, Leibniz was deeply anti-Spinozistic, superficially anti-Spinozistic, and deeply Spinozistic, all at the same time. The only thing that cannot be said, in my view, is that for Leibniz Spinoza did not matter.

It remains to acknowledge my debt to sources on Spinoza's life. All biographies of Spinoza begin with a lament about how little we know about his life. Since the point has already been made so many times, I am content merely to repeat it here: We know very little about Spinoza's life. Virtually all of the original sources for any biography of Spinoza—including the works of Lucas, Colerus, and Bayle—are collected in one slim volume: Freudenthal (1899). Among recent works, Nadler (1999) is the biography of reference. Nadler (2003) also offers a fascinating glimpse of life in the Amsterdam Jewish community that produced Spinoza.

Bibliography

Primary Sources

I have used standard abbreviations for citations from Spinoza's works. The meaning of abbreviations will be obvious from a glance at his collected works (e.g., "TTP" means *Tractatus Theologico-Politicus* and "E I P16" refers to *Ethics*, Part I, Proposition 16). Note that L refers to his Letters. I have used Shirley's translation in the main, with some minor modifications.

Opera, 2nd ed. Edited by Carl Gebhart. 4 vols. Heidelberg: C. Winters, 1972. (Original ed., Heidelberger Akademie, 1925).

Spinoza: The Collected Works. Edited by Edwin Curley. Vol 1. Princeton: Princeton University Press, 1985.

Spinoza, Complete Works. Edited by Michael Morgan. Translated by Samuel Shirley. Indianapolis: Hackett, 2002.

The standard, reference edition of Leibniz's collected works is that of the Berlin Akademie. The Akademie is expected to require another century or so to complete its edition, however, so the researcher must rely on a number of other editions of Leibniz's works. I have used the following abbreviations in the notes:

A   *Gottfried Wilhelm Leibniz: Sämtliche Schriften und Briefe*. Edited by Akademie der Wissenschaften, Berlin. Akademie Verlag, 1923–.

Du   *Leibniz: Opera Omnia.* Edited by L. Dutens. 6 vols. Reprint, Hildesheim, Ger.: Olms, 1989.

G   *Die Philosophischen Schriften von Leibniz.* Edited by C. I. Gerhardt. 7 vols. Reprint, Hildesheim, Ger.: Olms, 1965.

GM   *Mathematische Schriften.* Edited by C. I. Gerhardt. 7 vols. Reprint, Hildesheim, Ger.: Olms, 1962.

Klopp *Die Werke von Leibniz.* Edited by O. Klopp. 11 vols. Reprint, Hildesheim, Ger.: Olms, 1970.

TI   *Textes inédits.* Edited by Gaston Grua. 2 vols. New York: Garland, 1985.

English-language readers looking for Leibniz's principal texts, of course, need not throw themselves beneath the avalanche of his collected works. A number of handy collections exist. Where possible, I refer to these in the notes with the following abbreviations:

DSR   *The Yale Leibniz. De Summa Rerum: Metaphysical Papers, 1675–1676.* Translated by G. H. R. Parkinson. New Haven: Yale University Press, 1992.

LCC   *The Leibniz-Clarke Correspondence.* Edited by H. G. Alexander. Manchester: Manchester University Press, 1956.

LoC   *The Yale Leibniz. The Labyrinth of the Continuum: Writings on the Continuum Problem, 1672–1686.* Edited by Richard T. W. Arthur. New Haven: Yale University Press, 2001.

PE   *Philosophical Essays.* Edited by Roger Ariew and Daniel Garber. Indianapolis: Hackett, 1989.

PPL   *Philosophical Papers and Letters.* Edited by Leroy E. Loemker. 2 vols. Chicago: University of Chicago Press, 1956.

PT   *Philosophical Texts.* Edited by R. S. Woolhouse and Richard Franks. Oxford: Oxford University Press, 1998.

PW   *Political Writings.* Edited by Patrick Riley. Cambridge: Cambridge University Press, 1972.

Theodicy *Theodicy.* Edited by Austin Farrer. Translated by E. M. Huggard. Chicago: Open Court, 1990.

WoC   *Writings on China.* Edited by Daniel J. Cook and Henry Rosemont Jr. Chicago: Open Court, 1994.

Secondary Sources

Adams, Robert Merrihew. *Leibniz: Determinist, Theist, Idealist.* Oxford: Oxford University Press, 1994.

Aiton, E. J. *Leibniz: A Biography.* Boston: A. Hilger, 1985.

Allison, Henry E. *Benedict de Spinoza: An Introduction.* New Haven: Yale University Press, 1987.

Bagley, Paul J., ed. *Piety, Peace, and the Freedom to Philosophize.* Boston: Kluwer, 1999.

Balibar, Etienne. *Spinoza et la politique.* Paris: Presses Universitaires de France, 1985.

Barber, W. H. *Leibniz in France: From Arnauld to Voltaire.* Oxford: Oxford University Press, 1955.

Baruzzi, Jean. *Leibniz et l'organisation religieuse de la terre.* Paris: Alcan, 1907.

Bayle, Pierre. *Dictionnaire historique et critique.* 3 vols. Rotterdam, 1702.

Beck, Lewis White. *Early German Philosophy.* Bristol: Thoemmes, 1996.

Belaval, Yvon. *Leibniz: De l'age classique aux lumieres, lectures Leibniziennes.* Paris: Beauchesne, 1995.

Bell, Arthur Ernest. *Christian Huygens and the Development of Science in the Seventeenth Century.* London: E. Arnold, 1947.

Bennett, Jonathan. *A Study of Spinoza's Ethics.* Indianapolis: Hackett, 1984.

Bernard, Leon. *The Emerging City: Paris in the Age of Louis XIV.* Durham: Duke University Press, 1970.

Bossuet, Jacques-Bénigne. *Politics Drawn from the Very Words of the Holy Scripture.* Translated by Patrick Riley. Cambridge: Cambridge University Press, 1990.

Bouveresse, Renee. *Spinoza et Leibniz.* Paris: J. Vrin, 1992.

Brooks, Richard A. *Voltaire and Leibniz.* Geneva: Librairie Droz, 1964.

Brown, Stuart, ed. *The Young Leibniz and His Philosophy, 1646–1676.* Boston: Kluwer, 1999.

Bunge, Wiep van. *From Stevin to Spinoza.* Leiden: Brill, 2001.

Bunge, Wiep van, and Wim Klever, eds. *Disguised and Overt Spinozism Around 1700.* Leiden: Brill, 1996.

Cassirer, Ernst. *The Philosophy of the Enlightenment.* Princeton: Princeton University Press, 1979.

Centro Fiorentino di Storia e Filosofia. *The Leibniz Renaissance: International Workshop.* Florence: L. S. Olschki, 1989.

Clark, Ronald W. *Einstein: The Life and Times.* New York: World, 1971.

Clarke, Samuel. *A Demonstration of the Being and Attributes of God: More Particularly in Answer to Mr. Hobbs, Spinoza, and Their Followers.* Edited by E. Vailati. Cambridge: Cambridge University Press, 1998.

Condillac, Etienne Bonnot de. *Les Monades.* Oxford: Voltaire Foundation, 1980.

Cristofolini, Paolo, ed. *L'Heresie spinoziste: La discussion sur le Tractatus theologico-politicus, 1670–1677.* Amsterdam: Holland University Press, 1995.

Cubitt, Heather. *Holland in the Time of Rembrandt.* London: Longman, 1971.

Curley, Edwin. *Behind the Geometrical Method: A Reading of Spinoza's Ethics.* Princeton: Princeton University Press, 1988.

Curley, Edwin, and Pierre-François Moreau. *Spinoza: Issues and Directions.* Leiden: Brill, 1990.

Cutler, Alan. *The Seashell and the Mountaintop.* New York: Dutton, 2003.

Damasio, Antonio. *Looking for Spinoza: Joy, Sorrow, and the Feeling Brain.* Orlando: Harcourt, 2003.

Delahunty, R. J. *Spinoza.* Boston: Routledge, 1985.

Deleuze, Gilles. *Le Pli: Leibniz et le baroque.* Paris: Editions de Minuit, 1988.

———. *Spinoza: Philosophie practique.* Paris: Editions de Minuit, 1981.

Durant, Will and Ariel. *The Age of Louis XIV.* New York: Simon & Schuster, 1963.

Eliot, T. S. *Knowledge and Experience in the Philosophy of F. H. Bradley.* New York: Farrar Straus & Giroux, 1964.

Fischer. *Geschichte der neuern philosophie.* Heidelberg: C. Winter, 1897–1904.

Fleckenstein, J. O. *G. W. Leibniz: Barock und Universalismus.* Munich: Thun, Ott, 1958.

Frankfurt, Harry G., ed. *Leibniz: A Collection of Critical Essays.* Garden City, N.Y.: Anchor Books, 1972.

Freundenthal, Jacob. *Die Lebensgeschichte Spinozas in Quellenschriften, Urkunden und nichtamtliche Nachrichten.* Leipzig: Leipzig Veit & Comp., 1899.

Friedmann, Georges. *Leibniz et Spinoza.* Paris: Gallimard: 1962 (1st ed., 1946).

Garrett, Don. *The Cambridge Companion to Spinoza.* Cambridge: Cambridge University Press, 1996.

Gaukroger, Stephen. *Descartes: An Intellectual Biography.* Oxford: Oxford University Press, 1995.

Gebhardt, Carl. "Rembrandt und Spinoza." *Kantstudien* 32 (1927): 161–81.

Giraffi, Alessandro. *An Exact Historie of the Late Revolutions in Naples.* London, 1650.

Goetschel, Willi. *Spinoza's Modernity: Mendelssohn, Lessing, and Heine.* Madison: University of Wisconsin Press, 2004.

Grell, Ole Peter, and Roy Porter, eds. *Toleration in Enlightenment Europe.* Cambridge: Cambridge University Press, 2000.

Guhrauer, Gottschalk Eduard. *Gottfried Wilhelm, Freiherr v. Leibniz: Eine Biographie.* 2 vols. Breslau: F. Hirt, 1846.

Gullan-Whur, Margaret. *Within Reason: A Life of Spinoza.* London: Jonathan Cape, 1998.

Hall, A. Rupert. *Isaac Newton: Adventurer in Thought.* Oxford: Blackwell, 1992.

———. *Philosophers at War: The Quarrel Between Newton and Leibniz.* Cambridge: Cambridge University Press, 1980.

Hampshire, Stuart. *Spinoza*. New York: Penguin, 1987.

Harris, Errol E. *The Substance of Spinoza*. Atlantic Highlands, N.J.: Humanities Press, 1995.

Hart, Allan. *Spinoza's Ethics Parts I and II: A Platonic Commentary*. Leiden: Brill, 1983.

Hazard, Paul. *The European Mind, 1680–1715*. London: Hollis & Carter, 1953.

Hegel, G. W. F. *Lectures on the History of Philosophy*. Berkeley: University of California Press, 1990.

Hirsch, Eike Christian. *Der berühmte Herr Leibniz: Eine Biographie*. Munich: C. H. Beck, 2000.

Hofmann, Joseph E. *Leibniz in Paris, 1672–1676: His Growth to Mathematical Maturity*. Cambridge: Cambridge University Press, 1974.

Huizinga, Johann. *Dutch Civilisation in the Seventeenth Century*. New York: Frederick Unger, 1968.

Israel, Jonathan I. *The Dutch Republic: Its Rise, Greatness, and Fall, 1477–1806*. Oxford: Oxford University Press, 1995.

———. *Radical Enlightement: Philosophy and the Making of Modernity, 1650–1750*. Oxford: Oxford University Press, 2001.

Jacob, A. *Henry More's Refutation of Spinoza*. Hildesheim, Ger.: Olms, 1991.

Jolley, Nicholas. *Leibniz and Locke: A Study of the New Essays Concerning Human Understanding*. Oxford: Oxford University Press, 1984.

Jolley, Nicholas, ed. *The Cambridge Companion to Leibniz*. Cambridge: Cambridge University Press, 1995.

Jordan, G. J. *The Reunion of the Churches: A Study of G. W. Leibniz and His Great Attempt*. London, 1927.

Kashap, S. Paul, ed. *Studies in Spinoza*. Berkeley: University of California Press, 1972.

Kulstad, Mark. *Leibniz on Apperception, Consciousness, and Reflection*. Munich: Philosophia Verlag, 1991.

Lindo, E. H. *The History of Jews of Spain and Portugal*. 1848. Reprint, New York: Burt Franklin, 1970.

Lister, Martin. *A Journey to Paris in the Year 1698*. Edited by Raymond Phineas Stearns. Champaign: University of Illinois Press, 1967.

Loemker, Leroy E. *Struggle for Synthesis. The Seventeenth-Century Background of Leibniz's Synthesis of Order and Freedom*. Cambridge, Mass.: Harvard University Press, 1972.

Lough, John. *Locke's Travels in France, 1675–79. France Observed in the Seventeenth Century by British Travelers*. Cambridge: Cambridge University Press, 1995.

Malebranche, Nicolas. *Dialogues on Metaphysics and Religion*. Edited by N. Jolley. Cambridge: Cambridge University Press, 1997.

Mason, Richard. *The God of Spinoza: A Philosophical Study*. Cambridge: Cambridge University Press, 1997.

Meinsma, Koenraad Oege. *Spinoza et son cercle*. Translated by S. Rosenberg and J. P. Osier. Paris: J.Vrin, 1983.

———. *Spinoza und sein Kreis: Historisch-kritische Studien uber hollandische Freigeister.* Berlin: K. Schnabel, 1909.

Mercer, Christia. *Leibniz's Metaphysics: Its Origins and Development*. Cambridge: Cambridge University Press, 2001.

Meyer, R. W. *Leibniz and the Seventeenth Century Revolution*. Cambridge: Bowes & Bower, 1952.

Montag, Warren, and Ted Stolze, eds. *The New Spinoza*. Minneapolis: University of Minnesota Press, 1997.

Moreau, Pierre-François. *Spinoza: L'éxperience et l'éternité*. Paris: Presses Universitaires de France, 1994.

Müller, Kurt, and Gisela Krönert. *Leben und Werk von Gottfried Wilhelm Leibniz: Eine Chronik*. Frankfurt: Klostermann, 1969.

Nadler, Steven. *Malebranche and Ideas*. Oxford: Oxford University Press, 1992.

———. *Rembrandt's Jews*. Chicago: University of Chicago Press, 2003.

———. *Spinoza: A Life*. Cambridge: Cambridge University Press, 1999.

Nadler, Steven, and Daniel Garber. *Oxford Studies in Early Modern Philosophy*. Oxford: Oxford University Press, 2003.

Nietzsche, F. W. *Werke*. Edited by Karl Schlechter. Frankfurt: Ullstein, 1969.

Oldenburg, Henry. *The Correspondence of Henry Oldenburg*. Edited by A. R. and M. B. Hall. 13 vols. Madison: University of Wisconsin Press, 1965–.

Orléans, Charlotte-Elisabeth d'. *Lettres de Madame Palatine*. Paris: Le Club, 1961.

Price, J. L. *Culture and Society in the Dutch Republic During the Seventeenth Century*. London: Batsford, 1974.

Raphael, Chaim. *The Sephardi Story*. London:Valentine Mitchell, 1991.

Rescher, Nicholas. *The Philosophy of Leibniz*. Englewood Cliffs, N.J.: Prentice-Hall, 1967.

Rhys, H. H., ed. *Seventeenth Century Science and Arts*. Princeton: Princeton University Press, 1961.

Riley, Patrick. *Leibniz's Universal Jurisprudence*. Cambridge, Mass.: Harvard University Press, 1996.

Robinet, Andre. *G. W. Leibniz: Iter Italicum*. Florence, 1988.

Russell, Bertrand. *The Philosophy of Leibniz*. 1900. Reprint, London: Routledge, 1992.

Rutherford, D. *Leibniz and the Rational Order of Nature*. Cambridge: Cambridge University Press, 1995.

Sauval, Henri. *Histoire et recherches de antiquites de la ville de Paris.* 3 vols. Paris, 1724.

Schama, Simon. *The Embarrassment of Riches: An Interpretation of Dutch Culture in the Golden Age.* New York: Knopf, 1987.

Siebrand. H. J. *Spinoza and the Netherlanders: An Inquiry into the Early Reception of His Philosophy of Religion.* Assen, Netherlands: Van Gorcum, 1984.

Sleigh Jr., R. C. *Leibniz and Arnauld: A Commentary on Their Correspondence.* New Haven: Yale University Press, 1990.

Steenbakkers, Piet. *Spinoza's Ethica from Manuscript to Print.* Assen, Netherlands: Van Gorcum, 1994.

Stein, Ludwig. *Leibniz und Spinoza: Ein Beitrag zur Entwicklungsgeschichte der Leibnizischen Philosophie.* Berlin: Georg Reimer, 1890.

Strauss, Leo. *Spinoza's Critique of Religion.* New York: Schocken, 1965.

Studia Leibnitiana. Supplementa sviii (1978), *passim.* Esp. G. H. R. Parkinson, "Leibniz's Paris Writings in Relation to Spinoza," pp. 73–89.

Temple, Sir William. *Observations upon the United Provinces of the Netherlands.* Edited by Sir George Clark. 1673. Reprint, Oxford: Clarendon Press, 1972.

Totok, Wilhelm, and Carl Haase. *Leibniz: sein Leben, seine Wirken, seine Welt.* Hanover: Verlag für Literatur, 1966.

Tschirnhaus, Walther Ehrenfried von. *Medicina mentis et corporis.* 1695. Reprint, Hildesheim, Ger.: Olms, 1964.

Vailati, Ezio. *Leibniz and Clarke: A Study of Their Correspondence.* Oxford: Oxford University Press, 1997.

Valentiner, Wilhelm Reinhold. *Rembrandt and Spinoza.* London: Phaidon Press, 1957.

Walther, Manfred. *Das Leben Spinozas: Eine Bibliographie.* Hanover: Uni-Verlag Witte, 1996.

Weber, Theodor Hubert. *Spinozae atque Leibnizii philosophiae, ratione habita libri, cui nomen est "Refutation inedited de Spinoza."* Bonnae, formis C. Georgi, 1858.

Westfall, Richard S. *Science and Religion in Seventeenth Century England.* New Haven: Yale University Press, 1958.

———. *The Life of Isaac Newton.* Cambridge: Cambridge University Press, 1994.

Wilson, Catherine. *Leibniz's Metaphysics.* Manchester: Manchester University Press, 1989.

Wolfson, H. A. *The Philosophy of Spinoza.* 2 vols. 1934. Reprint, Cambridge, Mass.: Harvard University Press, 1983.

Woolhouse, R. S. *Descartes, Spinoza, Leibniz: The Concept of Substance in Seventeenth-Century Metaphysics*. London: Routledge, 1993.

Yovel, Yirmiyahu. *Spinoza and Other Heretics*. 2 vols. Princeton: Princeton University Press, 1989.

Zumthor, Paul. *La vie cotidienne en Holland*. Paris: Hachette, 1960.

Acknowledgments

I would like to thank the staff of the research institutions upon which I relied in preparing this book, including the New York University libraries, the New York Public Library, the Burke Library of the Union Theological Seminary, the Library of Congress, the British Library, the London Library, and the Royal Library of The Hague. I would also like to thank the many participants at the Young Leibniz Conference held at Rice University in April 2003, which I attended. Finally, I owe a debt of gratitude to Alane Mason, my editor, for her thorough and insightful edits as well as her enthusiasm for the subject; Andrew Stuart, my agent, who lent his support to the idea even while it occupied only half a sheet of paper; Richard Kaye for his helpful comments on the first drafts; Charles Gillispie for his words of wisdom; and Katherine, my wife, in equal measure for her comments on the text and her patience.

Index